The Ethics of Interdependence

New Millennium Books in International Studies

TITLES IN THE SERIES

The Ethics of Interdependence

Global Human Rights and Duties

William F. Felice

ROWMAN & LITTLEFIELD
Lanham • Boulder • New York • London

Published by Rowman & Littlefield
A wholly owned subsidiary of The Rowman & Littlefield Publishing Group, Inc.
4501 Forbes Boulevard, Suite 200, Lanham, Maryland 20706
https://rowman.com

Unit A, Whitacre Mews, 26-34 Stannary Street, London SE11 4AB, United Kingdom

British Library Cataloguing in Publication Information Available

Library of Congress Cataloging-in-Publication Data
Names: Felice, William F., 1950– author.
Title: The ethics of interdependence : global human rights and duties / William F. Felice.
Description: Lanham : Rowman & Littlefield, [2016] | Series: New millennium books in
    international studies | Includes index.
Identifiers: LCCN 2016007401 (print) | LCCN 2016025469 (ebook) | ISBN
    9781442266698 (hardcover : alkaline paper) | ISBN 9781442266704 (paperback :
    alkaline paper) | ISBN 9781442266711 (electronic)
Subjects: LCSH: Human rights—International cooperation—Case studies. | International
    relations—Moral and ethical aspects—Case studies. | International cooperation—Mo-
    ral and ethical aspects—Case studies. | Suffering—Political aspects—Case studies. |
    Suffering—Moral and ethical aspects—Case studies. | Globalization—Social as-
    pects—Case studies. | Globalization—Moral and ethical aspects—Case studies.
Classification: LCC JC571 .F4236 2016 (print) | LCC JC571 (ebook) | DDC 172/.4—dc23
LC record available at http://lccn.loc.gov/2016007401

Printed in the United States of America

Contents

Acknowledgments

There are a number of individuals who directly influenced the direction of this manuscript. It is a pleasure to thank them for their help and to publicly acknowledge their influence on my thinking. My gratitude to all of them is immeasurable.

I am especially indebted to the Rev. Dr. Kapya Kaoma for agreeing to be interviewed for this book. Rev. Kaoma is on the front lines of human rights struggles in Africa and a genuine hero. It is an honor to have his reflections on LGBT rights in Africa included in chapter 3.

Brent Pickett's first-rate feedback and thoughtful commentary enhanced and invigorated the entire manuscript. I am very grateful to Brent for taking the time to provide this critical support.

My colleague and friend Tony Brunello was also generous with his time, and his insightful comments were particularly useful.

Andrew Black brought his expertise on the US criminal justice system and restorative justice to his review of chapter 2 on mass incarceration in the United States. I so appreciate Andrew's astute feedback and input on these critical issues.

Fait Muedini carefully reviewed chapter 4 on women's rights in Saudi Arabia, provided valuable advice, and steered me to some excellent resources on this topic.

Jing Chen provided constructive insights and resources for chapter 5 on environmental rights in China. Jing's observations on this chapter were exceedingly helpful.

Many of the ideas developed in this book were presented at annual meetings of the International Studies Association. I am grateful to my ISA colleagues for providing substantial feedback and direction.

Todd Germann was a fountain of useful and creative ideas on the cover design. I am so appreciative of his generous time commitment to this project.

I wish to thank three people at Rowman & Littlefield who were instrumental in bringing this book to publication. Vice President and Editorial Director Susan McEachern has been a consistent source of support over many years, and this project benefited from her professionalism and skilled editorial supervision. Assistant Editor Audra Figgins and Assistant Managing Editor Janice Braunstein guided the manuscript through the production process. I am grateful to Susan, Audra, and Janice for their commitment to this project.

In addition, the peer reviews I received from Rowman & Littlefield, and from the editors of the New Millennium Books in International Studies, were exceedingly valuable and helpful. I am honored to be included in the New Millennium series.

While all of these people gave generously of their time, the responsibility for the contents of this book is entirely my own.

I wish to acknowledge with gratitude permission to draw on the following previously published works: "Introduction: A Study Guide to the Four Freedoms" (Carnegie Council on Ethics and International Affairs, 2005); and *The Global New Deal: Economic and Social Human Rights in World Politics*, 2nd ed. (Rowman & Littlefield, 2010).

I dedicate this book to my husband, Dale Lappe.

Abbreviations and Acronyms

ACLU	American Civil Liberties Union
AFDC	Aid to Families with Dependent Children
AI	Amnesty International
ANC	African National Congress
ATS	Alien Tort Statute
BJS	Bureau of Justice Statistics (US)
CCPR	Covenant on Civil and Political Rights
CCR	Center for Constitutional Rights
CDHRI	Cairo Declaration on Human Rights in Islam
CEDAW	Convention on the Elimination of All Forms of Discrimination against Women
CERD	Convention on the Elimination of All Forms of Racial Discrimination
CESCR	Covenant on Economic, Social and Cultural Rights
CRC	Convention on the Rights of the Child
ECOSOC	Economic and Social Council
EIA	Energy Information Administration (US)
HRC	Human Rights Council
ICJ	International Court of Justice

IGO	intergovernmental organization
IMF	International Monetary Fund
IO	international organization
LGBT	lesbian, gay, bisexual, and transgender
LGBTQIA	lesbian, gay, bisexual, transgender, questioning, intersex, and ally
NGO	nongovernmental organization
OHCHR	Office of the UN High Commissioner for Human Rights
PRWORA	Personal Responsibility and Work Opportunity Reconciliation Act
SMUG	Sexual Minorities Uganda
UDHR	Universal Declaration of Human Rights
UN	United Nations
UNHCHR	United Nations High Commissioner for Human Rights
WLUML	Women Living under Muslim Laws
WRI	World Resources Institute

Introduction

- Does a US citizen have a human rights duty to act to end the brutalization of gay men in Africa?
- Does a South African citizen have a human rights duty to speak out against the mass incarceration of African Americans in the United States?
- Does Brazil have a human rights duty to link its trade and investments with Saudi Arabia to the protection of women's rights inside the kingdom?
- Does Germany (or the United Nations Environment Program) have a human rights duty to pressure China to limit and phase out the burning of coal, which causes devastating environmental harm?

To many around the world, the answer to all of these questions is no. This conclusion is often based on the premise that the primary human rights duty of individuals and states is to focus on protecting human rights at home and not abroad. Instead of pressuring others about their human rights obligations, it is better to work to create a just society at home.

In fact, one of the most common questions I've been asked during my twenty-four years of teaching courses on human rights, ethics, and international relations, has been: "Since my primary moral duties are to my family, community, and country, why should I devote my limited resources and energy to protecting human rights abroad?" The American students raising these types of questions seem to reside on a solid honorable foundation as human rights violations and avoidable human suffering at home continue to haunt our country. US poverty levels remain tragically high, our prisons are bulging, our environment continues to be degraded, millions in the United

States face food insecurity and homelessness, discrimination against minorities continues apace, and on and on. There is an undeniable moral[1] duty for individuals to act to prevent such human suffering in their home states.

However, most individuals who make this localist argument will also acknowledge the ways in which "economic globalization" has created human rights duties beyond borders. Students, in particular, are often quick to criticize the actions of multinational corporations, such as Nike, Exxon, and Apple, for creating and perpetuating labor abuse and environmental degradation abroad. And yet, an ethical line continues to be drawn at the border. Even while accepting the moral and legal duties that flow from "economic interdependence," there remains a strong hesitancy to accede to the idea of "ethical interdependence." This diffidence often stems from a view of the world as fundamentally divided by geography, language, culture, religion, and politics. To these observers, economic globalization and financial integration, rather than pulling the world's peoples together, have contributed to pulling people apart, often resulting in national disintegration, fragmentation, and state failure at the local level. As a result, the world is seen as remaining divided into distinct civilizations with competing national and cultural priorities, unique and divergent views of justice and rights, and often opposing national interests. Given these wide differences between nations, and given the limitations of time, energy, and resources, it thus may appear foolhardy to try to end abuses in faraway lands; better to focus internally and use one's limited resources at home where they can make a positive difference.

The argument of this book is that this rigid distinction between the domestic and the foreign has appreciably weakened and no longer describes the reality of our ethically complex world. In fact, it is often ethically spurious today to make a division between foreign and domestic suffering. The economic, political, technological, environmental, and social links between the nations and peoples of the world are now so extensive that it is impossible to draw a clear line of ethical duty at any border. These ethical duties flow in all directions. If the actions of an individual, a nation, or a transnational organization create suffering in another nation-state, then ethical duties arise. When local actions create, or contribute to, suffering abroad, there is a strong level of "ethical interdependence" between the peoples of the world that requires a reformulation of our understanding of "rights," "duties," and "citizenship" in this new interdependent era.

Human rights realization depends upon the articulation of not only universal "rights" but global "duties" as well. These duties exist at the individual, national, and global levels.

- At the individual level, global duties revolve around consciousness and outer awareness of ethical interdependence. Such consciousness pushes individuals to expand their ethical circles of rights and responsibilities to include not only family and nation, but also humanity as a whole.[2]
- At the nation-state level, global duties involve the incorporation of international law, universal human rights, and global environmental accords into national policy formation. This governmental commitment is often undertaken with the knowledge that such a cooperative normative framework enhances national security.
- At the global level, institutions and "regimes"[3] of cooperation are pivotal to the creation of a world system responsive to conditions of ethical interdependence. Such global institutions give state and nonstate actors the ability to interact and engage one another, building mechanisms of trust and verification. Neutral global institutions are better positioned to apply human rights norms and laws fairly across boundaries and help to construct regimes of global governance responsive to the rights of the most vulnerable among us. The protection of the basic rights of citizens, including the right to life itself, around the world depends upon not only a caring national government, but also global institutions dedicated to upholding norms of humane governance and the protection of human rights.

The Ethics of Interdependence: Global Human Rights and Duties begins in chapter 1 with a "primer" on how the international community through the United Nations has articulated a clear corpus of international human rights law with corresponding global human duties. However, this global human rights regime is filled with conflicts between rights, in particular the clashes between individual and group rights. For example, in many parts of the world today there is a privileging of cultural and religious rights over the individual rights of women and the LGBT communities. Individual states have a lot of leeway in international law to prioritize particular human rights over other legitimate human rights claims, often perpetuating gross violations of human dignity. However, when a human rights threshold, as defined in chapter 1, is surpassed, urgent global action is needed to address unacceptable levels of human suffering. The concept of global citizenship is explored in this chapter as a possible framework to help address both the conflicts and inconsistencies found in human rights law and to be able to respond to violations that surpass the human rights threshold. A robust normative framework of global governance is seen as central to the actualization of human rights protection for all.

The ideas of ethical interdependence and global human rights and duties are then explored through the following four case studies: (1) mass incarceration in the United States, (2) LGBT rights in Africa, (3) women's rights in Saudi Arabia, and (4) environmental rights in China. In all four case studies the "human rights threshold" has been surpassed and these situations are illustrative of the ethics of interdependence.

These four case studies were selected for the following reasons. First, we begin with the United States because I am an American citizen and the responsibilities of global citizenship start at home. The mass incarceration of African American men is perhaps the most pressing human rights crisis confronting our country. The first human rights duty of those of us who live in the United States is to ensure that our own policies and practices comply with international human rights law.

As noted in chapter 2, the United States imprisons more of its racial and ethnic minorities than any other country in the world. While representing approximately 11 percent of the general adult population, African Americans constitute close to 50 percent of state and federal prisoners.[4] This tragic situation is a result of too many young African American males caught up in a police and judiciary system that often denies them basic human dignity and rights. The Universal Declaration of Human Rights (UDHR) states that "the recognition of the inherent dignity and of the equal and inalienable rights" of all people is "the foundation of freedom, justice and peace in the world." Many US citizens have historically felt an ethical duty to speak out and protest against the abuse of judicial procedures and prisoners in the former Soviet Union, Cuba, Iran, China, and elsewhere. Today, individuals from Latin America, Europe, and around the world who take human rights and duties seriously are speaking out against the mass incarceration of African Americans in the United States. These global citizens are pressuring their individual governments to forcefully confront the United States to change these practices.

LGBT rights in Africa and women's rights in Saudi Arabia were selected for the next two case studies because each of these situations dramatically illustrates the dialectical relationship between group and individual rights.

Chapters 3 and 4 attempt to define the human rights duties for individuals, nation-states, and international organizations concerned about LGBT rights in Africa and women's rights in Saudi Arabia.

As documented in chapter 3, thirty-eight out of fifty-four African countries criminalize "consensual same-sex conduct," making homosexuality illegal throughout 70 percent of the continent.[5] Yet homophobia in Africa is not indigenous to the continent but was introduced by colonialists and recently perpetuated by the actions of American missionaries. The United States and Europe thus have a considerable degree of ethical responsibility for the suffering of the LGBT community in Africa, and gay rights in the continent cannot be seen as solely a domestic concern of the various African states. European and American citizens concerned with human rights must ask whether the foreign policies of their nations contribute to or help to alleviate the abuse of homosexuals, especially gay men, in Africa.

The systematic oppression of women in Saudi Arabia, as detailed in chapter 4, has resulted in unequal treatment in marriage laws, divorce laws, property laws, employment, health care, domestic violence, union rights, freedom of movement, and public participation in the political process.[6] And yet the most powerful states in the world today often ignore this brazen apartheid system of discrimination against women in Saudi Arabia in order to maintain strong political and economic relations with this strategically located oil-rich regime. Through these political and economic policies the United States and other developed states bolster the current patriarchic Saudi regime. The ethical interdependence between the economic and security policies of the United States (and other nations) and the perpetuation of the Saudi ruling clique's treatment of women is impossible to ignore.

And finally, the last case study was chosen in order to examine the implications of the newly emerging human right to a healthy environment, often referred to as a key "solidarity right." The analysis of China's massive coal burning reveals global environmental interdependence and the need for solidarity between nations and peoples to create sustainable development and protect human health throughout our small planet.

China's actions, as the world's largest emitter of greenhouse gases into the atmosphere, cause serious suffering abroad. By 2011 China was burning almost as much coal as the rest of the world combined, 47 percent of global coal consumption. The United States contributes to this suffering by selling China over eight million tons of coal a year.[7] China is now the largest contributor of sulfur oxides and chlorofluorocarbons in the atmosphere. Pollution, of course, does not respect national boundaries, and China's aerial pollutants are transported to neighboring countries and across the Pacific Ocean and into the United States. The human rights duties of China, and to those countries like the United States that sell China coal, thus extend well beyond individual borders and include the impact of their policies globally.

In each of the case studies examined in this book (mass incarceration in the United States, LGBT rights in Africa, women's rights in Saudi Arabia, and environmental rights in China), a human rights threshold has been surpassed and human rights duties have emerged at the individual, nation-state, and global levels. The concluding chapter examines how a framework of global governance can help to conceptualize these human rights duties in this new era of ethical interdependence. In many fundamental respects, the United States has historically embraced this globalist approach to human rights and duties. The ethics illuminating Franklin Delano Roosevelt's (FDR) "four freedoms," for example, embody this cosmopolitan vision and the ethics of interdependence. In his famous 1941 speech, FDR called for "a world founded upon four essential human freedoms"—freedom of speech and expression, freedom of religion, freedom from want, and freedom from fear— "everywhere in the world."

Chapters of *The Ethics of Interdependence* end with the following resources:

1. Discussion questions, and
2. Websites of organizations working on the human rights issues discussed in the chapter.

Chapter One

Global Human Rights and Duties: A Primer

Scholars, diplomats, and activists continue to debate the meaning of the phrases "human rights" and "human duties."[1] This chapter is not intended to summarize these important philosophical, political, religious, and cultural disputes on the content and meaning of rights language. The goal here is rather to

- Provide an introductory framework for understanding how since World War II human rights and duties have been formulated by nation-states and civil society, working through international organizations (IOs) and nongovernmental organizations (NGOs), including contested and controversial rights claims and compliance difficulties.
- Explore the conflicts between individual and group rights—both affirmed by the international community—that have intensified with the strengthening of a global legal human rights regime.
- Examine whether the idea of global citizenship and a single moral community help to conceptualize a new framework for understanding the relationships between the individual, the nation-state, and the entire planet.
- Clarify the human rights duties on individuals, nation-states, and global actors such as IOs and NGOs.
- Articulate the criteria for a "human rights threshold" to be able to assess when urgent action is needed to address unacceptable levels of human suffering.

This primer on modern-day conceptions of human rights is intended to provide a reasonable account of the global duties and responsibilities of individuals, nation-states, and global actors codified in international law and reflective of the ethics of interdependence.

WHAT ARE "HUMAN RIGHTS"?

A human right can be defined as a claim on others to a certain type of treatment fundamentally linked to the alleviation of suffering.[2]

Human rights are not "things" that individuals "have" (like hands, ears, and toes) but socially constructed claims or entitlements that derive from legal and moral rules. One is entitled to these claims solely because he or she is a human being. Human rights are claims essential to protect human life, eliminate avoidable suffering, and enhance human dignity across cultures, political boundaries, and ideological divides. The central purpose of international human rights standards is to protect individuals and groups not only against the arbitrary exercise of nation-state power, but also from the suffering caused by the actions of nonstate actors as well, including global terrorist organizations, rapacious multinational corporations, and vicious individuals. In addition, human rights claims have been articulated to provide relief and protection from structural violence as well. The term "structural violence" refers to the denial of subsistence rights to the most vulnerable sectors as a by-product of economic globalization. The unintended consequences of the global reach of hefty economic institutions and actors has unfortunately often meant continued immiseration and suffering for many of the world's poor.[3] In essence, human rights are social constructions—claims for a certain type of treatment—that evolve and change as new sources of human suffering emerge with globalization in the twenty-first century. As such, human rights claims are not like the "ten commandments" written in stone; on the contrary, human rights claims evolve and change in order to address modern sources of human suffering.[4]

Human suffering is ubiquitous. Sentient beings in cultures around the world experience mild to intolerable forms of mental and physical suffering. Human rights claims are directed at preventing or ending avoidable, excessive, and unwarranted suffering. In our modern era, the sources of suffering are multifaceted. Intrusive, insensitive, oppressive, despotic, and unfair acts are committed not only by states but by individuals and other global institutions and organizations as well. As a result, the civil, political, economic, social, and cultural human rights obligations and duties apply not just to states but to all individuals and institutions that directly or indirectly contribute to the harm of groups and individuals. Human rights claims thus attempt to challenge avoidable, unwarranted suffering.

Human rights claims codified in international law include freedom from racial and equivalent forms of discrimination; the right to life, liberty, and the security of person; freedom from slavery or involuntary servitude; freedom from torture and cruel, inhuman, or degrading treatment or punishment; freedom from arbitrary arrest, detention, or exile; the right to a fair and public trial; freedom from interference in privacy and correspondence; freedom of movement and residence; the right to asylum from persecution; freedom of thought, conscience, and religion; freedom of opinion and expression; freedom of peaceful assembly and association; and the right to participate in government, directly or through free elections. [5]

In addition to these liberal rights based on "freedom," human rights law also embraces norms of "equality" through the promotion of economic, social, and cultural rights, including the right to social security; the right to work and protection against unemployment; the right to rest and leisure; the right to a standard of living adequate for the health and well-being of self and family; the right to education; and the right to the protection of one's scientific, literary, and artistic production. [6]

In response to the phenomenon of global interdependence, a new category of rights has emerged reflecting the norm of "fraternity." Individual states acting alone can no longer satisfy their human rights obligations. International cooperation is required to solve contemporary problems, leading to the establishment of "solidarity rights." Such claims include the right to peace; the right to a healthy and balanced environment; the right to humanitarian disaster relief; the right to political, economic, social, and cultural self-determination; and the right to participate in and benefit from "the common heritage of mankind" (including earth-space resources). These solidarity rights are often seen as collective human rights, which benefit individuals and groups. [7]

The codification of international human rights law surged after World War II. Beginning with the UN Charter, which included the respect for and promotion of human rights as a key purpose of the organization, the members of the United Nations drafted a series of core human rights resolutions and treaties. The UDHR, the first UN document to provide a clear "list" of human rights, was adopted nearly unanimously by the UN General Assembly in 1948. The UDHR includes both civil and political rights (i.e., freedom of speech and religion) and economic, social, and cultural rights (i.e., rights to work and social security). After the adoption of the UDHR, in 1966 the members of the United Nations adopted two key treaties: the International Covenant on Civil and Political Rights (CCPR) and the International Covenant on Economic, Social and Cultural Rights (CESCR). The UDHR, CCPR, and CESCR are often referred to collectively as the International Bill of Human Rights.

This work on norm creation and standard setting continued throughout the remainder of the twentieth century. This impressive corpus of international law includes protections for women, racial minorities, migrants, children, and refugees, and prohibitions against apartheid, torture, and genocide. These treaties are legally binding. States are required upon ratification to incorporate the human rights protections into their domestic legal systems.

In addition to this remarkable list of treaties, the UN also provides a forum for states to pass resolutions, declarations, charters of rights and duties, and final acts from international organizations and conferences on recommended human rights practices. These instruments are not "hard law"— that is, treaties or customary law—and are thus often referred to as "soft law." The term *soft law* is paradoxical because many of these instruments are not, strictly speaking, law. Yet their impact on state behavior can be significant in that they create an environment of strong expectations that states will gradually conform their conduct to meet the requirements of the adopted resolution or declaration. Soft law provides a means for articulating a new normative international program. Such a development makes it harder for governments to ignore these evolving concerns and continue a practice that is being declared immoral or unjust. Human rights resolutions, declarations, and conference statements can provide some generally agreed upon human rights rules as to what is permissible and impermissible. Soft law thus helps establish standards of accountability, when hard law fails.

All of these human rights documents in hard and soft law can be found at the website of the UN Office of the High Commissioner of Human Rights, at http://www.ohchr.org.

Contested Nature of Human Rights

Human rights are, of course, not without controversy due to differing political systems, legal traditions, philosophical orientations, and cultural practices around the world. There is a long-standing debate in the global community over the universality of human rights claims.

On the one side are those who argue for universality. These advocates maintain that basic rights, such as the right to a fair trial, habeas corpus, physical security, food, and water, must be upheld everywhere. From this perspective, while individual states, cultures, and peoples can determine their own path toward rights fulfillment, no state can "opt out" of these fundamental rights, which should be guaranteed to all.

On the other side are those who argue from a position of cultural relativism, promoting the belief that rights and duties flow from the political, religious, and institutional structures of a people's society and local culture. From this perspective, notions of justice, and right and wrong conduct, reflect specific cultural understandings and will thus differ throughout the world. As an empirical matter, it is absolutely true that we are a diverse human species composed of multiple cultures, languages, religions, and political systems. The debate is not over this reality, but rather what this reality implies. A strong cultural relativist will demand respect and acceptance of local autonomy and criticize attempts to impose global standards, such as universal human rights, as arrogant and insensitive to valid cultural beliefs. From this perspective, the International Bill of Human Rights and other human rights documents do not represent a transcultural globally agreed upon framework of rights and duties; and instead reflect the particular values and beliefs—such as liberalism and social democracy—of the strong states who were key in the drafting of these documents at the United Nations. It is therefore wrong for these human rights claims to be imposed on local societies and cultures by outsiders. Some go further and suggest that such attempts to foster global adherence to international human rights signify "cultural imperialism," since these documents reflect the particular values of the leading states disguised as universal norms, with such efforts to universalize human rights potentially harming local cultures, destroying cultural diversity, and leading to a cultural homogenization of our modern world. These debates today take place between developed and less-developed countries, religious communities, and indigenous peoples and nation-states.[8]

Furthermore, although lawyers and activists may proclaim that human rights claims have universal standing, in reality some states have an interest in protecting these rights while others do not; and the idea of human rights rooted in a philosophical vision based on human equality is not universally shared. An alternative approach, for example, articulated by Mahathir bin

Mohamad, the former prime minister of Malaysia from 1981 to 2003, presented the notion of "Asian values" in opposition to universal human rights. The "Asian values" approach prioritized the rights of families and communities and social and political stability over the rights of individuals. Different philosophical positions and religious views thus continue to challenge the human rights claims now codified in international law.[9]

The Islamic Republic of Iran, for example, announced in 1984 that it would not recognize the validity of any internationally recognized human rights that were contrary to Islam.[10] In 1990, in Cairo, Egypt, the Organization of the Islamic Conferences adopted the "Cairo Declaration on Human Rights in Islam" (CDHRI). Viewed by many as an Islamic response to the UDHR, the document affirms inequalities in religion, gender, sexuality, and political rights claimed to reside in Islamic law and tradition. Some Islamic scholars claim that the UDHR reflects a secular and Judeo-Christian tradition, which violates Islamic law. The CDHRI empowers states and not individuals and establishes a subordinated status to religious minorities. The CDHRI, signed by forty-five states, has been strongly criticized by numerous human rights NGOs, including the International Commission of Jurists.[11]

In contrast to the CDHRI, international human rights law categorically reflects a "universalist" approach stating that "everyone" has rights to liberty, equal protection, an adequate standard of living, will not be subjected to torture, and so on. No concessions are made in these documents to culture deviations. While the limitations clauses in the UDHR acknowledge compromises on rights for "morality, public order and the general welfare," no such compromise is articulated for culture. The universalism of modern international human rights law is based on the basic assumption that human beings are equal in human dignity. The history of the twentieth century is ripe with examples of the denial of such dignity to certain groups: Jews, blacks, indigenous peoples, women, gays, and so on. The universality of human rights is based on the claim that no matter what culture or background or race or religion one inhabits, our common humanity is more important than any perceived difference. There is only one moral community, one humanity.[12]

The former president of the International Court of Justice (ICJ) Dame Rosalyn C. Higgins eloquently articulated this universalist position as follows:

> It is sometimes suggested that there can be no fully universal concept of human rights, for it is necessary to take into account the diverse cultures and political systems of the world. In my view this is a point advanced mostly by

states, and by liberal scholars anxious not to impose the Western view of things on others. It is rarely advanced by the oppressed, who are only too anxious to benefit from perceived universal standards. The non-universal, relativist view of human rights is in fact a very state-centered view and loses sight of the fact that human rights are human rights and not dependent on the fact that states, or groupings of states, may behave differently from each other so far as their politics, economic policy, and culture are concerned. I believe, profoundly, in the universality of the human spirit. Individuals everywhere want the same essential things: to have sufficient food and shelter; to be able to speak freely; to practice their own religion or to abstain from religious belief; to feel that their person is not threatened by the state; to know that they will not be tortured, or detained without charge, and that, if charged, they will have a fair trial. I believe there is nothing in these aspirations that is dependent upon culture, or religion, or stage of development. They are as keenly felt by the African tribesman as by the European city-dweller, by the inhabitant of a Latin American shanty-town as by the resident of a Manhattan apartment. [13]

Compliance Difficulties

There are three components to the UN human rights system: (1) norm creation and standard setting, (2) permanent institutions, and (3) compliance procedures. As already outlined above, the United Nations has been highly successful in norm creation in the drafting of an impressive body of human rights law, including the UDHR, CCPR, CESCR, Convention on the Elimination of All Forms of Discrimination against Women (CEDAW), and Convention on the Elimination of All Forms of Racial Discrimination (CERD). International law now includes a clear list of internationally affirmed human rights. The United Nations has acted as a legitimating institution, helping states reach a moral consensus on the validity of human rights claims to alleviate suffering. The goal of this standard setting is to establish rules and norms of right and wrong conduct across cultural, national, political, religious, and ideological lines.

The United Nations has also been successful in establishing permanent human rights institutions. There are the UN Charter–based bodies, including the Human Rights Council (HRC) and organizations created by the UN's principle organs, such as the Commission on the Status of Women. In addition, there are treaty-based bodies, including the committees established to monitor state compliance with specific human rights treaties. Thus, for example, the CEDAW committee monitors the compliance of the obligations under the CEDAW to protect and improve the status of women in each country that has ratified the treaty. Through these institutions the United Nations engages in a "constructive dialogue" with member states pushing for full compliance with human rights obligations. States are under a legal obligation to follow through on their word and, upon ratification of a human rights treaty, incorporate these norms into their domestic legal and political systems. The primary means through which global human rights are enforced is thus through national legal and judicial systems.[14]

When this dialogue fails, these UN institutions can turn to the "mobilization of shame" and through traditional and social media bring to the world's attention a particular state's human rights failure. Through public committee meetings, press briefings, investigations, and the passing of resolutions and declarations, these institutions can put pressure on states to change their policies. Most states are concerned about their reputation and want to be viewed as law-abiding, human rights upholding members in good standing in the global community. Many states thus respond to such soft pressure and act to bring their policies into compliance with global human rights standards.

Yet, unfortunately, when a state fails to comply and bring its practice into alignment with international human rights standards, the United Nations and the international community face difficulties in enforcing these global norms. The weakest component of the UN's human rights system is its lack of enforcement capability.

This breakdown in mechanisms to make human rights compulsory, and ensure state compliance, can be seen through the "three Ps"—politicization, priority conflicts, and power limitations.

Politicization

Politicization refers to the political use of human rights. Instead of human rights standards being applied evenhandedly toward friend and foe alike, these norms are used solely or primarily to punish enemies, while human rights abuses of geopolitical or ideological allies are minimized or ignored. This duplicity is often justified as necessary to advance a nation-state's economic and geopolitical interests around the world. Human rights thus become secondary to other allegedly more important parochially defined national interests.

From 1946 to 2006, the UN Commission on Human Rights was plagued by member states abusing the institution to advance political agendas. This meant that for decades when some of the most serious human rights abuses were taking place in Burundi, South Korea, Argentina, Guatemala, the Sudan, and elsewhere, these regimes were more or less exempt from scrutiny by the commission. These governments were protected by the major powers with Cold War power politics determining foreign policy decision making. This meant that the actions of some of the most brutal regimes in the last quarter of the twentieth century, such as Pol Pot's reign of terror in Cambodia and Idi Amin's atrocities in Uganda, received only minimal rebukes. This politicization of the UN Commission on Human Rights led to its irrelevance in international relations as nations felt justified in ignoring the views of such a hypocritical body. Finally in 2006, the member states of the UN abolished the commission and replaced it with the HRC.

Measures were established to hopefully limit the politicization of the work of the HRC. The HRC meets year-round in Geneva, has mechanisms to recall a member that is involved in human rights violations, and stiffened the criteria for membership. In addition, the HRC runs the Universal Periodic Review, under which the human rights records of all of the 193 members of the United Nations are analyzed every four years. No one is exempt, including the United States and the other great powers; every member state of the United Nations is called upon to explain and defend their human rights practices. While the HRC has no real enforcement power, the hope is that by bringing the legitimacy of the United Nations, and to an extent acting as the world's moral conscience, nation-states will feel global pressure to adhere to the human rights that each member had earlier pledged to uphold.

Politicization, unfortunately, infects most individual nation-states' decision making regarding foreign policy priorities. For example, in its foreign policy the United States has often politicized human rights, as seen in the Kirkpatrick, Clinton, and Bush doctrines. In the 1980s the Reagan administration pursued the Kirkpatrick Doctrine, named after former US ambassador to the United Nations, Jeane Kirkpatrick. This policy differentiated between dictatorships of the Left, which were labeled totalitarian, versus dictatorships of the Right, labeled authoritarian. Since the right-wing dictators were supportive of capitalist economics and fundamentally anticommunist, the United States downplayed or ignored the violent human rights abuses in these authoritarian states. But, on the other hand, the United States would heap scorn on any human rights abuses committed by totalitarian dictatorships of the Left, bringing these cases to the United Nations for denunciation and action. In the 1990s, the Clinton Doctrine also led to a double standard and hypocritical approach to human rights. During the Clinton years, the United States was reluctant to raise human rights criticisms of economically powerful or geopolitically important states, such as China, India, Indonesia, Brazil, Russia, Israel, and Saudi Arabia. But the smaller states and the enemies of the United States, including Burma/Myanmar, Guatemala, Peru, Cuba, Iran, Libya, and North Korea, were harshly criticized by the Clinton administration for human rights abuses. And finally, in the "war on terror," former president George W. Bush declared that "You are either with us or against us" in the battle against America's enemies. In practice, this Bush Doctrine meant overlooking the human rights abuses of those states, like Saudi Arabia, Egypt, Israel, Azerbaijan, Eritrea, Uzbekistan, Kuwait, and Uganda, as long as they all joined the US coalition to fight terrorism. The Reagan, Clinton, and Bush administrations never seemed to understand how hypocrisy and double standards on human rights undermines America's moral standing in the world community and often negates any legitimacy for a US voice on human rights.

Priority Conflicts

Civil, political, economic, social, and cultural human rights claims are embedded in the International Bill of Human Rights and other central human rights treaties. These human rights conventions often represent compromises and purposeful ambiguity that is open to multiple interpretations. This opacity and vagueness was seen as necessary to get nation-states with differing values and political systems to sign on to these human rights accords. Yet such haziness and imprecision has meant that it has been difficult for nation-states at the United Nations to agree on either human rights priorities or a road map for rights fulfillment. Instead, there has been conflict between nation-states over the prioritization of rights.

Northern, developed nation-states, for example, have primarily pursued a human rights agenda that prioritizes civil and political rights and traditional capitalist notions of private property and the free market. Economic and social rights are not a priority as seen by the fact that the United States has yet to ratify the CESCR. For the developing and less-developed countries, on the other hand, economic and social human rights are the clear priority as millions of their citizens suffer from a denial of basic needs, including food, water, education, and health care. To many in these countries, civil and political rights only make sense if at the same time efforts are made to fulfill economic and social rights as well. In the oft-quoted words of Leopold Senghor, the former president of Senegal: "[H]uman rights begin with breakfast."[15] The "right to vote" is only meaningful if the "right to food and water" is protected as well. Many developing nations thus call for the "right to development" to be included in the International Bill of Human Rights while developed states remain skeptical of such an approach.

These conflicts over human rights prioritization have weakened the implementation of a global human rights agenda. On the one hand, Northern developed nation-states pursue a liberal approach to human rights based on limiting state power in order to protect individual freedoms. On the other hand, the less-developed countries will often see human rights fulfillment contingent upon a strong, activist, interventionist state to provide economic development and basic needs to its citizens. The result is often deadlock and a lack of a unified global agenda on human rights fulfillment.

Power Limitations

Yet even when politicization is overcome and there is agreement among rich and poor states on the need for action regarding a particular human rights violation, what power does the United Nations possess to enforce this mandate? As noted above, the primary tool at the UN's disposal is the "mobilization of shame" and deterrence through exposure. With its ability to bring harsh policies into the public sphere, the international community, through IOs and NGOs, has been able to shine a bright light on human rights abuses. Since most states value their reputation, such exposure can help bring about change.

However, when this "constructive dialogue" and "soft" pressure fails, the United Nations has attempted to force change by bringing economic sanctions against the country violating human rights. Economic sanctions are based on a theory of relative depravation. By imposing significant economic costs, the target state is faced with a choice of either complying with these international human rights norms or suffering. The sanctions imposed against the former apartheid regime in South Africa, for example, are often pointed to as providing significant help to the African National Congress (ANC) in their ultimately successful effort to bring down that racist regime. However, sanctions are a blunt instrument and can often create unintended consequences on the target society such as hurting the most vulnerable members (children, the poor) who feel the brunt of the economic turmoil such harsh actions can create.

The United Nations and the international community have few instruments of power beyond "deterrence through exposure" and sanctions; and it is here that the limitations of power become apparent. There is little currently that the international community can do when a nation ignores the pleas and economic pressure of outsiders to correct their internal policies. In fact, member states of the United Nations are protected from outside interference by Article 2, Section 7 of the UN Charter, which denies the right of the United Nations to intervene in the internal affairs of sovereign states. The case studies in this book of the United States, Saudi Arabia, China, and key African states demonstrate the difficult challenge for IOs like the United Nations and for global citizens to devise means to effectively pressure states to change internal policies that violate fundamental human rights of their citizens.

And, as reviewed in the next section, human rights implementation and enforcement also hinges upon reconciling the perceived conflicts between group and individual rights embedded in international human rights law.

CONFLICTS BETWEEN RIGHTS

The fundamental premise behind the modern conception of human rights is the idea that individuals—not states, ethnic groups, religious communities, or other groupings—are morally primary. Rights and duties have a global scope and are not confined to geographical boundaries and nation-state's borders. Since it is the individual rather than the state that is endowed with human rights in a worldwide civil society, rights claims to alleviate suffering do not fundamentally hinge on state consent.

Yet individual human rights protection often depends on the establishment and defense of certain group rights, or "collective human rights." There is a symbiotic relationship between individual and group rights. Certain rights are collective in nature even though the individual is the ultimate beneficiary. This synergetic relationship is seen in the following assertions: the protection of minority cultures must be guaranteed if an individual is to enjoy his or her culture; freedom of association must be guaranteed for an individual to enjoy the right to join a trade union; the right of a religion to practice communal group worship is essential for an individual to enjoy his or her freedom of religion; and many of the world's indigenous peoples are threatened with extinction without special group rights and protections. In these instances, individual rights can only be fully realized through an understanding and protection of group rights.

In *Taking Suffering Seriously*, I explored in detail the danger of human rights focusing solely on the rights of the individual while ignoring group suffering. There is not a "level playing field" within most nation-states due largely to structural violence and a history of discrimination based on culture, race, class, gender, and sexuality. Individual human rights often are not that helpful when an entire group is in a structurally disadvantageous position. For example, as a group African Americans do not enjoy the same rights as whites in the United States. The statistics are well known. Despite the advances in civil rights legislation, the proportionate ratio of blacks to whites below the poverty line is still what it was in 1959, approximately three to one. Individual rights focus almost solely on the right of the individual African American to be upwardly mobile in a class-based society. Collective human rights (group rights) focus on the rights of the entire group of African Americans to have basic needs met, including health care, employment, and housing. Until these group rights are met, individual rights for African Americans too often remain empty promises. [16]

Examine the need for protecting the collective/group rights to culture and religion. The denial of cultural and religious rights in the former Yugoslavia in the 1990s led to ethnic cleansing and monstrous violence. Richard Falk, for example, has contended: "It is at least arguable that if the collective human rights of the Serb minorities in Croatia and Bosnia had been credibly protected, the horrifying Balkan ordeal [of the 1990s] . . . could have been avoided." [17] A regime of human rights protection must therefore include group protections based on culture, ethnicity/race, gender, and sexuality. For individual rights to be real for many oppressed groups in the world, group claims to justice must at the same time be addressed. Unfortunately, it often serves ruling elites and majority ethnic groups to ignore the group dimensions to human suffering.

However, this attempt to address group suffering, by calling for the protection of certain collective rights, should not mean a denial of individual human rights. In fact, a group is only worth defending if it respects the individual rights of each of its members and the human rights of individuals outside that group. Therefore, claims of a racist, skinhead community for autonomy would not be considered as in any way comparable to the claims of an oppressed ethnic or national minority for emancipation. Both individual and group rights are indispensable and essential. [18]

Yet how are conflicts between group and individual rights to be resolved? What if the claims of one group pose a fundamental challenge to individual dignity and rights? Religion and culture often provide a clear example of the conflicts between the rights affirmed in international law. On the one hand, the UDHR in Article 1 affirms that all human beings are equal in rights. On the other hand, Article 18 of the UDHR proclaims that everyone has a right to freedom of religion. But what if a religion or culture denies that women, nonbelievers, or homosexuals are equal in rights? It seems impossible in this case for both sets of rights (freedom of religion and human equality in rights) to be respected because the implementation of one human right requires the violation of another human right. Which right should trump? Who decides?

The right of a people to have their culture and religion protected is essential to preserve our multiethnic global community. Without such protections, indigenous languages, affirmative traditions, and constructive practices, for example, are threatened with extinction as more powerful communities and groups assert global dominion.[19] Yet in global politics today religion and culture too often trump other rights. While human rights abuses committed by states are now often criticized, abuses committed by religions or cultures are just as often tolerated and accepted as uncontestable. As reviewed below, according to Madhavi Sunder, religion and culture represent the "New Sovereignty."[20] While religious communities are not monolithic, and in fact basic doctrine remains highly contested, fundamentalist views when merged with elite interests often create an environment toxic to the rights of women, homosexuals, nonbelievers, and competing religions. Yet under the banners of "freedom of religion" and "the right to culture," misogynist and homophobic elites are able to consolidate state power. The case studies in chapter 3 on discrimination toward gays in Africa, and in chapter 4 on Saudi Arabia's discrimination toward women, are emblematic of this sacrifice of fundamental human rights in the name of elite interpretations of religion and culture.

Another example of the conflict between rights can be seen in the UN affirmation of both a people's right to self-determination and a people's right to development. In the name of self-determination, self-defense, and liberty, astounding quantities of military weapons are purchased around the world. However, these military expenditures often impede economic development. High levels of military spending can hinder economic growth and threaten financing for social welfare programs. These nations risk denying their people basic economic rights in the name of military preparedness to protect the right to self-determination and security. In this example there seems to be a direct trade-off between rights to subsistence and rights to security. Since both are legitimate rights claims, which one "trumps" the other? How is this to be determined? How does a society go about accommodating different values?[21]

To make human rights the "cornerstone" of ethical action demands that one think deeply about moral duty. Given the acute philosophical and political differences that exist around the world, it is astonishing that the international community was even able to draft an impressive corpus of international human rights law and create a viable global human rights regime. This human rights law is, of course, made by governments, often in consultation with NGOs, with the application of these norms often deemed too controversial by specific nations. To move beyond "lip service" to actual human rights protection depends upon addressing the conflicts between rights.

Article 29 (2) of the UDHR acknowledges the conflict between rights:

> In the exercise of his [or her] rights and freedoms, everyone shall be subject only to such limitations as are determined by law solely for the purpose of securing due recognition and respect for the rights and freedoms of others and of meeting the just requirements of morality, public order and the general welfare of a democratic society.

In other words, limitations of rights "determined by law" can be made in a democratic society in order to protect the overall rights and freedoms of the society. Liberal principles[22] of autonomy and self-governance legitimate a people's right, through democratic institutions, to determine the appropriate "trade-offs" between rights. Through democratic structures the government determines how to balance rights to life, security, liberty, and equality. As much as is possible, decisions regarding rights should be made at the state and local level. This idea corresponds to the principle of "subsidiarity"—that is, decisions and governance is to occur at the lowest possible and appropriate level.

But what are democratic states to do when the human rights of some conflict with those of others? Are there guidelines for determining the trade-offs between rights? One approach, for example, is to prioritize rights and attempt to calculate what combination of protections creates the best overall defense of human rights. For example, Henry Shue presents a compelling case for "basic rights" to security, subsistence, and liberty. He argues that all other human rights are contingent upon these rights being respected. All people are entitled to make minimum reasonable demands to have basic rights met. Shue writes, "Basic rights are the morality of the depths. They specify the line beneath which no one is to be allowed to sink."[23] From this perspective, governments have a duty to guarantee a minimum of liberty, security, and subsistence. For human beings to function in today's world, these basic rights must be respected.

Other scholars have pointed to different principles to guide nation-states in human rights policymaking. For example, Michael Freeman summarizes a more "utilitarian" approach: while the government should always try to respect all rights, "when some sacrifice is unavoidable, . . . distribute the sacrifice fairly." In this framework, the human rights of some are not sacrificed for the good of all; rather, everyone collectively experiences the denial of certain rights. While useful, this approach doesn't really help resolve conflicts between equally important rights.[24]

"Rule-utilitarianism" offers an approach to resolving these rights conflicts. "Rule-Utilitarianism says we ought to live by those rules that best promote the common good. It would tell us not to violate the human rights of one person to protect the human rights of others because this would violate a justified rule, and rule-Utilitarianism says that this should not be done even if, in the short run, it did more good than harm."[25] This approach represents a utilitarian calculation of rights outcomes; thus utilizing deontological principles for consequentialist objectives. Yet critics could argue that this approach (as all utilitarian theories) sacrifices the rights of some for the good of the community.

In the end, it appears that nation-states have a lot of leeway in international law to determine the appropriate trade-offs between human rights, which seems correct and in-line with democratic principles of self-governance. A people should be able to determine the proper balance between rights for their specific community and culture. But what happens when the national government goes too far in denying basic rights to liberty, security, and subsistence? How are claims of individual positive identity (minority rights, indigenous rights, LGBT rights, women's rights) and ecological balance (environmental rights) to be protected and secured when local cultures, religions, and governments deny the legitimacy of these foundational human rights? When global human rights norms and standards conflict with local governance and local religious prejudices, how are these conflicts to be resolved? How do we reconcile "norms and standards, which originate outside the will of democratic legislatures" with liberal principles of autonomy and self-governance?[26] Conceptions of "global citizenship" have been developed to articulate a framework for understanding how global human rights and duties intersect at the local level.

WHAT IS "GLOBAL CITIZENSHIP"?

The concepts of national citizenship and national sovereignty are in flux due to the challenges presented by global economic, environmental, and technological forces. A nationalist perspective alone is often unable to shed light on some of the world's most pressing problems. For example, terrorism, economic stagnation, national debt, environmental destruction, natural resource scarcity, migration, religious resurgence, and war can only be understood within a global framework. In fact, an expanding consensus has emerged regarding energy resources and the environment articulating that human survival depends upon designing global, not merely national, solutions on the basis of global environmental sustainability.

Citizenship has traditionally referred to the geographically bounded nation, and the rights, privileges, and responsibilities of the people born or migrated to that state. Yet today, due to economic and ethical interdependence, global rights, responsibilities, and privileges have emerged. The idea of "global citizenship" attempts to capture this new reality. However, notions of global citizenship are not new. In the economic realm, Adam Smith, Friedrich Hayek, Karl Marx, and Milton Friedman all argued for various forms of economic globalization embracing the idea of duties beyond borders. The World Trade Organization (WTO) today holds a particular model of neoliberal economic globalization and enforces these global trade rules, including rights for economic actors such as multinational corporations, in countries around the planet. In the moral, legal, and political realms, Montesquieu, Voltaire, Hume, Jefferson, and (most prominently) Kant argued for a concept of ethical cosmopolitanism framed around international law. Cosmopolitanism, the idea of a single moral community, is also the major premise behind the modern concept of universal human rights that transcend national and cultural boundaries.

Combining "global" and "citizenship" brings this idea of a single moral community into focus and creates a new framework for understanding the relationship between the individual, the state, and the entire planet. Globalism and nationalism can be mutually reinforcing and do not have to exist in tension and conflict. This is the view of Kwame Anthony Appiah, who argues for a "rooted" approach to cosmopolitanism that holds out the possibility that local loyalties and universal responsibilities can coexist harmoniously and facilitate dialogue and interaction across cultures. Appiah writes: "So cosmopolitanism shouldn't be seen as some exalted attainment: it begins with the simple idea that in the human community, as in national communities, we need to develop habits of coexistence: conversation in its older meaning, of living together, association."[27]

An ethic of global citizenship is based on the human rights idea that individuals—not states or other groupings—are morally primary. Human rights have a global scope, cannot be confined solely to compatriots, and extend beyond borders creating duties at the individual, nation-state, and global levels.[28] At the individual level, global citizenship reflects a person's individual awareness and acceptance of human rights duties at home and abroad. At the nation-state level, this awareness moves a country to accept human rights duties and act as good international citizens. And at the world level, global laws and institutions to promote and protect human rights are essential for the creation of a strong and viable human rights regime.

Individual Level

As Luis Cabrera notes, global citizenship as a global ethic at the individual level "focuses on transforming individual attitudes, rather than the institutions in which individuals are embedded." There are at least two broad ways of envisioning global citizenship as a global ethic: "what is" and "what ought to be." The first "what is" attempts to identify a global ethic through the recognition of a common moral core that exists across cultures and nations. For example, theologian Hans Küng examines the ethical agreements and commonalities in the world's major religions to determine a global ethic. Küng concludes that the global ethical core in these religions includes the golden rule (treating others as you would want to be treated), nonviolence, a just economic order, tolerance, and gender equality. Yet such commitments are clearly often at odds with the practices of these religions, and thus a very thin consensus on the meaning of this global ethical core seems to exist.[29]

An additional method for developing a common ethical core begins with what "ought" to be, rather than what "is." Richard Falk identifies a process he calls "globalization from below," which "consists of an array of transnational social forces animated by environmental concerns, human rights, hostility to patriarchy, and a vision of human community based on the unity of diverse cultures seeking an end to poverty, oppression, humiliation, and collective violence." Falk's ideal is the "citizen pilgrim," a practitioner of global citizenship committed to systemic transformational politics to alleviate suffering.[30]

Key at the individual level is awareness, consciousness of the necessity for a global way of thinking. Hans Schattle notes that some advocates for global citizenship worry that this consciousness is in short supply. Oscar Arias, Nobel Peace Prize laureate and former president of Costa Rica, lamented to Schattle: "I don't think people are ready to accept the term of a global citizen. People are not aware that we live in a more interdependent and interconnected world, a globalized world." Political consciousness for most individuals is tied to the nation-state, not global politics or world systems. Nationalist consciousness can unfortunately tend toward attitudes of exclusivity and difference over commonality and cooperation.[31]

The well-known NGO Oxfam defines a global citizen as someone who

- Is aware of the wider world and has a sense of their own role as a world citizen.
- Respects and values diversity.
- Has an understanding of how the world works.
- Is passionately committed to social justice.
- Participates in the community at a range of levels, from the local to the global.
- Works with others to make the world a more equitable and sustainable place.
- Takes responsibility for their actions.[32]

At the core of global citizenship at the individual level is awareness and consciousness of global interconnectedness, interdependence, and mutual vulnerability, which creates a deeper understanding of global rights, responsibilities, and duties. One gains not only new insights about one's self and one's country, but a deeper appreciation of others, which can bridge divides, overcome stereotypes, and open conversations based on mutual respect. Global citizenship at the individual level is thus based on recognition of the universality of the human experience and the common needs and challenges confronting all of humanity.[33]

Nation-State Level

The second level, good international citizenship, requires that leaders of nation-states work multilaterally to uphold principles and instruments of international law and human rights. Nation-states are thus expected to adhere to agreed upon norms of right and wrong conduct in their foreign policy.[34]

Then-senator Barack Obama projected this perspective before an audience of some two hundred thousand in Berlin on July 24, 2008, stating: "Tonight I speak to you not as a candidate for president, but as a citizen, a proud citizen of the United States, and a fellow citizen of the world." Obama continued:

> Yes, there have been differences between America and Europe. No doubt, there will be differences in the future. But the burdens of global citizenship continue to bind us together. A change of leadership in Washington will not lift this burden. In this new century, Americans and Europeans alike will be required to do more—not less. Partnership and cooperation among nations is not a choice; it is the one way, the only way, to protect our common security and advance our common humanity.[35]

After his election, President Obama returned to the language of world norms and common global principles in his 2009 speech in Egypt where he said:

> I've come here to Cairo to seek a new beginning between the United States and Muslims around the world, one based on mutual interest and mutual respect, and one based upon the truth that America and Islam are not exclusive and need not be in competition. *Instead, they overlap, and share common principles—principles of justice and progress; tolerance and the dignity of all human beings.*[36] (Emphasis added)

After the terrorist attacks in Paris in November 2015, President Obama stated:

> Once again we've seen an outrageous attempt to terrorize innocent civilians. This is an attack not just on Paris, it is an attack not just on the people of France, but this is an attack on all of humanity and the universal values we share.[37]

The president thus speaks of "universal values," describes himself as a "citizen of the world," and notes the overlapping principles of justice, tolerance, and dignity between the United States and others around the world. In essence, President Obama is referring to the ethics of interdependence found in the international human rights norms embraced by different religions and by individuals and states with divergent politics.

Despite the rhetorical commitment of government leaders to global human rights standards and international law, individual national interest for short-term advantage too often takes priority over acting as a good international citizen. Individuals who have embraced the ethics of interdependence can, of course, pressure their nation to uphold human rights commitments, but there are few interstate mechanisms or global institutions with effective power to compel these states to follow through on their word. Even though it has limited power, the UN human rights system (described above) has at least provided a vehicle for individuals and groups in civil society to press nations to act on global norms of right and wrong conduct. The challenge for human rights advocates is to demonstrate that a state's national interest is synonymous with acting as a good international citizen. In other words, to demonstrate that when states act as global international citizens they are also acting in their own national interest. When this is accomplished, the nation-state system becomes a means to achieve a universal framework of global citizenship.[38]

Individual citizens often pressure their nations to accept these global responsibilities and human rights duties, many of which have been articulated in international human rights law. For example, the UDHR proclaims that "[e]veryone is entitled to all the rights and freedoms set forth in this Declaration . . . [with] no distinction . . . made on the basis of the political, jurisdictional or international status of the country or territory to which a person belongs."[39] Clearly the rights and duties articulated in the UDHR, as well as the CCPR and the CESCR, are based upon an ethic of global citizenship, the idea that individuals—not states or other groupings—are morally primary. In 2016 there are 168 states parties to the CCPR, and 164 to the CESCR.[40] This high level of state ratification of these human rights treaties indicates that these nations have in theory accepted the importance of "good international citizenship" as the fundamental moral framework for organizing the international system.

The Scandinavian countries of Norway and Sweden are often raised as examples of nations embracing principles of "good international citizenship" in their foreign policy. These nations have often prioritized working multilaterally and cooperatively with the United Nations to achieve foreign policy goals. These nations are thus perceived as consistently acting in the long-term interests of the international system overall and for the protection of the human rights of individuals beyond their borders.

The foreign policy of the United States, on the other hand, has too often veered away from multilateralism. International law, including key human rights treaties and environmental accords, has not been a priority for the United States. For example, the United States has not ratified the following treaties: CESCR, CEDAW, Convention on the Rights of the Child (CRC), American Convention on Human Rights, and many others. This neglect continues. For example, in the 2012 foreign policy presidential debate between President Obama and Governor Romney, and in the 2016 early US presidential primary debates, human rights were barely mentioned and multilateral approaches to global issues were hardly discussed. Neither Democrats nor Republicans articulate "good international citizenship" as a central foreign policy goal.

US policy has too often been unilateral in implementation with a focus on short-term gain rather than long-term sustainability. The George W. Bush administration, for example, walked away from multilateral efforts to control global warming (Kyoto Protocol), eliminate land mines (Ottawa Treaty), prosecute war crimes and crimes against humanity (International Criminal Court), opposed a ban on nuclear weapons testing, opposed the enforcement mechanisms in the biological weapons treaty, and acted unilaterally in relation to Iran and North Korea.[41] Former Bush administration officials and conservative analysts argue that transnationalism and attempts to articulate mechanisms of global governance through human rights law prioritizes international legal norms "over" the US Constitution and US political processes inflicting "further harm on federalism and democratic accountability."[42]

In many respects, the rush to war in Iraq in March 2003 exemplified the unilateralist, neoconservative American approach to foreign policy. As David Reiff of the Council of Foreign Relations wrote:

> Here is the pessimists' case: Whatever else it may eventually accomplish, the war in Iraq seems to have put the final nail in the coffin of the dream of global citizenship that began more than half a century ago with the founding of the United Nations. Instead of a world order grounded, however imperfectly, in the idea of collective security, the war has made plain one of the central new realities of the post-9/11 world: The most powerful nation on earth, the United States of America, has decided to turn the international system on its head. . . . To say this is not to demand that people stop dreaming of a better world. Many of us may still aspire to the idea of global citizenship and long for the day when the words "international community" would not be cause for a bitter smile or a sardonic shrug. But it is important to understand how far we are from that day and to act accordingly.[43]

Global Level

Advocates for "institutional global citizenship" aim to construct global institutions to promote and protect peace and safeguard human rights. Cabrera argues that it "is not the fact of state interdependence . . . that give rise to individual duties to create or transform institutions. Rather, it is the potential for appropriately conceived institutions to better secure human rights—to provide comprehensive rights coverage and obtain compliance—that will generate such duties."[44] Functionalists[45] and federalists[46] have for decades argued for a global institutional approach to address the suffering caused to the vulnerable and impoverished groups, historically by imperialism and colonialism, and today by rapid economic globalization. The World Order Models Project, for example, in the 1980s and 1990s presented a "systems-transforming" alternative to the current statist world system based on norms of peace, economic well-being, social justice, ecological balance, and positive identity. Mainstreaming these normative values into the work of IOs and NGOs was seen as central to creating a world system that respects, protects, and fulfills individual and collective human rights.[47]

Cabrera summarizes the "need for rights-protecting institutions of fully global scope." In the absence of such institutions

> own-case and related biases will continue to affect judgments . . . about fair terms of global trade and investment, loan and aid conditionalities, responsibility to address climate change, and myriad other issues with implications for rights protections. The promotion of integration between states, and the creation of broader political communities, should provide some means for challenging such biases.[48]

For example, the Office of the High Commissioner for Human Rights in Geneva, Switzerland, is to act with neutrality in its judgments of human rights violations within UN member states; and the UN Environment Program is to act with scientific objectivity in its evaluation of the causes of global environmental dangers. These IOs are not burdened with individual nation-state biases and can focus on the survival needs of the global community overall. There is clearly a need for neutral global institutions working to respect, protect, and fulfill international human rights and environmental law.[49]

Regional and international organizations represent a multilevel system of global governance operating, as previously mentioned, on the principle of "subsidiarity"—that is, decisions and governance is to occur at the lowest possible and appropriate level. In other words, central authority should have a "subsidiary" function and perform only those tasks that can't be done more efficiently at the local level. [50]

But when "subsidiarity" disappoints and the state fails to act, human rights law has attempted to open up avenues for individuals to have standing within global accountability structures to challenge the actions of their home state. Through "individual complaint procedures" individuals who have exhausted all domestic remedies, and yet continue to suffer human rights abuses, can appeal directly to these international organizations and treaty bodies. These international bodies then serve as suprastate institutions to push individual nations to uphold their global commitments. Individual complaint procedures have been adopted by many of the treaty bodies monitoring human rights compliance, including the CCPR, CESCR, CEDAW, CERD, and others. These procedures are responsive to the victims of human rights abuse and provide a framework at the global institutional level to protect citizens' rights. [51]

Individuals and groups within civil society can now file complaints not only against their governments, but also toward the actions of multinational corporations, [52] international financial organizations, trade organizations, and powerful individuals. The impetus for these actions is the local community, the individual citizen. This "bottom-up" approach to global institution building has been surprisingly successful. In case after case, the voices of those denied basic human rights protection have been heard through these individual complaint mechanisms. [53]

WHAT IS A HUMAN RIGHTS "DUTY"?

A duty can be either a legal obligation (e.g., to pay taxes) or an ethical obligation (e.g., to tell the truth). In some respects these two types of duties are essentially different. A legal duty is usually enforced by an external authority, whereas an ethical duty is usually an internal, self-motivated obligation. Nevertheless, human rights duties often encompass both legal and ethical obligations. [54] Murder, for example, is both immoral and illegal. Acting to protect human rights in most cases will require ethical and legal action, whereas an abuse of human rights usually entails both illegal and immoral behavior. A "right" claimed by one person implies a "duty" by someone else to take or not take a particular action. [55]

The preamble to the African Charter on Human and Peoples' Rights, adopted in 1981 by the Organization of African Unity, is explicit: "Considering that the enjoyment of rights and freedoms also implies the performance of duties on the part of everyone."[56] And the American Declaration of the Rights and Duties of Man, adopted in 1948 by the Organization of American States, says in its Preamble: "The fulfillment of duty by each individual is a prerequisite to the rights of all. Rights and duties are interrelated in every social and political activity of man. While rights exalt individual liberty, duties express the dignity of that liberty. Duties of a juridical nature presuppose others of a moral nature which support them in principle and constitute their basis."[57]

As outlined above, through a lens of global citizenship, human rights duties exist on the following three levels:

1. Duties on individuals
2. Duties on nation-states
3. Duties on global institutions and organizations

Duties on Individuals

Individuals have duties to exercise rights responsibly; as well they have more general duties toward the community by respecting the rights, reputations, and freedom of others. An individual's personal right to "freedom" is qualified when it infringes on the rights of others. For example, as is widely acknowledged, the right to freedom of expression does not allow one to shout "fire" in a theater or to slander or libel someone else.[58] Freedom of the press does not allow journalists to promote violence (as occurred in Rwanda in 1994). There is thus an individual responsibility and duty in regard to the protection and fulfillment of human rights. In addition, certain groups of individuals—parents, doctors, police—have certain duties in relation to their exercise of power over others. Doctors have a legal duty not to participate directly or indirectly in torture.

Article 29(1) UDHR states: "*Everyone has duties to the community in which alone the free and full development of his personality is possible.*" The phrase "duties to the community" refers to both legal obligations (paying taxes, military service) and moral obligations (respect for the rights of others, nondiscrimination). These "duties to the community" are of central importance to the creation of a society that protects the individual human rights of its citizens. We all have these duties. While the government has the overall duty to create the laws and institutions to protect human rights, individuals have duties to uphold these rights. These general duties are elaborated in many other human rights treaties. For example, both the CCPR and the CESCR include the following: "Realizing that the individual, having duties to other individuals and to the community to which he belongs, is under a responsibility to strive for the promotion and observance of the rights recognized in the present Covenant."[59]

Duties on Nation-States

International human rights law has created certain duties on nation-states. A distinction has been drawn between "negative" duties (prohibitions against certain actions) and "positive" duties (requirements to act). For example, certain civil and political rights create negative duties on nation-states—not to torture, not to discriminate, and so on. Certain economic and social rights create positive duties on nation-states—to establish schools and an education system, create affordable housing, and so on. However, since most human rights require both positive and negative duties and measures, this distinction is now rarely made. For example, protection against torture and cruel and inhumane treatment requires not just a prohibition in law, but education and training of police and punishment of offenders.[60]

Yet "nation-states" do not "act." It is rather the individuals in positions of authority within states that act to promote, protect, and fulfill human rights law. It is thus these government officials who are required by law to uphold international human rights treaties. For each human right codified in international law, it is possible to identify a corresponding duty on individual government officials and authorities. It is not enough for these officials to merely announce support of a particular human right. The government must also enact legislation and procedures to give effect to the proclaimed rights. Laws must be in place therefore to protect free speech, the right to organize, and so on. It is the government official, for example, who is responsible to prevent torture and guarantee that the state bureaucracy treats people humanely.

Duties on Global Institutions and Organizations

Human rights duties extend beyond the individual and the nation-state to include IOs, NGOs, and other global actors, including multinational corporations. For example, under the leadership of former UN secretary-general Kofi

Annan, and former high commissioner of human rights Mary Robinson, efforts were made to mainstream human rights throughout the entire UN system. Annan appealed to all UN-specialized agencies and affiliated organizations to consider how their work was linked to the corpus of internationally recognized human rights in international law. In one of his last acts as secretary-general, Annan called for basing new reforms at the United Nations on three notions of freedom: freedom from want, freedom from fear, and freedom to live a life with dignity. [61]

Robinson explicitly linked human rights law to the development policies of IOs such as the World Bank and the World Trade Organization. She suggested that decisions as to appropriate priorities in the quest for development "can be made easier by using the language and standards of human rights and placing the decision-making process firmly in the context of the government's international human rights obligations. These obligations stretch also to international organizations." [62] The CESCR Committee furthermore asserted that development activities that do not contribute to respect for human rights are not worthy of the name. [63]

In addition, the CESCR Committee has explored the human rights implications of the policies of the World Bank and the International Monetary Fund (IMF). States reporting to the CESCR Committee are systematically asked whether they consider the human rights implications of their own voting behavior inside the World Bank and the IMF. In other words, the attempt is being made to hold these powerful IOs and international financial institutions accountable to fulfill human rights duties. [64]

This conception of human rights duties, embracing IOs, NGOs, and other global actors, was also articulated and deepened by the Commission on Global Governance in their influential 1995 report *Our Global Neighborhood*, which was discussed at the UN's fiftieth anniversary session. The commission proposed a common world ethic with international values including respect for life, liberty, justice, and equality. Their report became a central guide to further discussions on global governance and multilateral cooperation. The commission suggested that documents like the UDHR needed to be supplemented for two reasons.

> First, as presently conceived, rights are almost entirely defined in terms of the relationship between people and governments. We believe it is now important to begin to think of rights in broader terms by recognizing that governments are only one source of threats to human rights and, at the same time, that more and more often, government action alone will not be sufficient to protect many

human rights. This means that all citizens, as individuals and as members of different private groups and associations, should accept the obligation to recognize and help protect the rights of others.

Second, rights need to be joined with responsibilities. The tendency to emphasize rights while forgetting responsibilities has deleterious consequences. Over the long run, rights can only be preserved if they are exercised responsibly and with due respect for the reciprocal rights of others.[65]

A HUMAN RIGHTS THRESHOLD

The idea of a "threshold effect" has been utilized in psychology, physics, management, and many other fields of study as well. In medicine a threshold is passed when a disease or syndrome appears without warning after a long period of inconspicuous and unobtrusive growth. Or after years of mismanagement and overextension in the financial and banking sector, a threshold will be passed and investor confidence will quickly dissipate. A threshold effect, in other words, refers to a "radical change of state within a system whether a physical system like the human body or an abstract (conceptual) system such as an economy that often manifests suddenly when a critical limit is crossed."[66]

Urgent action is often required when such a threshold is passed. When a disease passes a threshold and suddenly appears, the medical community will mobilize and attempt to stem the new threat's harm to humans. When a threshold is passed in the financial community leading to a banking crisis, the governments of the world mobilize to prevent a collapse of the world's banks.

Applying the "threshold effect" to human rights violations helps sort out the duties for global citizens. When a "radical change of state" within a community, nation, or region has occurred and the most fundamental rights are violated, a "human rights threshold" has been passed requiring urgent action. This threshold framework provides a way to prioritize and focus on the most pressing human rights duties.

Human rights abuses occur daily in every society and all deserve amelioration. Yet when the level of suffering passes a significant "threshold" (or benchmark), certain duties should lock in for global citizens at the local, national, and world levels. What are the criteria to determine that this threshold has been achieved?

Guidelines for determining when a "human rights threshold" has been surpassed, and local, national, and global human rights duties become essential, include both "qualifying criteria" and "implementing criteria." Qualifying criteria refer to guidelines to determine if the nature of the human rights violation has surpassed the benchmark when human rights duties would emerge. Implementing criteria are linked to the absolute necessity for outsiders to follow the lead of local, indigenous leaders. Human rights duties should "lock in" when there is a combination of (a) any one of the four qualifying criteria with (b) local, indigenous leadership in control—that is, the implementing criteria. Specifically this criteria can be defined as follows:

1. Qualifying Criteria

    - The widespread scale of the suffering.
    - The severe nature of the violation creating extreme human deprivation.
    - The radical departure and clear violation of established global human rights norms and laws.
    - The growing mutation and metastasizing of the violations and the suffering of victims across a nation, region, or the globe.

2. Implementing Criteria

    - The articulation of a strategy of change by the victims; listening to the victims' voices and accepting their leadership.

Qualifying Criteria

The Widespread Scale of the Suffering

When the scale of human suffering becomes widespread throughout a nation or region, a human rights threshold is surpassed, and the need for action becomes palpable. At a certain point, for example, it was unbearable for global citizens to ignore the crimes of the former apartheid government in South Africa due to the widespread scale of the suffering inflicted on the nation's black community. The brutality of apartheid shocked the peoples of the world, a threshold was surpassed, and mobilizations occurred at the local, national, and global levels to isolate the regime and end a system of governance premised on racial discrimination. It is impossible for global citizens at the local, national, and world levels to ignore such vast levels of human suffering.

The Severe Nature of the Violation

All human rights violations causing pain and suffering should be challenged and hopefully ameliorated. But since it is impossible to act everywhere, it is imperative that a method be developed to prioritize and focus attention and action on the most pressing cases. The "human rights threshold" criteria would thus apply only to the most grave and severe situations of abuse. And the serious nature of these violations can be shocking. For example, the rabid homophobia throughout parts of Africa, supported by major political and religious leaders, has created a climate of terror for gay men, who are intimidated, assaulted, and in some cases killed due to their sexuality. Rights to security and freedom are denied to the LGBT community throughout the continent. These human rights violations are extreme and the human rights threshold for effective action has thus been surpassed.

The Radical Departure from Human Rights Norms and Laws

Since World War II, the global community has codified some basic norms of behavior in international human rights law. The nations and peoples of the world have overwhelmingly approved the International Bill of Human Rights (UDHR, CCPR, and the CESCR). Additional human rights treaties binding the peoples of the world include the rights of women, children, the disabled, and migrant workers. The world's nations and peoples have also agreed to prohibit torture and cruel and unusual punishment, and to abolish genocide and apartheid. These globally affirmed documents provide both the moral and legal criteria to determine the content of human rights violations. They provide a yardstick to evaluate whether practices of individuals, states, and global actors infringe on human dignity. When these universally agreed upon norms and laws are massively ignored, leading to widespread suffering, the human rights threshold has been surpassed.

The Growing Mutation and Metastasizing of the Violations

Harmful diseases require swift and sure responses. To ameliorate suffering, radical measures, both traditional and modern, are often taken when cancer cells metastasize and grow inside the body. When the HIV virus is detected, treatments and drug regimens are administered to contain the disease and educational measures are enacted to prevent the virus from spreading to others. When Ebola is identified, the World Health Organization and Doctors Without Borders mobilize to prevent the disease from spreading. The human rights threshold is similarly designed to mobilize action and administer treatments to prevent human suffering from mutating and metastasizing further into the national and global body politic. When certain violations continue to grow or spread, containment actions become imperative. Coal burning on a global scale is jeopardizing the right to health for millions around the world. An individual nation may have the sovereign right legally to pursue a "dirty" energy policy, but the ethical implications of these actions affect others outside its borders. A human rights threshold is thus passed when the violations mutate and grow beyond the control of an individual state.

Implementing Criteria

Listening to the Voices of the Victims and Following Their Leadership

When a human rights threshold is surpassed, any action taken in response to the gross violations of human rights must be led by the victims and the local organizations on the ground fighting and organizing for change. The voices of the victims must be heard and local leadership followed. Again the example of the struggle against apartheid in South Africa is illustrative. The ANC provided the leadership to the campaign to end apartheid. Outside the country, the most effective means to assist this effort to end apartheid was to work with the ANC and follow their leadership. This "inside-outside" strategy is essential. It is counterproductive for outsiders to "preach" human rights to a foreign community. On the other hand, it can be productive for outsiders to listen to the victims and follow their lead. The universal framework of global human rights and duties can thus be responsive to cultural rights of autonomy and self-determination.

The next four chapters document clear cases where the human rights threshold has been surpassed and human rights duties should "lock in" at the individual, nation-state, and global levels. In each of these cases we find widespread suffering, severe violations leading to extreme human deprivation, radical violations of international human rights law, a growing metastasizing of the violations, and victims leading efforts for change. These four case studies are as follows:

- Chapter 2: Mass Incarceration in the United States
- Chapter 3: Homophobia and Anti-Gay Violence in Africa
- Chapter 4: Saudi Arabia and the Rights of Women

- Chapter 5: Environmental Rights in China

DISCUSSION QUESTIONS

1. Human rights are defined in this chapter as claims on others for a certain type of treatment fundamentally linked to the alleviation of suffering. How would you define suffering? Physical pain? Mental stress? Are there parameters to a definition of suffering that would help clarify and legitimate certain human rights claims?

2. As an individual, do you feel bound by certain human rights duties? Do these duties for you extend beyond family and nation to include the alleviation of suffering abroad?

3. If a conflict emerges between a religious belief and an internationally recognized human right codified in international law, which norm should prevail? Why?

4. Is it possible to hold multinational corporations and international financial institutions to human rights standards? How would this be accomplished?

5. The term "responsible sovereignty" has been used to indicate a "bounding" of sovereign power to act "responsibly" and uphold international human rights norms and standards. In what ways has "responsible sovereignty" eclipsed "absolute sovereignty" in international relations? In what ways have the sovereign power of states been affected by the global human rights regime that has consolidated since World War II?

6. If the forces eroding national sovereignty and empowering interconnectedness continue, is there a further stage of human rights law and standards? If so, what might it look like?

Chapter Two

Mass Incarceration in the United States

According to the latest data available from the US Bureau of Justice Statistics (BJS), the total US correctional population (individuals on probation, parole, in prison or jail) was approximately 6.851 million people in 2014, larger than the individual population of thirty-seven US states. This was the equivalent of about 1 in 36 US adults, or 2.8 percent of the adult resident population.[1] The BJS reported that black males were 6 times and Hispanic males 2.5 times more likely to be imprisoned than white males. In fact, black males ages eighteen to nineteen were almost 9.5 times more likely than white males of the same age group to be in prison.[2] Sociologist Becky Pettit finds that 37 percent of young black males ages twenty to thirty-four without a high school diploma were in prison or jail on any given day in 2008.[3]

An explosion of imprisonment occurred in the United States between 1975 and 2009, with incarceration rates growing an average of 4.7 percent annually. By 2009 there were 2.3 million people housed in US prisons and jails, a figure that has remained relatively stable to today. The BJS reports that in 2012 there were around 2.2 million prisoners, including 1.25 million incarcerated in state prisons, 217,800 in federal prisons, and 744,500 in local jails.[4] The US incarceration rate is now about 768 per 100,000 American citizens.[5]

Between 1980 and 2010, the federal prison system experienced an eightfold increase in its prison population. Inmates under the jurisdiction of the Federal Bureau of Prisons went from 24,000 in 1980, to 145,416 in 2000, to roughly 210,000 in 2010. This rate of growth exceeded that of the US residence population overall. While in 1980 there were 11 federal prison inmates per 100,000, by 2010 this rate was 67 per 100,000.[6]

The United States is currently the world's leader in incarceration. The United States outranks every other country for which there is data on incarceration, including Russia, Rwanda, China, and Iran. The International Centre for Prison Studies at the University of Essex collects and compares incarceration rates from around the world. These statistics reveal that the United States locks up a higher fraction of its population than any other advanced industrialized country. In fact, no other industrialized country comes close to the high US rate. The total incarceration rates per 100,000 citizens between 2008 and 2011 in leading developed states were as follows: United States 743; Spain 159; United Kingdom 152; Portugal 116; Italy 111; France 102; Germany 85; Sweden 78; Denmark 74; Finland 59. Even US neighbors Canada and Mexico have much lower incarceration rates. The United States locks up its citizens 6.4 times that of Canada and 3.7 times that of Mexico.[7]

Michelle Alexander points out that the most striking feature of mass incarceration in the United States is its racial dimension:

> No country in the world imprisons so many of its racial or ethnic minorities. The United States imprisons a larger percentage of its black population than South Africa did at the height of apartheid. In Washington, D.C., our nation's capital, it is estimated that three out of four young black men (and nearly all those in the poorest neighborhoods) can expect to serve time in prison. Similar rates can be found in black communities across America.[8]

The statistics regarding the racial dimension to US incarceration rates are startling:

- While representing approximately 11 percent of the general adult population in 2004, African Americans constituted close to 50 percent of state and federal prisoners.[9]
- While representing approximately 13 percent of the general adult population in 2004, Hispanics constituted around 20 percent of state and 25 percent of federal prison inmates.[10]
- If present trends continue, one in three African American men will serve time in prison. More black men are imprisoned today than at any other point in our nation's history.[11]

- This mass incarceration of people of color, according to Alexander, "is a big part of the reason that a black child born today is less likely to be raised by both parents than a black child born during slavery."[12]
- The Pew Research Center on the States reports that while one in one hundred American men is behind bars, the number for African American men is one in nine. [13]
- According to Pettit, while 5 percent of white men born between 1975 and 1979 spent a year in prison before reaching age thirty-five, the corresponding figure for black men born in the same period is an astounding 28 percent. "The risks of spending time in prison for this birth cohort were significantly higher among high school dropouts: 28 percent of white and 68 percent of black dropouts had spent at least a year in prison by 2009."[14]
- Black men were more likely to go to prison than to complete college. Pettit writes: "Spending time in prison has become more common than completing a four-year college degree or military service among young black men. And young, black, male high school dropouts are more likely to spend at least a year in prison than they are to get married. In short, among low-skill black men, spending time in prison has become a normative life event, furthering their segregation from mainstream society."[15] As widely reported, by 2000 more African American men were in jail and prison than were in higher education. [16]
- Julia Sudbury documents the impact on women. "Whereas in 1970 there were 5,600 incarcerated women, by June 2001, 161,200 women were held in U.S. prisons and jails, representing a staggering 2,800 percent increase." Although making up only 9 percent of those incarcerated nationally, "the rate of population growth for incarcerated women outstrips that of men."[17]
- During the late twentieth century, African American women were incarcerated at rates six to seven times those of white women, representing the fastest growing incarceration rates. Between 1990 and 2000, the number of women prisoners more than doubled. "Despite comparable female populations, the number of women incarcerated in the United States is ten times the total number of women incarcerated in Western European countries."[18]

As this chapter will demonstrate, the "human rights threshold" criteria explored in chapter 1 have been surpassed with the mass incarceration of African Americans in the United States. The targeting of young black males has led to severe violations of basic human rights norms and laws and has metastasized into America's most severe human rights crisis. This wide- spread suffering has directly impacted millions of families throughout the entire African American community. Community leaders have mobilized to articulate changes in public policy, judicial procedures, and legal reforms to bring an end to this system of racially based injustice.

HOW DID WE GET HERE?

To many Americans the explosion in our prison population is thought to have come about due to an increase in crime and deviant behavior often linked to either drug use or illegal immigration. Throughout the 1980s and 1990s politicians and the media fed this message and contributed to a perception of a need for "law and order." Fighting crime overtook other social issues (unemployment, poverty, environmental protection, and so on) as the government's highest priority. However, as Ruth Wilson Gilmore notes, "by the time the great prison roundups began, crime had started to go down."[19]

In fact, some criminologists argue that the increase in crime rates reported by the FBI were illusory. What occurred was that more local police depart- ments were reporting to the FBI and participating in the data collection effort. As a result, the numbers of crimes being reported was growing, not necessarily because more crime was being committed but that the agencies were reporting them for the first time. In addition, victims of certain catego- ries of crimes (for example, sexual assault) were more likely than before to actually report the crime, and the police were more likely to include these acts as actual offenses. While certain violent crimes, including homicides, were increasing, the "overall increases in crime, in particular property crime and poorly reported violent crimes, were certainly overstated by improve- ments in coverage of the UCR [FBI Uniform Crime Report] statistics."[20]

But what about the so-called drug epidemic? Didn't the police crackdown on the sale and use of illegal substances contribute to a decline in crime? After the widening growth in the use of drugs in the early 1970s, it is certain- ly true that the government launched a rancorous "War on Drugs." Drug arrests leading to incarceration in state and federal prisons surged 975 per- cent between 1982 and 1999. Americans were told drug use was "exploding" in the minority communities in the 1980s leading to gang violence and ram- pant drug dealing. The claim was that such conditions demanded a strong police response to regain control and stop the violence.[21]

Yet Gilmore notes that according to BJS statistics, "illegal drug use among all kinds of people throughout the United States declined drastically starting in the mid 1970s."[22] Despite this decline in drug use, the media continued to sensationalize the issue capitalizing on public fears of a crack epidemic flowing out of the inner city and into white middle-class America. As a result, Andrew Black writes that "between 1985 and 1989, the percentage of Americans who believed that drugs were the most serious problem facing the nation rose from 2% to 38%."[23]

Even incidents of property crime had peaked in 1980, pushing down the overall crime rate. The economic boom of the Clinton years in the 1990s was accompanied with annual reports on the long-term drops in crime. If crime rates didn't really go up, why did the "crackdown" continue so rapaciously? What was being controlled? Who was being arrested? What was really happening? Why have we become the world's leader in incarceration? To address these questions it is necessary to examine the impact of poverty, race, and politics on the formulation of the public policies that came to be known as the "War on Drugs" and the "War on Crime." The exploration of these issues in this chapter is thus organized as follows:

1. Poverty and Economic Globalization
2. Race and the New Jim Crow
3. Politics and the War on Drugs
4. Policy and the War on Crime

POVERTY AND ECONOMIC GLOBALIZATION

The explosion of arrests and the massive incarceration of minorities occurred at a time when the United States was forced to restructure its economy due to the disruptive impact of economic globalization. As economic globalization deepened in the late twentieth century, the US economy seemed to work against the interests of the bottom third of the population. From the 1980s to 2016 the following trends in human development in the United States took place during the period of mass incarceration.[24]

1980s: According to US government statistics, the US standard of living for the middle class and poor declined from the mid-1970s through the 1980s and it became harder to climb out of poverty. The Census Bureau reported that the percentage of full-time workers with low earnings grew sharply in the 1980s. The bureau defined low earnings as $12,195 per year, expressed in

1990 dollars (thus adjusted for inflation). At the end of the 1970s, 12.1 percent of all full-time employees earned below the equivalent of $12,195; by 1990 that figure had risen to 18 percent.[25]

The number of American children living in poverty grew by more than 1 million during the 1980s, and in 1989 about 18 percent of children in the United States lived in families with incomes below the federal poverty line, including 39.8 percent of all African American children, 38.8 percent of Native American children, 32.2 percent of Hispanic children, 17.1 percent of Asian American children, and 12.5 percent of Caucasian children.[26]

1990s: The real (inflation-adjusted) wage rates for the majority of workers in the vast middle class eroded in the 1990s with the median worker's wage falling 5 percent between 1989 and 1997.[27] According to the Congressional Budget Office, the gap between the rich and the poor more than doubled from 1979 to 2000. By 2000, the richest 1 percent of US citizens had more money to spend after taxes than the entire bottom 40 percent of the population.[28]

Economic inequality in the United States skyrocketed in the 1990s. The proportion of the nation's income received by the poorest fifth of US families declined dramatically, while the proportion held by the richest families increased. The respected Gini Index calculates that economic inequality in the United States worsened dramatically from 1980 to the beginning of the new century. Consider that in 1980 the top 5 percent of all families received 14.6 percent of the nation's aggregate income. By 2001, this elite group of 5 percent was getting 21 percent of all income. On the other side, the already small share of the nation's income going to the bottom fifth of families fell by 20.8 percent during these years.[29]

2000s: These trends have continued in the first two decades of the twenty-first century. According to the 2008–2009 *American Human Development Report*, the United States ranked forty-second in global life expectancy and first among the world's twenty-five richest countries in the percentage of children living in poverty.[30] In addition, fundamental deprivations in food and housing are far too prevalent. Over the course of a year, at least 1.35 million children in the United States are, at some point, homeless. Sarah Burd-Sharps, Kristen Lewis, and Eduardo Borges Martins summarize: "More families with children are homeless today than at any time since the Great Depression. For the hungry and homeless, the American Dream is especially elusive. It is hard to dream on an empty stomach, with no roof over your head or living in fear of violence."[31]

The typical American household by 2014 had been getting much, much poorer. Whereas in 2003 the inflation-adjusted net worth for the typical household was $87,992, by 2013 it was only $56,335, or a 36 percent decline. This figure represents the median point in wealth distribution with an equal number of households whose worth is higher and lower.[32] Joseph Stiglitz reported that median incomes in 2014 were lower than they were a quarter century earlier and that almost a quarter of American children younger than five lived in poverty. Furthermore, the incomes of those with only a high school diploma in 2014 declined by 13 percent over the previous thirty-five years.[33] And Thomas Piketty dramatically documents the magnitude of inequality in the United States with respect to labor and capital. Looking to the future, Piketty projects that the United States "may set a new record around 2030 if inequality of income from labor . . . continue[s] to increase as they have done in recent decades. The top decile would then claim about 60 percent of national income, while the bottom half would get barely 15 percent."[34]

For the past four decades the United States has faced high levels of unemployment, homelessness, and drug addiction. To address these rising groups of undesirables the government shifted its positions on both welfare and prisons. On the one hand, the triumph of neoliberal economics led to the privatization of public goods and the unraveling of welfare protections financed by the state. Big government was seen as part of the problem and thus we witnessed a rollback of basic social protections for the poor and vulnerable. On the other hand, in order to address the social unraveling accompanying the new dire economic conditions, there was a need to increase the capacity of our policing and prisons. Thus, while social service programs were cut, the government was willing to spend lavishly to enhance the penal system.

The increase in incarceration rates coincided with the increasingly dire economic conditions faced by most Americans. There is potentially a relatively straightforward connection between these labor market changes and the increase in incarceration. If one's opportunities for legitimate advancement in the formal economy are weak, or nonexistent, then criminal income-generating prospects become more appealing. As Raphael and Stoll summarize: "[T]he likelihood of engaging in criminal activity (or stated in the language of modern microeconomics, supplying one's time to criminal pursuits) should increase as potential earnings in legitimate employment decline."[35]

Academic studies present considerable evidence that higher unemployment leads to an increase in property crimes; with the opposite true as well, with property crime decreasing with increasing wages. It seems axiomatic that if young people see they can earn more money selling drugs than working in a legitimate job, they will more likely engage in criminal activity.[36]

Yet instead of mobilizing resources to address job creation, poverty prevention, affordable housing, and other programs to protect the vulnerable, the United States went in the opposite direction based upon the idea of a limited government. Welfare and social protections were claimed to create "dependency" by the poor on the government. Critics alleged that social welfare programs, instead of helping individuals rise out of poverty, created disincentives to find work. Unemployment was viewed as a personal failure and not a systemic weakness of the market economy. Citizens were expected to assume individual responsibility and not rely on universal rights and state duties to protect them. This conservative ideology led to a major push to remove or redesign existing welfare programs.

One of the most dramatic examples of the rollback in social protections for the vulnerable occurred in 1996 with the enactment of the Personal Responsibility and Work Opportunity Reconciliation Act (PRWORA).[37] President Clinton designed this statute to "end welfare as we know it." The PRWORA abolished the Aid to Families with Dependent Children (AFDC) program, a federal entitlement to subsistence aid for eligible families. To replace AFDC, PRWORA established the Temporary Assistance to Needy Families (TANF) program, which neither guaranteed assistance to needy families nor required the states to do so. The overall purpose of PRWORA was not to reduce poverty, but rather to end the alleged dependency of families on public aid. Those most negatively affected were poor women and children, indigent elderly, and immigrants.[38]

Severe limitations on the rights of the poor are codified in PRWORA. For example, an examination of this radical restructuring of US social welfare policy in relation to the legal obligations found in the CESCR is instructive. Many of the provisions of PRWORA are in violation of the legal duties of states articulated in the CESCR. While the United States has not ratified this treaty, many of the features of CESCR are now considered emerging customary international law principles. Examine the following:

- Benefits under PRWORA are not guaranteed to all eligible recipients, but limited by the number of applicants and the amount of appropriation.

While this limitation was imposed, the United States continued to spend billions of dollars on esoteric military projects (such as the costly and unreliable missile defense system).[39] This is a clear violation of Article 2.1 of the CESCR, which calls on states to utilize the "maximum of its available resources" to progressively achieve the full realization of the economic and social rights of its citizens. It is also a violation of Article 10, which calls for the "widest possible protection and assistance" for the family, particularly the "care and education of dependent children," and Article 11, which recognizes the right of everyone to an adequate standard of living including "adequate food, clothing and housing, and to the continuous improvement of living conditions."

- Individual states could interpret PRWORA as requiring recipients to accept whatever job is offered them and canceling their benefits if they decline. This is a clear violation of Article 6.1 of the CESCR, which recognizes the right "of everyone to the opportunity to gain his [or her] living by work which he [or she] freely chooses or accepts." Article 6.2 requires state parties to take steps including "technical and vocational guidance and training programs, policies and techniques to achieve steady economic, social and cultural development and full and productive employment under conditions safeguarding fundamental political and economic freedoms to the individual."

- PRWORA imposes a five-year limit on benefits for most recipients and is a deliberate retreat from a legal guarantee of subsistence benefits to families in need. This is a clear violation of Articles 2.1, the commitment to seek to achieve progressively "the full realization of the rights recognized in the present Covenant by all appropriate means," and 5.2, limiting derogations from the Covenant.

There is a popular mistaken belief in the success of these Clinton welfare reform policies. Following implementation of these reforms, there was a drop in the numbers of families on welfare, an increased supply of single mothers in the labor force, and a decline in child poverty. The robust economy of the 1990s contributed significantly to these improvements. But these trends did not last. The labor supply of less-educated single mothers has returned to earlier levels; and poverty and births outside of marriage rebounded. Pushing the poor off welfare by replacing cash assistance with limited state-run programs has hurt the poorest of the poor. As a result, the poorest Americans

have a limited safety net to help them through the Great Recession that
continues from 2008 to today.[40]

The denial of cash assistance to low-income families with children,
through a federal entitlement program, is popular with many Americans. This
pervasive view is often based on the belief that such aid to the poor encour-
ages dependency and bad behavior. Yet according to reports from MIT and
the World Bank, there is no evidence to support this conclusion. In fact, these
reports suggest that cash assistance can be of great assistance to the poor. The
MIT study examined seven cash-transfer programs around the world and
found "no systematic evidence that cash transfer programs discourage work."
The World Bank found that, contrary to popular myth, the poor did not use
cash transfers for things like alcohol and tobacco. Furthermore, US academic
studies demonstrate that welfare payments did not increase single mother-
hood (and ending welfare did not reduce it). On the other hand, welfare
provides significant benefits. These studies show that welfare cash aid to
help poor children improves a child's longevity, education, nutritional status,
and eventual income in adulthood.[41]

Article 25(1) of the UDHR declares: "Everyone has the right to a standard
of living adequate for the health and well-being of himself and of his family,
including food, clothing, housing and medical care and necessary social services, and the right to security in the event of unemployment, sickness,
disability, widowhood, old age or other lack of livelihood in circumstances
beyond his control." The respect for human dignity thus includes a minimum
level of subsistence necessary to support the continuation of human life at a
decent level. The US government does not accept the *legal* duty to guarantee
citizen access to basic subsistence. The United States thus limits its responsibility to provide sufficient methods and resources so that all citizens are
guaranteed the right to subsistence. As a result, when economic conditions
worsen, the poor are often left to fend for themselves. For example, while
Clinton talked about "moving people from welfare to work," PRWORA had
"absolutely no jobs component."[42]

The economic decline of America since the 1970s does not in itself explain the mass incarceration that took place at the same time. Yet it is impossible to understand why the mass arrests took place without also understanding these underlying conditions that created insecurity, misery, and suffering
for millions of Americans. The moral philosophy of radical individualism
stands behind both the severe cutting of welfare programs and the expansion
of our nation's prisons. Many Americans became convinced that the severe

poverty impacting millions was a consequence of individual failure. "Welfare queens" and irresponsible unwed mothers, the "undeserving poor," were often viewed as a moral virus on society. And, of course, racial bias emerged as welfare was too often falsely perceived by many whites as primarily benefiting blacks and working against the work ethic and family values. Conservative commentators thus argued that the "culture of dependency" had to be severed. [43]

To be clear: there is no preordained systemic need for capitalism to destroy social welfare programs and create what has been termed a "prison-industrial complex." Other paths were open and remain feasible. The decisions to create social insecurity and mass incarceration were instead the product of political decision making by individuals in positions of authority and power.

RACE AND THE NEW JIM CROW

Most white US citizens probably hope that "justice is blind" and that the rules and laws of society are applied more or less fairly with "no one above the law." Such sentiment would argue against either a class or racial dimension to incarceration. The legitimacy of the judicial system overall is often not questioned by white Americans. Crime is often seen as a normal part of society with some delinquents unfortunately resorting to criminality.

But this is too facile and misleading as it ignores the impact of America's ugly racial history on current punitive policies toward people of color and the severity and cruelty of our criminal justice system. Racial and class bias in sentencing exists, and there is disproportionate policing and punitive measures directed at the poor African American community. In fact, it is only through the prism of race that it is possible to understand how it is that the United States became the leading incarcerator among the world's democracies.

"Old-fashion" racism is not at work here. As Alexander notes, "politicians and law enforcement officials today rarely endorse racially biased practices, and most of them fiercely condemn racial discrimination of any kind." [44] Notorious earlier forms of racial discrimination are now seen as an affront to our new ethic of colorblindness. Yet *de jure* legal equality and new social norms of etiquette have, unfortunately, not created *de facto* equality in the administration of the criminal justice system in America. Race to a large degree still determines who gets arrested and who doesn't.

Alexander explains how a "formally colorblind criminal justice system" achieves racially discriminatory results. The first step is to give law enforcement officials "extraordinary discretion regarding whom to stop, search, arrest, and charge for drug offenses, thus ensuring that conscious and unconscious racial beliefs and stereotypes will be given free rein." This unbridled discretion has (inevitably) created huge racial disparities in arrests. The second step, according to Alexander, is to "[c]lose the courthouse doors" to any claims by defendants that the criminal justice system operates in a racially discriminatory fashion. And the clincher: "Demand that anyone who wants to challenge racial bias in the system offer, in advance, clear proof that the racial disparities are the product of intentional racial discrimination—i.e., the work of a bigot." In an era of "colorblindness" this evidence will almost never be available.[45]

For example, despite the colorblind rhetoric, the design of the War on Drugs effectively guaranteed that those swept up and arrested were largely black and brown.[46] Yet defenders of the current system would insist that this is a result of crime rates, not discrimination. Their claim is that the violent crime rates, as a product of the drug culture, in African American communities is the reason so many black men are in jail. This is not true. Alexander and others have documented how violent crime rates are not responsible for mass incarceration. In fact, violent crime rates have fluctuated and often have little relationship to incarceration rates.[47]

What has occurred is unfortunately distressingly simple. As Alexander summarizes: "What is painfully obvious when one steps back from individual cases and specific policies is that the system of mass incarceration operates with stunning efficiency to sweep people of color off the streets, lock them in cages, and then release them into an inferior second-class status." In particular, the "enemy" in the War on Drugs has been identified by race.[48] As Cornel West writes, "There is no doubt that if young white people were incarcerated at the same rate as young black people, the issue would be a national emergency."[49]

According to Glenn Loury we have become a more punitive society as demonstrated by "the likelihood that a person who is arrested will be subsequently incarcerated. Between 1980 and 2001, there was no real change in the chances of being arrested in response to a complaint: the rate was just under 50 percent. But the likelihood that an arrest would result in imprisonment more than doubled, from 13 to 28 percent." Many experts, including

Alfred Blumstein and Loury, contend that "none of the growth in incarceration between 1980 and 1996 can be attributed to more crime."[50]

Criminologists continue to document the many ways in which this increase in imprisonment was unrelated to an increase in crime. For example, Jeffrey Fagan, Valerie West, and Jan Halland examined the arrest records in New York City. Their study shows that the incarceration rates were highest in the city's poorest minority neighborhoods and often not those neighborhoods where crime rates were the highest.[51]

In the imagination of large segments of the public, media, and the police, "black" became associated with dangerous crime, delinquency, and personal failure. Young African American males, in particular, were seen as lacking personal responsibility and motivation to get educated and get ahead in society. Instead, these young black males turned to crime. And thus, the purpose of incarceration shifted from rehabilitation to punishment.

Joy James describes the construction of a new "racial formation"—the savage, the prisoner. Incarcerated individuals and communities are "unique among the outcasts—the outlaw community viewed not as (anti)hero but as (sub)human. Prisoners become 'non-citizens'" and "debased from all other racial formations in society."[52]

And Alexander documents the ways in which former black prisoners are victimized for the rest of their lives. She describes this process as the "new Jim Crow" at work in America. It is socially permissible to discriminate, exclude, and have contempt for former "criminals." As she writes:

> [W]e use the criminal justice system to label people of color "criminals" and then engage in all the practices we supposedly left behind. Today it is perfectly legal to discriminate against criminals in nearly all the ways that it was once legal to discriminate against African Americans. Once you're labeled a felon, the old forms of discrimination—employment discrimination, housing discrimination, denial of the right to vote, denial of educational opportunity, denial of food stamps and other public benefits, and exclusion from jury service—are suddenly legal. As a criminal, you have scarcely more rights, and arguably less respect, than a black man living in Alabama at the height of Jim Crow. We have not ended racial caste in America: we have merely redesigned it.[53]

It should startle all Americans to learn that we are the only country in the world that so ferociously disenfranchises people released from prison. While some countries have limited postprison disqualifications, no country relegates individuals who've served their sentences to a lower, secondary caste as we do in the United States. The United Nations Human Rights Committee has labeled US disenfranchisement policies discriminatory and a violation of international law.[54]

Across the United States, felons' right to vote is revoked not just while they serve their sentence, but after they have done their time and returned home. This shameful practice particularly impacts the African American community where, as already documented, imprisonment rates are highest. Many children in these communities thus grow up with parents who cannot cast a ballot. According to the research organization The Sentencing Project, an estimated 5.85 million individuals were unable to vote in the November 2014 US election due to felony convictions. Three-fourths of these individuals had completed their sentences and were living back in their communities. The highest rates of disenfranchisement were in the South, with the state of Florida at the top. The Florida statistics are alarming: nearly one in four African American Floridians cannot vote because of felony convictions.[55]

Pamela S. Karlan notes that prisoners, and offenders who have served their sentences or alternative punishments, can vote in countries all over the world, including the Czech Republic, Canada, South Africa, Denmark, France, Israel, Japan, the Netherlands, and Zimbabwe. "Israel sets up polling places in prisons and detention centers, and its laws even permitted the man who assassinated Yitzhak Rabin to vote for his successor."[56]

South African Justice Albie Sachs who spent time in jail during the apartheid era put it this way:

> The vote of each and every citizen is a badge of dignity and of personhood. Quite literally, it says that everybody counts. In a country of great disparities of wealth and power it declares that whomever we are, whether rich or poor, exalted or disgraced, we all belong to the same democratic South African nation; that our destinies are intertwined in a single interactive polity.[57]

POLITICS AND THE WAR ON DRUGS

In response to social instability and a perceived rise in crime, a new consensus emerged in both political parties focused on individual responsibility. The government was said to be "part of the problem," and the key for stability and growth was to allow the market to work free of state interference. Delinquency and crime was linked to individual behavior and not to market failure. The government should thus on the one hand cut back on social welfare programs that "rewarded" bad behavior, but, on the other hand, should invest more in prisons, police, and security overall. The "right to security" trumped all other human rights, including the right to health, education, and food. In fact, what were formerly seen as "public goods," including education and criminal justice, became subject to "privatization." Democrats and Republicans were united in this effort. To many observers, the War on Crime and the War on Drugs had unfortunately spiraled into a War on the Poor.[58]

President Ronald Reagan in 1983 in "Remarks at a Conservative Action Committee Dinner" stated:

> It is abundantly clear that much of our crime problem was provoked by a social philosophy that saw man as primarily a creature of his material environment. The same liberal philosophy that saw an era of prosperity and virtue ushered in by changing man's environment through massive Federal spending programs also viewed criminals as the unfortunate products of poor socioeconomic conditions or an underprivileged upbringing. Society, not the individual, they said was at fault for criminal wrongdoing. We were to blame. Well, today, a new political consensus utterly rejects this point of view. The American people demand that government exercise its legitimate and constitutional duty to punish career criminals—those who consciously choose to make their life by preying on the innocent.[59]

President George H. W. Bush devoted his entire first televised address in 1989 to the problem of illegal drugs. In dramatic fashion, the president displayed on camera a bag of cocaine purchased "in the shadow of the White House," and went on to announce the creation of a national drug czar to administer the federal government's antidrug policy.[60] The role of the military was also expanded to combat drug trafficking. In an address to law enforcement officials, Bush called on the country to "raise our voices to correct an insidious tendency—the tendency to blame crime on society rather than on the criminal. . . . I, like most Americans, believe that we can start building a safer society by first agreeing that society itself doesn't cause the crime—criminals cause the crime."[61]

Bush's speeches and the White House mobilization on the issue had a dramatic impact. In response to this message from the White House, the media followed with weeks of coverage of the drug problem facing the nation. And public opinion polls shifted with the majority identifying drugs and drug abuse as the nation's primary problem.[62]

A similar phenomenon occurred during the first Clinton administration with the passage of the 1994 Violent Crime Control and Enforcement Act.

During the decade prior to the passage of this bill, only 10 percent of the public identified crime or violence as the nation's most important problem. Following the media coverage surrounding the Violent Crime Act, this figure shot up to over 50 percent. Public opinion subsequently called for greater punishments signifying a "shift in perspective on the nature of criminal offending from a social theory emphasizing poverty and racial discrimination, and other environmental determinants of crime toward a vision of crime as the rational choice of the calculating offender."[63]

Linda Evans argues that while the War on Drugs provided the public rationale for both Nixon's War on Crime and Reagan's increased spending on policing and prisons, these "wars" were in actuality designed to maintain social order.

> As economic conditions deteriorate, the strategy for social control is to put poor people away before they pose a serious threat to social order. The goal is to incarcerate and immobilize people oppressed by these social conditions—those at the bottom, the helpless, the hopeless—before they organize to demand change. Communities of color that are already ravaged by drug addiction, poverty, and related violence have been further decimated by the war on drugs and mass imprisonment. These social conditions, compounded by intensive policing and punitive penal policies, have severely compromised the ability of people in these communities to organize and take action against economic and social injustice.[64]

The War on Drugs was aimed at the African American community and targeted low-level street dealers and young men in the inner city. Despite the steady decline in marijuana and cocaine use since 1979, the war was declared in 1983 and focused on lower-class African Americans in decaying urban America. The racial results speak volumes:

- In 1975 the ratio of black to white arrest rates for drug-related offenses was 2 to 1. By 1990 this ratio was 5 to 1, even though drug usage among whites and blacks remained the same.[65]
- The War on Drugs ignored white teenagers and targeted black teens. The drug arrest rates for white minors actually dropped during the aggressive War on Drugs. Black minors, on the other hand, faced a hostile state. The arrest rate of black juveniles for drug infractions had dropped to a ratio of 185 arrests per 100,000 in 1981. By 1989, at the height of this war, this figure rocketed to 460 per 100,000. Young black men in the ghetto were clearly the chosen police targets.[66]

POLICY AND THE WAR ON CRIME

Until the mid-1970s the US prison population had remained relatively stable in relation to the overall population for over a half-century. Prison sentences since the 1920s were governed by a set of practices that criminologists refer to as "indeterminate sentencing," through which judges specified a minimum and maximum sentence (e.g., five to ten years, or fifteen to life). Actual time served within this range would be determined by parole boards examining the inmates' behavior while incarcerated, such as evident remorse, evidence of rehabilitation, and so on. Sentences were thus individualized and there were incentives for prisoners to take the steps needed to hasten their release. The longest prison sentences would thus be reserved for those who committed the most serious crimes and continued to pose a threat to society.[67]

The "tough on crime" political message coming from the Republican and Democratic parties challenged the idea that "hardened criminals" could be rehabilitated. Some argued that the justice system had become soft on dangerous criminals. Sensationalized accounts of criminality filled the press. The actions of judges came under scrutiny with many bemoaning the low rate that convicted offenders were sentenced to prison. Calls were made to strengthen the power of prosecutors and to limit the role of judges and parole boards in determining the length of sentences and release decisions.

Yet calls for a crackdown on crime came not only from the white community but from African Americans themselves, who were engaged in a battle against violence inside their own communities. For example, according to Michael Fortner, concentrated poverty in black communities in the urban cities led to major problems like drug addiction and crime that "degraded the social and civic health of black neighborhoods." Fortner continues: "After the Harlem riots of 1964 (which erupted following the shooting of a 15-year-old black male by a white cop), polls showed that many African-Americans in New York City still considered crime a top problem facing blacks in the city, while few worried about civil rights and police brutality."[68]

In 1969, the NAACP in Manhattan warned of the "reign of criminal terror" with Harlem victimized by "marauding hoodlums." The civil rights organization proposed that certain criminals, including muggers, pushers, and vagrants, be subject to steep criminal sentences. The NAACP went on to state: "We favor the use of whatever force is necessary to stop a crime or to apprehend a criminal." By 1973, "nearly three-quarters of blacks and Puerto Ricans favored life sentences for drug pushers."[69]

As a result of this pressure from the black and white communities, harsher judicial policies were rapidly implemented. Raphael, Stoll, Wacquant, and other scholars summarize some of these major changes in sentencing practices at the state and federal levels that fundamentally altered the criminal justice system, including:

• The shift from indeterminate to determinate sentencing.

In contrast to the indeterminate sentencing described above, "determinate sentencing," introduced state by state between 1978 and 1984, either fixed sentences or established a relatively narrow minimum and maximum range. Furthermore, the power of parole boards was constrained and curtailed in an attempt to ensure that the sentence served was the one determined by the judge. [70] At the beginning of the twenty-first century, twenty-two states utilized determinate sentencing while another twenty-two had a "mixed regime" (of determinate and indeterminate). This reduction of "correctional discretion" and, in particular, the weakening of the power of parole boards, significantly lengthened the sentences and the harshness of the punishments handed down. [71]

• Truth-in-sentencing laws.

Truth in sentencing is based on the idea that every convict should serve a minimum portion of his or her sentence before becoming eligible for parole. These policies were adopted in the mid-1980s in response to the perception of leniency in "indeterminate sentencing." "Good behavior," for example, would no longer be considered as a factor to reduce the minimum portion of the convict's sentence. [72]

The Violent Crime Control and Law Enforcement Act of 1994 pushed this effort along by providing funds to local police throughout the country on the condition that states have a "truth-in-sentencing" provision that violent offenders were required to serve a minimum of 85 percent of their sentence. [73] This federal effort worked. The "minimums" now vary from 75 percent (four states) to 85 percent (30 states) to 100 percent (4 states). [74]

• Repeat offender laws.

Leaning on a broadly understood baseball analogy ("three strikes and you're out"), in the 1990s laws were adopted in two dozen states and the federal government for the mechanical and automatic implementation of sanctions after the accused had committed three specially designated felonies. Washington became the first state, doing so in 1993, to enact the repeat offender "three strikes and you're out" law. By 2000 one-half of all states had these provisions in their sentencing systems.[75] These laws are intended to severely punish serial criminal offenders. Unfortunately, these laws and policies were too often not focused on egregious actions and varied greatly by jurisdiction. California, in particular, enacted a cruel version of "three strikes and you're out." California listed over five hundred offenses, with some as minor as shoplifting in a store, as qualifying for the third strike and triggering mandatory lifetime imprisonment.[76] Until recently, all third strikers (those with two prior felony convictions) in California were given automatic sentences of twenty-five years to life.

• Mandatory minimum sentences.

Mandatory minimum sentences were created by direct acts of the US Congress. These laws established compulsory sanctions for specific offenses. According to Raphael and Stoll:

> Between 1975 and 2002, every state adopted some form of mandatory minimum sentencing targeted at a specific offense. Nearly three-quarters of all states and the federal government enacted mandatory minimum sentences for possession or trafficking of illegal drugs. Mandatory minimum penalties are also often encountered for violent offenses, offenses involving weapons, carjacking, offenses victimizing minors and offenses committed in close proximity to schools. Federal law is riddled with mandatory minimum sentences.[77]

The Anti-Drug Abuse Act of 1986 has gained special notoriety and disrepute due to its targeting of particular drug users (income-poor African American males) over other drug users (income-rich white males). The act specified a five-year mandatory minimum penalty for trafficking offenses involving at least five grams of crack cocaine (which was seen as a ghetto drug). Yet a drug dealer of powder cocaine to the white community would receive the same minimum of five years for trafficking only if the sales equaled at least five hundred grams of powder cocaine. Five grams versus five hundred grams. In addition, 1988 federal legislation applied the five-year mandatory minimum to possession offences and "conspiracy" to commit drug crimes. In 2010 Congress recognized some of the unjust disparity in these acts and raised the minimum amount of crack needed to trigger the determinate, mandatory five-year sentence. But the disparity in punishment between crack and powder cocaine remains large, approximately 28 to 1.[78]

As a result of these policies, the United States, according to Robert Ferguson, "punishes more frequently and more heavily than other modern democracies. The incarceration rate in Europe is 1 out of 1,000; the United States imprisons 1 out of 143 and for longer periods under poorer conditions. The richest country in the world is one of the worst in housing the people it punishes."[79]

Most Americans hope and probably believe that the justice system is based upon principles of fairness, such as "the punishment should be proportional to the crime" and "the same punishment for the same crime." Yet, as Ferguson points out, "differences in sentencing for the same crime occur all the time."[80] And, as we have already seen, a person's race and ethnicity is often the basis to the differential in the administered punishment.

Even Supreme Court Justice Anthony M. Kennedy argues that "our resources are misspent, our punishments too severe, our sentences too long . . . [with much in the system] unwise and unjust." Kennedy maintains that our current prison system actively seeks "to degrade and demean the prisoner," and asserts that "a purpose to degrade or demean individuals is not acceptable in a society founded on respect for the inalienable rights of the people." Kennedy continues: "Out of sight, out of mind is an unacceptable excuse for a prison system that incarcerates over two million human beings in the United States." "When the door is locked against the prisoner, we do not think about what is behind it." "We have a greater responsibility. As a profession, and as a people, we should know what happens after the prisoner is taken away."[81]

HUMAN RIGHTS DUTIES AND MASS INCARCERATION IN THE UNITED STATES

Human rights duties flow from international human rights law directly to individuals, states, and global actors, including international organizations, multinational corporations, and NGOs. What are the human rights duties for those concerned about mass incarceration in the United States? Are there human rights duties for those outside the borders of the United States who are concerned about the emergence of the "new Jim Crow" inside America? Or is this simply a national issue for US citizens?

Duties on Individuals

Individuals have duties to respect the rights and freedom of others. Human rights at the individual level begin with an acknowledgment of both the local and global duties that emerge due to ethical interdependence. Many individuals now work with transnational organizations with global agendas focusing on women's rights, LGBT rights, environmental rights, civil rights, political rights, and the elimination of world poverty. These individuals act with a sense of duty beyond borders to alleviate suffering.

Protecting the civil and political rights of individuals around the world has long been a focus of Amnesty International (AI) and other global human rights organizations. AI calls on individuals around the world to speak out against the violations of the civil and political rights of individuals in all countries of the world, including the United States. In their most recent annual report, for example, AI points to the following violations in US prisons:

> Incarceration rates remained at historically high levels. Thousands of prisoners across the USA remained in isolation in "super-maximum security" prisons. They were confined to cells for 22–24 hours a day without adequate access to natural light, exercise or rehabilitation programs. Conditions in such facilities violated international standards and in some cases amounted to cruel, inhuman or degrading treatment. [82]

In addition, AI points to the "excessive use of force" by the police across the United States:

> At least 42 people across 20 states died [in 2012] after being struck by police Tasers, bringing the total number of deaths since 2001 to 540. Tasers have been listed as a cause or contributory factor in more than 60 deaths. Most of those who died after being struck with a Taser were not armed and did not appear to pose a serious threat when the Taser was deployed. [83]

But why should individuals from other countries be concerned about prison conditions and the excessive use of force by the police in the United States? The AI vision answers that question: "Our vision is a world in which every person—regardless of race, religion, ethnicity, sexual orientation or gender identity—enjoys all of the human rights enshrined in the UDHR and other internationally recognized human rights standards." The UDHR states that "the recognition of the inherent dignity and of the equal and inalienable rights" of all people is "the foundation of freedom, justice and peace in the world." AI thus attempts to unite people from all over the world to fight for human rights everywhere—including in the world's most powerful states.[84]

During the Cold War, many US citizens felt an ethical duty to speak out and protest against the gulag, the former Soviet Union's main penal system. In addition to common criminals such as robbers and thieves, the gulag held political prisoners and innocents trapped by the Soviet secret police. Peasant mothers, alleged to have stolen small amounts of food to feed their hungry children during the famine of the 1930s, were sentenced to up to ten years in prison. Telling an innocent joke about the Communist Party led to sentences of up to twenty-five years. The outrageous, cruel, inhumane, and arbitrary punishments shocked the world and concerned individuals on every continent spoke out, organized, and protested against these civil and political rights violations in a country far away. These individuals pressured their governments to more forcefully challenge the leadership of the USSR to end this mass incarceration and the brutal treatment of its own citizens.[85]

Tragically, US prisons today can be characterized as inhuman, racist, and cruel. Too many young African American males are caught up in a police and justice enforcement system that denies them basic human dignity and rights. Prison conditions throughout America fail to meet basic standards of decency. As Robert Ferguson writes:

> The standard joke—inmates are in control of the asylum—is the reality that every prisoner must learn to live with today. Organized gangs, predatory inmates, endemic violence, simmering personal disputes, indifferent or abusive prison guards, insufficient surveillance, ethnic wars, dysfunctional cellmates, serious overcrowding, rampant disease, certifiable insanity, wretched physical circumstances, and a merciless pecking order make every jail sentence a daily ordeal of danger, humiliation, and insecurity. . . . Just as worrisome is the magnitude of the situation, a magnitude on such a scale that it begins to define the country itself.[86]

Rape and sexual abuse is widespread throughout the local, state, and federal prison system. From its most recent surveys, the BJS documents that in 2011 and 2012, 3.2 percent of all people in jail, 4.0 percent of state and federal prisoners, and 9.5 percent of those held in juvenile detention report having been sexually abused in their current facility the preceding year. The senior BJS statistician and lead author of these reports, Allen J. Beck, stated that the new findings indicate that nearly two hundred thousand people were sexually abused in American detention facilities in 2011. And finally, the studies confirm that most of the sexual abuse in detention was committed by corrections staff, not inmates. [87]

Such conditions should shame and shock people everywhere. Not only is "punishment as retribution" out of control, but it is also "out of mind." Once these prisoners are sent off to jail, we look away. Yet listen to a summary of the bipartisan Ford Foundation 2006 report *Confronting Confinement*:

> American prisons are dangerously overcrowded, unnecessarily violent, excessively reliant on physical segregation, breeding grounds of infectious disease, lacking in meaningful programs for inmates, and staffed by underpaid and undertrained guards in a culture that promote abuse. [88]

Individuals from around the world have accepted the human rights duty to expose the violations of basic human rights occurring in US jails. For example, in 2015 filmmakers in France released *In the Land of the Free*, which documents human rights abuses in America's prisons, with a focus on the heightened levels of cruelty created by decades of solitary confinement. Amnesty International publicized the case of Louisiana prisoner Albert Woodfox, who spent over four decades in solitary confinement for a murder he claimed he did not commit. Amnesty noted that there was no physical evidence linking him to the crime and that his conviction had been overturned three times. Despite the fact that a judge ordered his unconditional release, Louisiana authorities continued to block his release. Individuals from around the world responded to Amnesty's plea for global citizens to write letters to Louisiana's attorney general on behalf of Albert Woodfox. In addition, an International Coalition to free Albert Woodfox actively worked to publicize his case and bring global pressure for his release. These individuals from many different countries understood the ethics of interdependence and accepted the human rights duty to act with resolve to pressure the US judiciary to end these egregious actions. [89]

As a result of these global efforts, Louisiana prosecutors finally agreed to a plea agreement in February 2016, which granted Albert Woodfox his freedom and he walked out of prison a free man. In the end, Mr. Woodfox was kept in solitary confinement longer than any other prisoner in the country, and probably longer than any in American history. His freedom is a testament to the collective power of individuals accepting the human rights duties of global citizenship and working effectively through the worldwide human rights movement. [90]

Duties on Nation-States

Individuals in positions of authority within states are to act to promote, protect, and fulfill human rights law. State officials are required by law to uphold international human rights treaties. The state must enact legislation and procedures to give effect to the proclaimed rights.

For example, the United States ratified the CCPR in 1992 under the administration of President George H. W. Bush. The CCPR is one of the fundamental instruments of international human rights law designed to provide a range of protections, including the right to life and human dignity; equality before the law; freedom from torture, ill-treatment, and arbitrary detention; the right to a fair trial; and minority rights. Upon ratification by the US Senate, the United States is legally required to take administrative, judicial, and legislative measures to protect these rights. Under the "Supremacy Clause" of the US Constitution, which gives ratified treaties the status of federal law, the CCPR became the "supreme law of the land."

In March 2014 the United States submitted a report on compliance with the CCPR to the Human Rights Committee in Geneva. After reviewing this report and other evidence on US practices, the Human Rights Committee stated that it continued "to be concerned about racial disparities at different stages in the [US] criminal justice system, as well as sentencing disparities and the overrepresentation of individuals belonging to racial and ethnic minorities." The committee called on the United States to "address racial disparities in the criminal justice system, including by amending regulations and policies leading to racially disparate impact at the federal, state and local levels. The [U.S.] should ensure the retroactive application of the Fair Sentencing Act and reform mandatory minimum sentencing statues." The committee also remained concerned about the documented cases of "racial profiling" and called on the United States to "train state and local law enforcement personnel on cultural awareness and the inadmissibility of racial profiling." And finally, the committee was concerned about the extensively "reported cases of excessive use of force" by the police and called for improved investigations and, where warranted, prosecutions and sanctions of those responsible for these abusive practices.[91]

The American Civil Liberties Union (ACLU) has taken the lead in pressuring the US government to come into compliance with the CCPR. The ACLU documents the astounding racial disparities in drug sentencing and the tragedy of drug offenders staying locked up for lengthy sentences—and often forever under the "three strikes and you're out" penalties for petty drug crimes. The United States can end these practices. The ACLU, for example, continues to challenge the constitutionality of laws that impose disproportionate mandatory sentences of life without parole for simple possession of drugs. The ACLU also outlines how the United States can ensure that prison conditions are constitutional and "consistent with health, safety, and human dignity." The programs and policies exist for the United States to end the existing "cruel, inhuman, and degrading conditions of confinement" and increase "public accountability and transparency of jails, prisons, and other places of detention," and expand "prisoners' freedom of religion, expression, and association." According to the ACLU, the US government has a legal and moral duty to adopt these policies and come into compliance with the international human rights law that on paper they have committed the country to uphold. [92]

In 2014 the ACLU launched an eight-year political campaign across the United States to bring about changes in criminal justice policies. With funding assistance from George Soros's Open Society Foundation, the campaign's goal is to slash incarceration rates that have tripled since 1980. The campaign has received support from a coalition of liberal, conservative, and libertarian leaders who all agree that the policies behind the War on Drugs have become counterproductive and are causing extensive damage to the African American community. [93]

In response to political pressures from the UN's Human Rights Committee, the ACLU and others, the United States in 2014 began to address some of the pressing issues surrounding punishment and justice. US Attorney General Eric Holder announced the Department of Justice's total support for retroactively reducing the sentences of some prisoners locked up on federal drug offenses. In a statement, Holder said:

> Under the department's proposal, if your offense was nonviolent, did not involve a weapon, and you do not have a significant criminal history, then you would be eligible for a reduced sentence in accordance with the new rules approved by the Commission [on Sentencing] in April. Not everyone in prison for a drug-related offense would be eligible. Nor would everyone who is eligible be guaranteed a reduced sentence. But this proposal strikes the best balance between protecting public safety and addressing the overcrowding of our prison system that has been exacerbated by unnecessarily long sentences. [94]

The harshest penalties would then be reserved for the most serious criminals. This new plan could potentially shorten the prison times for as many as twenty thousand currently incarcerated individuals by an average of twenty-three months.[95]

Holder's actions indicate that the Obama administration would like to "roll back" the mandatory minimum sentences enacted as part of the War on Drugs that, as we have seen, targeted poor minorities and nonviolent offenders. US prisons are bulging and the DOJ is looking for a way to reduce the prison population. The DOJ estimates that 50 percent of federal inmates are incarcerated on drug offenses. Since African Americans constitute only 13 percent of the country's population, but 37 percent of the federal prison population, Holder views this as a civil rights issue.[96]

Inimai M. Chettiar, director of the Justice Program at the Brennan Center for Justice at NYU School of Law, would like the Obama administration to go further and calls on the president to create a National Commission on Mass Incarceration. Chettiar points out that there is broad bipartisan support for prison reform and widespread acknowledgment that mass incarceration is "a 10-ton elephant we can not afford to ignore." Chettiar writes: "One of the mandates of National Commission on Mass Incarceration would be to identify solutions premised on achieving a clear, measurable nationwide goal—for example, cutting the country's incarcerated population by 25% before 2025. This would require policy recommendations at the federal, state and local level. In particular, 'front-end' reforms that slow the flow of people into prisons will have the greatest impact by preventing unnecessary incarceration in the first place." Chettiar concludes: "A report from the National Commission on Mass Incarceration, like its predecessor from the Kerner Commission [The National Advisory Commission on Civil Disorders], would help illustrate to the general public that our criminal justice policy has reached a critical point—and that we can't afford to wait for reform."[97]

In November 2014, California voters approved, by a wide margin, Proposition 47, a ballot measure that redefined many lower-level felonies, including possession for personal use of hard drugs, as misdemeanors. Conservatives, including Newt Gingrich, and liberals, including George Soros, joined together in support of Proposition 47. Bipartisan support may be emerging in support of sentencing and probation reforms intended to drastically reduce incarceration rates.[98]

Perhaps the facts are getting through. For example, multiple studies have documented how crime has gone down faster in those states that *reduced* their prison population. California voters in 2012 voted to scale back the notorious "three strikes and you're out" law. By February 2015 this led to the release of more than 2,008 prisoners, many of whom had been serving life in prison for minor offences such as petty theft. The predictions that this would lead to an increase in crime were proved erroneous. In fact, after being free for an average of more than eighteen months, only 4.7 percent of the former life prisoners returned to prison for new crimes. The comparative figure over the same period for all inmates released from California prisons is about 45 percent returned for new crimes. [99] With the passage of Proposition 47, many more low-level drug and property offenses—including shoplifting and writing bad checks—will be converted from felonies to misdemeanors. This should result in the sentences of more than ten thousand people to be reduced on average by a whole year, saving the state millions of dollars annually. [100]

Since 90 percent of those incarcerated are in state and local facilities, actions to end mass incarceration will need to occur at the state level. In recent years, New Jersey, California, and New York have reduced their prison populations by about 25 percent, with no increase in crime. [101]

In July 2015, President Obama, left-leaning Democrats, and libertarian-leaning Republicans were pressuring Congress to revise four decades of federal policy and sentencing laws. Proposals included "safety-valve" provisions to give judges discretion to sentence low-level drug offenders to less time in prison than the required mandatory minimum term if they met certain criteria; allowing low-risk prisoners to participate in a recidivism program to earn up to a 25 percent reduction of their sentence; and creating more alternatives for low-level drug offenders. Incarceration rates are now seen as a national crisis across the political spectrum. Changes in the federal sentencing laws should help. [102]

While visiting a federal prison in Oklahoma in July 2015, President Obama stated: "These are young people who made mistakes that aren't that different than the mistakes that I made, and the mistakes that a lot of you guys made. The difference is they did not have the kinds of support structures, the second chances, the resources that would allow them to survive those mistakes." The president went on to talk about community investment and early childhood education in lower-income minority communities as vehicles to stop crime before it starts. Obama also commuted the sentences of forty-six people, most serving twenty years or more for nonviolent drug crimes. The message and tone coming from the Obama White House was thus significantly different from the Reagan/Bush years. Hopefully these words will translate into new federal policy.[103]

In addition, the US government has a moral responsibility to enact public policy to end the rape and sexual abuse in our prisons. Successful reform policies at juvenile detention facilities that have led to a decrease in sexual abuse include education, therapy, rehabilitation programs, and shorter sentences combined with smaller facilities located closer to the juveniles' home communities. Given that we know such policy changes can dramatically reduce instances of rape and sexual violence inside our prisons, we have a human rights duty to implement these reforms.[104]

Duties on Global Institutions and Organizations

Human rights duties extend beyond the individual and the nation-state to include IOs, NGOs, and other global actors. The monitoring of human rights practices coordinated out of the Office of the High Commissioner for Human Rights in Geneva is one attempt by the United Nations to embrace this duty and create structures to hold nation-states and global organizations accountable to human rights law.

For example, the United States has signed and ratified the CERD and thus must defend its record on racial discrimination to the human rights committee monitoring states' compliance with this treaty. This body—the CERD Committee—issued a scalding report in 2014 on the US failure to comply with its duties and obligations under the CERD. The CERD Committee highlighted the huge gaps between the rhetoric of the Obama administration and the reality of continuing practices that discriminate and impact minorities in the United States. The committee reviewed documents presented by the US government, NGOs, including the ACLU, and heard testimony from victims, including moving comments from the parents of Trayvon Martin, the seventeen-year-old African American high school student fatally shot by George Zimmerman in 2012 in Stanford, Florida.

According to the ACLU, the CERD Committee report provides a "blueprint to end discrimination and promote equal opportunity" and includes calls to

- End racial profiling by adopting the End Racial Profiling Act and swiftly revising the 2003 Justice Department Guidelines on the Use of Race by Federal Law Enforcement Agencies.

- Stop the militarized approach to policing, which has had a disproportionate impact on communities of color and to immigration law enforcement, which has led to killings at the border, mandatory detention of immigrants, and deportation without adequate access to justice.
- Develop a comprehensive plan to reduce school segregation and address the school-to-prison pipeline.
- End racial disparities in the criminal justice system at the federal, state, and local levels.[105]

This UN report was compiled and issued as another unarmed African American young man was shot and killed by police in Ferguson, Missouri. Following this killing, law enforcement officials carried out a violent and militarized crackdown on the nonviolent protestors. Jamil Dakwar, director of the ACLU Human Rights Program, notes that "[w]ere they depicting a foreign crisis, these images would have been condemned by the U.S. State Department and policymakers as evidence of human rights violations. But when they come out of our own backyard, we don't call them human rights abuses. They are, at best, labeled police misconduct and civil rights concerns."[106]

Dakwar goes on to explain that the "world is tired of U.S. double standards when it comes to human rights."[107] Images of teargas, rubber bullets, and militarized police remind the world of countries condemned by the United States for their poor human rights records, including Egypt, Venezuela, Cuba, Iran, Turkey, and Bahrain. The events in Ferguson demonstrate a deep level of hypocrisy when the United States doesn't apply the same human rights standards to its own behavior.

It is thus necessary for international human rights organizations, like the CERD Committee, to speak out about mass incarceration and police brutality inside the United States and in other countries around the world. These global human rights bodies can act with even-handedness and apply basic human rights standards equally to the practice of all nations. Every nation violates some human rights of its citizens. It often takes an outside voice of experts, who are not politically invested in the country, to be able to accurately access state practice in regards to human rights fulfillment. These global human rights organizations are thus positioned to come to the aid of victims of state oppression—from gays in Africa—to women in Saudi Arabia—to environmental activists in China—and to African Americans mistreated in the US judicial system. All countries benefit when unbiased eyes evaluate their human rights practices. All nations should welcome this level of inspection, engage in a constructive dialogue with global human rights bodies, and be open to changing practices that create needless suffering.

California: Success at the Ballot Box

What are the human rights duties for US citizens who understand the depths of the crisis facing America due to the mass incarceration of African Americans? What actions can be taken to alleviate the suffering of innocents incarcerated due to racial profiling and bias in sentencing? The people of California provide a dramatic example of how effectively educating and organizing can bring about positive change through the ballot box.

With a notable 58 percent of the vote, California citizens in November 2014 approved Proposition 47, a sentencing reform measure, which could dramatically affect the lives of tens of thousands currently behind bars. Conservatives and liberals joined together to support this ballot initiative, which reduces dozens of nonviolent property and drug crimes from felonies to misdemeanors. Such a reclassification of convictions could lead to a potential freeing of thousands of prisoners. The hope is that the funds that would have been spent on their incarceration will now be used for mental health and drug treatment programs. This proposition was supported not only by the California Catholic bishops, tech industry leaders, and justice reform groups, but also included prominent figures across the political spectrum from Jay-Z to Newt Gingrich.[a]

According to Matt Ford, Prop 47 could lead to forty thousand felony convictions reduced to misdemeanors and about seven thousand inmates able to petition the courts for release. This potentially could mean that approximately one in five inmates serving time in the state would be affected, saving California hundreds of millions of dollars each year. In addition, a former inmate's prospects for housing, employment, and government assistance improve drastically without a "felony" conviction hanging over his or her head. Prop 47 thus reduces and eliminates both unreasonably hard sentences and the accompanying lifelong stigmas.[b]

Proposition 47 came after two other significant reforms in California: laws were approved in 2011 to divert low-level offenders from state prisons to county jails and in 2012 a ballot initiative scaled back a "three strikes" law. The combination of all these reforms profoundly impacted the state's prison and jail population, which fell by thirteen thousand, thus relieving severe overcrowding. Prior to these reforms, authorities had been releasing as many as ten thousand from jail each month due to a bed shortage regardless of the risk. With the release of these low-level offenders, authorities can now make smarter and more thoughtful decisions about whom to release.[c]

And although crime rates vary throughout the state, these reforms have not led to an overall upsurge in criminality, as some in law enforcement had argued. In fact, the 2015 crime rate in San Diego County is at a record low. The recidivism rate of those released due to Proposition 47 is less than 4.7 percent, compared to the state average of 45 percent.[d]

Mass incarceration came about due to public support generated by political officials under the banners of the "war on crime" and the "war on drugs." The citizens of California have demonstrated that the public can also recognize when a policy has failed and a new direction is needed.

[a] Lauren McCauley, "California Voters Pass 'Historic Mass Incarceration Reform," *Common Dreams*, November 5, 2014. Available at http://www.commondreams.org/news/2014/11/05/california-voters-pass-historic-mass-incarceration-reform (accessed March 18, 2015).

[b] Matt Ford, "Californians Vote to Weaken Mass Incarceration," *The Atlantic*, November 5, 2014. Available at http://www.theatlantic.com/politics/archive/2014/11/california-prop-47-mass-incarceration/382372 (accessed March 18, 2015).

[c] "California's Prison Experiment," *New York Times*, November 13, 2015.

[d] Erik Eckholm, "California Convicts Are Out of Prison after Third Strike, and Staying Out," *New York Times*, February 26, 2015.

DISCUSSION QUESTIONS

1. During the Cold War, many Americans spoke out against the maltreatment of prisoners in the former Soviet Union. These US citizens felt a duty to pressure the US government to pursue a forceful foreign policy aimed at improving the lives of those individuals imprisoned in the USSR. Given the treatment of young African American males by the

US justice system, do citizens of other countries have a human rights duty to act on behalf of those facing cruel treatment in US prisons?

2. The United States has ratified both the CCPR and the CERD. The treaty bodies monitoring state compliance with their obligations in each treaty have found that the United States has a poor record in relation to protecting the fundamental human rights of the African American community. Do such UN actions make a difference in US policy formation? Explain why or why not.

3. In what ways does a "new Jim Crow" system of discrimination and exclusion exist in the United States? If it does exist, how can it be ended?

4. Since declining economic opportunities and falling incomes helped create a wave of mass incarceration, to what extent should policy aimed at reversing those trends be the focus of reform efforts?

WEBSITES

The American Civil Liberties Union (ACLU) works in the courts, legislatures, and communities to defend individual rights and liberties in all communities in the United States. Website: https://www.aclu.org.

The W. Haywood Burns Institute for Juvenile Justice, Fairness & Equity works to reduce racial and economic disparities in more than forty jurisdictions nationally and provides support to organizations that provide alternatives to detention. Website: http://www.burnsinstitute.org.

The Constitution Project promotes justice in federal and state sentencing systems by advocating for increased judicial discretion in sentencing decisions and improved procedural fairness and due process in the sentencing process. Website: http://www.constitutionproject.org.

The Innocence Project assists prisoners who could be proven innocent through DNA testing to free the staggering numbers of innocent people who remain incarcerated. Website: http://www.innocenceproject.org.

The NAACP Legal Defense and Education Fund (LDF) is considered by many to be America's first and foremost civil and human rights law firm. Website: http://www.naacpldf.org.

The Sentencing Project works for a fair US criminal justice system through reforms in sentencing policy to end unjust racial disparities and practices and through the promotion of alternatives to incarceration. Website: http://www.sentencingproject.org.

Chapter Three

Homophobia and Anti-Gay Violence in Africa

The persecution and violence against LGBT individuals throughout Africa is extreme. According to Amnesty International, thirty-eight out of fifty-four African countries criminalize "consensual same-sex conduct," making homosexuality illegal throughout 70 percent of the continent.[1] Waves of antigay violence have swept through country after country. Gay men have been arrested in Cameroon, Kenya, Malawi, Senegal, Sierra Leone, and Nigeria. Homosexuals can be put to death if convicted of "sodomy" or "indecent" sexual activities in Mauritania, Somalia, and Sudan. Gay African refugees face brutal violence and rape throughout the continent.[2]

In one infamous incident, in 2011 a leading Ugandan newspaper published the names and photographs of one hundred alleged homosexuals on its front page with the headline "Hang Them!" The consequences were immediate. The house of a transgender man, whose name was on the list, was stoned by a crowd, which shouted, "We will kill you!" Uganda's well-known gay activist, David Kato, received death threats and was murdered three months later. Others on the tabloid's list were harassed and threatened, even by family members, most of whom learned that their son was gay from the article. Two years earlier, in 2009, an "Anti-Homosexuality Bill," also known as the "Kill the Gays" bill, was introduced in the Ugandan parliament. The original provisions of the bill called for the death penalty for individuals who engaged in "aggravated homosexuality," including those who were labeled "serial offenders."[3] Although the death penalty provision was eventually removed, the bill signed into law by President Yoweri Museveni of

73

Uganda in February 2014 imposed harsh sentences for homosexual acts, including life imprisonment in some cases. The Ugandan law calls for life terms for repeat convictions on the charge of "aggravated homosexuality" along with fourteen-year sentences for the "promotion or recognition" of homosexual relations. The law punishes "conspiracy to commit homosexuality" or "aiding and abetting homosexuality" with seven years in prison.[4] Immediately following President Museveni's signing of this bill, a Ugandan newspaper published a list of what it claimed to be the country's "200 top" gays. This front-page story, under the headline "Exposed! Uganda's 200 Top Homos Named," once again identified people who had not come out publicly, raising fears, yet again, of a witch hunt and violence against these individuals.[5] A Ugandan court invalidated the bill in August 2014 stating the measure was illegal since there was no quorum present in the parliamentary session when it was passed. Yet the measure still enjoys widespread support throughout the country and homosexuality remains illegal. A long-standing law from the colonial era criminalizes sex acts "against the order of nature" and thus the police still can arrest men who love men. Homophobia remains at a fever pitch in Uganda.[6]

In Cameroon the penal laws are extremely harsh toward LGBT individuals. People found guilty of "sexual relations with a person of the same sex" can be sentenced up to five years imprisonment. Even texting one's love can lead to prison. In 2012, Jean-Claude Roger Mbede was found guilty of homosexual conduct for sending a text to another man saying, "I'm very much in love with you." Mr. Mbede, not sure he could withstand his three-year jail sentence, stated, "I am not sure I can put up with the antigay attacks and harassment I underwent at the hands of fellow inmates and prison authorities on account of my perceived and unproved sexual orientation. The justice system in this country is just so unfair." Many observers perceive Cameroon as the most repressive country in Africa for its prosecution of same-sex couples.[7]

Conditions for the LGBT community in Nigeria are similarly dire. In January 2014 Nigerian president Goodluck Jonathan signed into law the "Same-Sex Marriage Prohibition Bill," which prohibited the "public show of same sex amorous relationship [*sic*] directly or indirectly." Gay people can now be arrested for holding a meeting or joining a homosexual club or organization with penalties of up to fourteen years in jail. If a gay man kisses or hugs his partner in public, under this bill, he could face up to ten years in prison. Commentators noted that the motivation for the law seemed strictly political, since Nigeria already has a law making homosexual sex illegal and gay people were not demanding to be married. Furthermore, in parts of northern Nigeria where Islamic Sharia law is enforced, gays and lesbians can be legally stoned to death.[8] In lobbying for the anti-gay bill, religious fundamentalists fomented a climate of fear intimidating legislators from even hearing from the opponents of the legislation. Some commentators viewed the anti-gay bill as a diversionary tactic to distract attention from the lack of progress in providing basic health care, education, and infrastructure. The tragic end result of this effort was the fueling of bigotry and hatred toward the LGBT community in Nigeria.[9]

The LGBT community in Ghana faces a climate of discrimination, humiliation, and violence. In 2011, the president of Ghana, John Atta Mills, "doubled down" on his country's discriminatory laws, declaring that he would never legalize homosexuality, despite pressures from the international community. When British prime minister David Cameron suggested that Britain would cut foreign aid to those countries that fail to respect gay rights, President Atta Mills responded by declaring that Ghana's "societal norms" were different from those in the United Kingdom and that Cameron had no right to tell Ghana what to do.[10] By 2016 conditions for gays and lesbians had not improved. The current president of Ghana, John Mahama, announced that he "does not subscribe to homosexualism and will not take any step to promote homosexualism in Ghana." And the minister of justice, Marietta Appiah-Oppong, stated categorically that the constitution of Ghana does not recognize gay rights and "unnatural carnal knowledge is a criminal offence."[11]

The list of African leaders lining up to denounce homosexuality seems endless. The current Liberian president and Nobel Peace Prize winner, Ellen Johnson Sirleaf, defended her country's anti-gay law, which makes homosexuality a misdemeanor offense with those found guilty subject to one year in prison. "We like ourselves just the way we are," Johnson Sirleaf stated. "We've got certain traditional values in our society that we would like to preserve." She was emphatic that she would not act to decriminalize homosexuality, and when pressed on this issue responded: "I have just said to you, we gonna maintain our traditional values."[12] British colonial laws prohibiting homosexuality remain in effect in Zambia and Malawi. In Malawi Steve Monjeza and Tionge Chimbalanga were arrested after expressing their intention to marry and were sentenced to a fourteen-year prison term. It took the intervention of UN secretary-general Ban Ki-moon on the couple's behalf to get the late Malawi president Binguwa Mutharkia to pardon the couple.[13]

Human Rights Watch, Amnesty International, and OutRight Action International (formerly the International Gay and Lesbian Human Rights Commission) have gathered testimony from the victims and documented many cases where individual gays and lesbians throughout Africa have been subjected to extreme abuse, discrimination, harassment, and violence.[14] In addition, the US State Department now includes violence against the LGBT community in their annual human rights report.[15]

Tragically, the "human rights threshold" criteria explored in chapter 1 have been surpassed with the abuse of gay Africans across the continent. The widespread suffering constitutes clear violations of established global human rights norms and law. In addition, there is a growing mutation and metastasizing of homophobia led by religious leaders. Fortunately, as will be shown below, South Africa is taking the lead to bring about change—listening to the victims and projecting a new, more inclusive, vision of African identity.

AFRICAN LEADERS AND AMERICAN CHRISTIAN PROSELYTIZERS

African political leaders and anti-gay religious advocates claim that they are defending "African values." Same-sex relations have been denounced as a "Western vice" that arrived with the white colonialists. In addition, the HIV/AIDS epidemic was also seen as a product of the West. In 1995 Zimbabwe president Robert Mugabe equated homosexuals with "pigs and dogs." By 1999 homosexuals to Mugabe had become "gangsters," and in 2000 he declared that homosexuality was "an abomination, a rottenness of culture," which Britain's "gay government" was imposing upon Africans. He urged his Zimbabwean citizens to defend themselves against this new form of Western imperialism. In 1999, Uganda president Yoweri Museveni joined the homophobic chorus and ordered the police to look for gays and arrest them, stating: "God created Adam and Eve as wife and husband but not for men to marry fellow men." Museveni went on to claim that the "homosexuals are the ones provoking us." Scholars note that this theme of the West imposing homosexuality on Africa was then promoted not just by the governments of Zimbabwe and Uganda, but also by the king of Swaziland, the presidents of Namibia, Kenya, and Zambia as well as by leading church officials from around the continent. These leaders consistently preached that it was the West and the homosexuals who were the provocateurs, the aggressors. In September 2000 Namibian president Sam Nujoma declared homosexuality to be one of the two top enemies of the government. In response, the Namibian minister of home affairs urged police recruits to "arrest on sight gays and lesbians and eliminate them from the face of Namibia."[16]

The US Christian Right has been in the forefront in promoting homophobia, reconstructing African history, and creating strong sexual politics in Africa. Key figures from the Christian Right actively promoting a homophobic agenda in Africa include well-known Baptist pastor and best-selling author Rick Warren; the prominent Holocaust revisionist Scott Lively; and the leader of the New Apostolic Reformation movement Lou Engle. These US religious leaders actively organized and funded influential African religious organizers to denounce any movement toward LGBT equality in Africa. In a carefully documented study, Evangelical Rev. Dr. Kapya Kaoma from Zambia followed the work of "renewal movements" in three denominations—the Episcopal Church (TEC), the United Methodist Church USA (UMC), and the Presbyterian Church USA (PCUSA). Kaoma demonstrates the ways these movements partnered with African religious leaders to destabilize progressive movements within the church and promote homophobia in Africa. The impact has been profound. Kaoma summarizes: "Involvement of African clerics in this U.S. 'culture war' has had the effect of slowing, if not stopping altogether, the recognition by these churches of the full equality of LGBT people."[17]

Since the American conservatives often find themselves in the minority of their denomination at home, Kaoma's research demonstrates how they have come to depend upon African religious leaders to legitimize their extreme positions. In fact, these American religious leaders have argued that the West's commitment to human rights is an "imperialist" attempt to "manipulate Africans into accepting homosexuality, which they characterize as a purely Western phenomenon." How do they do this? According to Kaoma: "Through their extensive communications networks in Africa, social welfare projects, Bible schools and educational materials, U.S. religious conservatives warn of the dangers of homosexuals, and present themselves as the true representatives of U.S. evangelicalism, so helping to marginalize mainline churches." The "collateral damage" of this strong role pursued by US evangelicals in promoting homophobia in Africa is the growing persecution and violence against LGBT people throughout the continent.[18]

Despite the revelations of these activities by the human rights community and criticisms from leading states, including the United States and the United Kingdom, the work of the Christian Right in Africa in the promotion of animosity toward the LGBT community continues. By 2013, Roman Catholics, Mormons, and right-leaning evangelicals had expanded their overall infrastructure on the African continent "with new institutions and campaigns that are reshaping national political dynamics and even laws based on an American template." According to Kaoma:

> Within the past five years [2008–2012], the Roman Catholic Human Life International (HLI), the Pat Robertson–founded American Center for Law and Justice (ACIJ-USA), and Family Watch International (FWI), led by a Mormon, have launched or expanded their work in Africa dedicated to promoting their Christian Right worldview. A loose network of right-wing charismatic Christians called the Transformation movement joins them in fanning the flames of the culture wars over homosexuality and abortion by backing prominent African campaigners and political leaders. [19]

Tragically, these efforts have been "successful in painting African campaigners for LGBT rights as dupes of neocolonial forces trying to impose an alien philosophy on the continent."[20] Key African religious and political figures pragmatically organize around the false claim that homosexuality was introduced by white colonists in order to gain political power.

HISTORICAL OVERVIEW OF HOMOSEXUALITY AND HOMOPHOBIA IN AFRICA

Definitive academic studies document the historical presence of homosexuality throughout Africa over hundreds of years. These studies also verify the decisive role of European colonialists in the creation of homophobic norms and attitudes.[21] It is homophobia, and not homosexuality, that was imposed by the colonialists, imperialists, and Christian and Muslim religious proselytizers on the continent. Homosexuality is as indigenous to African society as it is to all other civilizations and peoples on all continents of our planet.[22]

In his conclusive study of sexuality in Africa, Marc Epprecht, for example, assembles voluminous evidence to demonstrate that southern African peoples have consistently, from the earliest of times to the present, engaged in accommodating all manner of sexual expressions. There is a tradition in Africa of same-sex involvement. There is a tradition of acceptance of different sexualities. Fear and hatred of homosexuals is not an African value. Epprecht documents evidence of same-sex sexuality across time throughout southern Africa.[23]

Kenyan legal scholar Makau Mutua supports Epprecht's analysis, and notes that as a natural condition, similar to race, gender, disability, or ethnicity, homosexuality has always been present in Africa. Mutua identifies a further contradiction in the arguments of those who use religion to claim that homosexuality is un-African. Mutua documents how hatred against gay people did not originate in African culture, but was rather a product of contact with foreign religions, in particular Christianity and Islam. Mutua describes how homosexuality existed in Africa prior to Christianity and Islam. Homophobia, on the other hand, only emerged on the continent as a consequence of contact with these outside religions.[24]

Yet some noted Islamic scholars tend to reverse this analysis.[25] Instead of recognizing the role of religion in the rise of homophobia in Africa and elsewhere, these scholars claim the opposite and charge those who argue for gay rights with attacking Muslims with a "liberal," "neo-colonialist agenda." For example, Tariq Ramadan, professor of contemporary Islamic studies at Oxford University, writes: "Muslims are now being called upon to condemn the Qur'an, and to accept and promote homosexuality to gain entry into the modern world. . . . It reveals a new dogmatism—and a whiff of colonialism, not to mention xenophobia—at the heart of so-called modern, progressive thought."[26] But Ramadan is wrong: homosexuality is indigenous to Africa, and all of the world's civilizations, and not a product of foreign "modern, progressive thought."[27]

Epprecht's research also reveals the ways Africans were able historically to carry on same-sex relations without attracting the attention of the colonialists and demonstrates that same-sex relations were not just a product of circumstance or structures. For example, some have asserted that homosexual activity grew in contexts like mines and prisons where there was an absence of women. However, Epprecht shows how homosexuality was present in rural areas and urban settlements, challenging this functionalist argument. He further demonstrates that there was a greater tolerance for same-sex relations among the working class and poor majority in Africa, compared to the educated elite and colonial leadership.[28]

Furthermore, even "the claim that same-sex sexual behavior is un-African appears to have originated in the West rather than Africa itself." This argument appealed to colonialists who often used biblical and "family values" arguments in "making the case for the 'natural' right to rule of heterosexually virile, bourgeois, white men, both within Europe and beyond."[29]

In fact, the "dogmatic revulsion against same-sex behaviors, acts, relationships, and thought [that is, homophobia] was introduced into the region
by European colonialists and preachers." The people of Africa were encour-
aged by whites from the North to equate "homophobic constructions of sexuality, sensuality, and gender with civilization."[30]

UNITED STATES: LGBTQIA

By 2016 a remarkable global political divide, cloaked in the language of
culture, had emerged between the United States and many African nations
over homosexuality. While country after country in Africa moved to uphold,
reinforce, and strengthen old colonial laws against homosexuality, the United
States was moving in the opposite direction. During the first decades of the
twenty-first century, the LGBT community in the United States experienced
enormous progress toward equality in civil society, in marriage, and in the
military. In fact, the US movement can no longer be limited to LGBT. The
new "millennial generation" is more radical, calling for an end to gender
roles defined through a binary lens of male/female. "The core question,"
according to Michael Schulman, "isn't whom they love, but who they are—
that is, identity as distinct from sexual orientation." And thus, "identity" in
the "post-post-post-gay-rights" era has become more complicated.[31]

While Africa struggles to accept the legitimacy of LGBT, America is
moving toward an unwieldy rubric of LGBTQIA—Lesbian, Gay, Bisexual,
Transgender, Questioning, Intersex, Ally. There is an LGBTQIA Resource
Center at the University of Missouri, Kansas City; LGBTQIA discussion
groups at Vassar College; and further LGBTQIA activities at Lehigh University and Amherst College. In fact, more and more colleges are responding to
this new generation. According to a 2012 survey by Campus Pride, transgender students could room with their preferred gender at 203 campuses; a
person could change his or her name and gender in university records at 49
schools; and hormone therapy was covered at 57 schools. The University of
Iowa in 2012 became the first to add a "transgender" checkbox to its college
application.[32]

When President Barack Obama announced his support for same-sex marriage in 2012, 51 percent of Americans approved of his position, compared
with 45 percent who disapproved.[33] In the 2012 US elections, Maine and
Maryland became the first states to vote in favor of same-sex marriage and
Tammy Baldwin became the first openly gay senator to be elected to the US

Senate. In Minnesota, voters rejected an initiative to enshrine in the state's constitution a definition of marriage as being solely between a man and a woman.[34] Following a landmark US Supreme Court decision in June 2013, gays and lesbians could legally get married in the District of Columbia and thirteen states. In addition, the Supreme Court ruled that the federal Defense of Marriage Act (DOMA) was invalid and that married same-sex couples were entitled to some federal benefits.[35] The Supreme Court in 2015 declined to hear appeals from five states that sought to keep their marriage bans in place. As a result, gay marriage became legal across the country, including in the state of Florida, bringing the total number of states with federal recognition of gay marriage to thirty-six, plus the District of Columbia.[36]

And finally, in a historic decision in June 2015, the US Supreme Court—in *Obergefell v. Hodges*—reaffirmed the scope of the Constitution's guarantee of equal protection under that law and legalized same-sex marriage in all fifty states. Justice Anthony Kennedy wrote: "The right to marry is a fundamental right inherent in the liberty of the person, and under the Due Process and Equal Protection Clauses of the Fourteenth Amendment couples of the same sex may not be deprived of that right and that liberty." In explaining the court majority's decision, Justice Kennedy noted the Constitution's ability to evolve and the court itself "has recognized that new insights and societal understandings can reveal unjustified inequality within our most fundamental institutions that once passed unnoticed and unchallenged." Kennedy wrote of the "transcendent importance of marriage," and that "through its enduring bond, two persons together can find other freedoms, such as expression, intimacy, and spirituality. This is true for all persons, whatever their sexual orientation. There is dignity in the bond between two men or two women who seek to marry and in their autonomy to make such profound choices."[37]

Yet discrimination on the basis of sexual orientation remains present across America. At the beginning of 2016, thirty-one states lacked comprehensive laws that would protect gay and transgender Americans. As a result, across America, LGBT individuals continue to be fired from their jobs, evicted from their homes, denied lines of credit, suspended from schools, bullied and harassed, and denied legal protections. A sizable minority, strongly influenced by conservative religious dogma, continues to oppose LGBT rights across the United States, especially in the southern states.[38]

Local and Global Conversations?

How do we have local and global conversations on these issues? While an emerging majority in the United States appears to be supportive of LGBT rights, including same-sex marriage, a sizable minority within the country continues to argue, primarily based on narrow interpretations of religious texts, that homosexuality is a sin and gay marriage an abomination. In many countries in Africa, on the other hand, the majority appears to agree with those who misrepresent African history and culture to depict homosexuality as foreign to native cultures. As a result, there is widespread popular support for the criminalization of homosexuality throughout the continent, while a significant, and growing, minority in Africa organize for LGBT rights. Furthermore, this broadening divergence in attitudes concerning homosexuality seems to have grown wider in recent years.

For decades African leaders have claimed the centrality of heterosexuality to African culture and rejected homosexuality as threatening to "African values." This socially constructed articulation of African culture is now widely accepted throughout the continent, with LGBT rights portrayed as "foreign" and as a "neocolonial ideology." Homophobia in Africa has thus now become part of the culture and cannot be understood as solely the product of either colonization or missionary religious proselytizing. A negative view of homosexuality is now widely accepted as indigenous and culturally based across the African continent. Fundamental cultural change to recast "African values" to accommodate multiple sexualities will have to come from indigenous leadership inside the culture.

Yet, as documented above, homophobia in Africa is actually not indigenous to local cultures; instead, European colonialism and modern-day evangelical proselytizing have contributed significantly to the construction of heterosexuality, and fear of homosexuality, as central to African culture. There is thus a degree of moral responsibility in the West for the intense suffering caused by extreme homophobia in Africa. In other words, there exists a high level of ethical interdependence between continents and peoples on this issue.

But does this articulation of an ethic of interdependence help provide a framework for a global dialogue on LGBT human rights? Is the normative structure of universal human rights and duties a useful way to think about individual and nation-state rights and responsibilities in regard to LGBT issues at home and abroad? These questions will be explored through an examination of human rights duties at the individual, nation-state, and global levels.

HUMAN RIGHTS DUTIES AND LGBT RIGHTS IN AFRICA

Duties on Individuals

As outlined in chapter 1, individuals have duties to the community to uphold and realize affirmed human rights. We are now more aware than ever of the degrees of global interconnectedness, interdependence, and mutual vulnerability. This awareness can lead to a deeper understanding of global rights, responsibilities, and duties.

Individuals living in the developed Northern countries, with a new cognizance of the history of sexual politics in Africa, should feel a profound sense of responsibility for the growth of homophobia on the continent. As we have seen, "Africans" are no different from "Europeans" or "North Americans" in their sexual desires and sexual practices. The continent is certainly as complex and diverse as any other on our planet. Racial and sexual stereotypes of African heterosexuality are more often than not promoted for political reasons and are not only historically false, but dangerous and hurtful.[39] As we have seen, it is far more historically accurate to note the ways in which homophobia, not homosexuality, was brought to Africa by the European colonialists and promoted today by proselytizing American evangelical missionaries. It is thus difficult to ignore the global duties that emerge for citizens in the United States and Europe to help end this hateful and violent climate of repression toward the LGBT community in Africa. Since the creation and promotion of homophobia came to a large degree from the developed North, citizens of those states have a human rights duty to help eradicate this climate of hate.

Where does this human rights duty come from? Why, for example, do those living today have ethical and moral responsibility for the actions of their ancestors? Why should an individual living today feel any moral "duty" for deeds undertaken by colonial powers decades before he or she was born? The answers to these questions rest in the recognition of the legacy of this history on current conditions of oppression and injustice in the world today.

Just as slavery created the institutionalization of racism, colonialism contributed significantly to the global institutionalization of homophobia. Just as the unequal treatment of blacks did not end when slavery was abolished, the discrimination against gays remained vibrant long after the end of colonialism. Citizens from Europe and America should feel alarmed at the ways in which prejudice and violence against gays became institutionalized in national laws and cultural practices around the world following the end of colonialism.

In addition, in a democracy it is vital for citizens to accept individual moral responsibility and engage in a process of ethical reasoning in order to hold the government accountable. Individual citizens are able to evaluate the morality of their nation's actions in the world, both historically and in current events, and act accordingly. We are able to investigate whether the foreign policy of our nation contributes or alleviates human suffering abroad. Our individual actions, and the foreign policy of our nation, can be evaluated through a normative lens of fundamental human rights. When one's consciousness includes a global way of thinking, and an understanding of the dynamics of our interconnected and interdependent world, it is impossible not to apply ethical reasoning to the global system as a whole. Through this framework of global human rights, an ethical duty emerges to help end the ongoing oppression of the LGBT community in Africa.

But what is to be done? It is definitely not helpful, and more often than not counterproductive, for Europeans or Americans to lecture, patronize, and judge Africans from afar. As Damian Ugwu wrote:

> The truth is that the battle cannot be won primarily in the streets and conference halls in New York or Geneva but here in Lagos and Abuja. This is not to say that support from international NGOs, activists and diplomats is not important—far from that. The point being canvassed here is that local activists need to be empowered to drive the process. They need offices, computers and, more importantly, the training and skills to drive the process. They must be allowed to take the lead.[40]

Attempts to "drive the process" from rich, highly developed countries, ignoring the vital role of local leadership, can backfire. In fact, activists and scholars note that pressure from the outside on Uganda emboldened evangelical fundamentalists and their allies. It also served to support the thesis that homosexuality came from the North. And such an approach ignores the cases where the gay rights movement in Africa has had remarkable success. South Africa, in particular, since its liberation in 1994 from apartheid and white rule, has taken global leadership on gay rights by enshrining freedom from discrimination based on sexual orientation in its national constitution. Former South African president Nelson Mandela met with gay activists and endorsed principles of equality for gays and lesbians. As well, the South African courts have affirmed the interconnectedness of oppressions based upon race, gender, and sexuality, making the country far more progressive and liberal than most other nations. In addition to South Africa, gay rights organizations operate in Botswana, Swaziland, Namibia, Zimbabwe, and elsewhere. The courageous individuals in these organizations, primarily black Africans, facing severe repression and dangers, demonstrate to the world the sexual diversity existing on the continent. In addition, South Africa, the Central African Republic, Rwanda, and Sierra Leone joined with more than eighty countries in signing a joint UN statement condemning "acts of violence and related human rights violations based on sexual orientation and gender identity."[41]

Citizens around the world, concerned about the suffering and abuse of the gay population in parts of Africa, could mobilize support for South Africa's work in support of LGBT rights at the United Nations. Individuals and organizations outside of Africa can continue to back the work of Sexual Minorities Uganda (SMUG), the Centre for the Development of People in Malawi, Gay and Lesbian Memory in Action in South Africa, the Coalition of African Lesbians, and other African NGOs promoting the rights of LGBT. Assistance can also be given to the African Program of OutRight International based in Johannesburg, South Africa. These LGBT movements across the continent are being led and directed by Africans. The reality of moral interdependence implies an ethical duty for citizens from around the world to actively promote these African efforts to end homophobia across the continent.

In sum, morality is ultimately not just what we think or feel, but what we do. An individual who sees herself as a global citizen will not be satisfied with only an intellectual understanding of the connections between her country and homophobia in parts of Africa. Moral behavior to her means acting on this knowledge as well. One clear avenue for such moral action is to support the individuals and organizations in Africa fighting for LGBT rights. A second path for action is to push a human rights agenda at the national level.

Duties on Nation-States

As previously outlined, global human rights duties at the national level requires leaders of states to uphold principles and instruments of international law and human rights. "Good international citizenship" thus entails a state's commitment to defend the International Bill of Human Rights, for example, the UDHR, CCPR, and CESCR.

National legal systems provide a means for individuals and organizations to pursue legal routes to hold individuals and governments accountable to these global norms. In the United States, for example, the Alien Tort Statute (ATS), approved by Congress in 1789, has been used by US courts to hear human rights cases brought by foreign citizens for conduct committed outside the United States. The statute reads: "The district courts shall have original jurisdiction of any civil action by an alien for a tort only, committed in violation of the law of nations or a treaty of the United States" (28 U.S.C.; 1350). Since the 1980 *Filartiga v. Pena-Irala* case, US courts have held that the "law of nations . . . has always been part of the federal common law," and that the contemporary law of nations prohibits state-sanctioned torture. The right to be free from torture is now *jus cogens* (i.e., a preemptory norm) and a principle of customary international law. In addition to torture, US courts have found that cruel, inhuman, or degrading treatment, genocide, war crimes, crimes against humanity, summary execution, prolonged arbitrary detention, and forced disappearances are actionable under the ATS.[42]

Working with the Center for Constitutional Rights (CCR), SMUG, a nonprofit umbrella organization made up of various Ugandan LGBT organizations, filed a federal lawsuit in the United States in March 2012 based on ATS. The lawsuit against US evangelist Scott Lively alleged that he had waged a decade-long campaign to persecute gays in Uganda. As mentioned, Lively is president of the conservative evangelical Abiding Truth Ministries (classified as a hate group by the Southern Poverty Law Center). Since 2002, Lively has traveled often to Uganda to organize a movement to not only strip away rights for LGBT people, but to silence and demonize gay people as well. In March 2009, Lively held a three-day conference in Uganda titled "Seminar on Exposing the Homosexual Agenda" attended ·by key government officials and religious leaders. At the conference, Lively linked homosexuality with pedophilia, stating: "When [homosexuals] see a child that's from a broken home, it's like they have a flashing neon sign over their head." Lively helped draft the "Kill the Gays Bill" (described above) by contributing portions of the bill intended to criminalize LGBT rights and deprive gay activists of freedom of assembly. SMUG is suing Lively "for the persecution they have faced as a result of his involvement in a conspiracy to deprive them of their rights based on their sexual orientation and/or gender identification." The lawsuit states that Lively's work in Uganda "ignited a cultural panic and atmosphere of terror that radically intensified the climate of hatred in which Lively's goals of persecution could advance."[43]

The CCR/SMUG case against Lively is a clear example of the use of national legal systems to enforce international human rights law. The US Supreme Court, however, in April 2013 made it more difficult to use the ATS to prosecute human rights cases. In a unanimous decision, the justices limited aspects of the extraterritorial application of the law.[44] Yet, according to the CCR, Lively, as a US citizen, should still be held accountable under the ATS for his actions in violation of the "law of nations." The CCR argues that the "extraterritoriality" issue behind the Supreme Court's decision does not apply in this case. The CCR writes that as an American national, "there is a strong national interest in ensuring that the United States does not become a safe harbor for its own citizens who have committed serious human rights violations abroad." The case continues to move forward through the US courts.[45]

The overwhelming majority of the world's nations have pledged to uphold the norms and obligations found in the International Bill of Human Rights. Citizens in these countries can use this legal framework to hold their states accountable. In addition, since World War II there has been a notable growth in support for the legal principle of "universal jurisdiction." There exists now an impressive list of actions prohibited by *jus cogens* (preemptory norms), including torture, cruel and inhumane treatment, crimes against humanity, and a prohibition on aggressive war. While these norms are violated too often with impunity, it is still the case that most nations strive to uphold these norms most of the time. This worldwide human rights legal framework thus provides citizens globally with a viable vehicle through which to pursue an agenda based on the alleviation of suffering.

Duties on Global Institutions and Organizations

As noted in chapter 1, human rights duties at the world level focus on the construction of laws and institutions to promote universal norms and human rights. The emergence of rights-based institutions, in particular, is seen as critical to holding state and nonstate actors accountable to uphold human rights law and respond to conditions of ethical interdependence.

Not one of the major international human rights treaties mentions "sexual orientation" or "gender identity." International human rights law makes special references to race and sex, and has focused on specific groups including refugees, children, women, ethnic minorities, indigenous peoples, migrant workers, and the disabled. Yet the rights of LGBT individuals have been purposely left out of this body of law. A political coalition of key states and major religions has blocked efforts within the UN system to raise the profile of LGBT rights.[46]

The UN human rights institutions have interpreted the general provisions of equal rights in human rights law to include the protection and support of the LGBT community. For decades, UN treaty bodies, other UN agencies, and UN rapporteurs have stated that the general commitments to equal rights and nondiscrimination in existing international human rights law prohibit discrimination on the grounds of sexual orientation or gender identity. As the former UN high commissioner for human rights Navi Pillay stated: "The case for extending the same rights to lesbian, gay, bisexual and transgender (LGBT) persons as those enjoyed by everyone else is neither radical nor complicated. It rests on two fundamental principles that underpin international human rights law: equality and nondiscrimination."[47]

In the last few years, the United Nations has taken even more affirmative action regarding LGBT rights, including the following:

- In 2006, the International Lesbian and Gay Association and two other LGBT NGOs gained consultative status with the Economic and Social Council (ECOSOC). In addition, other NGOs including Amnesty International, Human Rights Watch, and the International Commission of Jurists were actively engaged with LGBT issues in their work at the United Nations.[48]
- In 2008, sixty-six countries agreed to a UN General Assembly Declaration calling for the universal decriminalization of homosexuality and condemned homophobic discrimination and violence. This was the first time that the UN General Assembly had addressed LGBT issues.[49]
- In 2011, the UN HRC passed resolution 17/19 on supporting equal rights for all, regardless of sexual orientation or gender identity. This resolution was introduced by South Africa and was the first-ever UN resolution on the human rights of the LGBT community.[50]
- In 2011, eighty-five countries signed a statement condemning "acts of violence and related human rights violations based on sexual orientation and gender identity." The statement called "on states to take steps to end acts of violence, criminal sanctions and related human rights violations committed against individuals because of their sexual orientation or gender identity." Unfortunately, only four African nations—the Central

African Republic, Rwanda, Sierra Leone, and South Africa—signed the statement.[51]

- In 2012, the Third Committee of the UN General Assembly passed a resolution condemning extrajudicial, summary, or arbitrary executions (A/C.3/67/L.36), including individuals targeted because of their sexual orientation or gender identity.[52]
- In 2012, the HRC held a panel discussion and debate on "Human Rights, Sexual Orientation and Gender Identity" at its nineteenth session. This historic debate, sponsored by South Africa and Brazil, became divisive as a bloc of Middle Eastern, African, and other states walked out. This walkout was the first by a major grouping of nations in the HRC. And it came after appeals by UN secretary-general Ban Ki-moon and UN human rights high commissioner Navi Pillay for governments to protect the rights of gays and lesbians.[53]

High Commissioner Pillay reported to the Human Rights Council in 2012 that 76 countries among the UN's 192 members had laws criminalizing homosexual behavior. By addressing this issue, Egypt accused Pillay of promoting homosexuality despite reservations of some member states. In response, Pillay said that some states would argue that homosexuality or bisexuality "conflict with local cultural or traditional values, or with religious teachings, or run counter to public opinion." Pillay stated that although people were "free to disapprove of same-sex relationships" and had "an absolute right to believe whatever religious teachings they choose," universal human rights always trumped tradition and culture.[54]

Due to South Africa's leadership, the African group's reaction to this effort was slightly more tempered than in the past. Representing the African group, the Senegalese delegate stated that homosexuality was not covered by global human rights accords and called the debate an "attempt to try to hijack" human rights discourse and "an act of contempt towards the universality of human rights." Yet he went on to cite precedents from African law that protect the human rights of individuals. "Thanks to South Africa's leadership on the matter," said Dawn Cavanagh of the Coalition for African Lesbians, "the African bloc position against lesbian, gay, bisexual and transgender rights is breaking up. This is hugely encouraging."[55]

The global divide over LGBT rights has, however, blocked progress. There is still no specific piece of international law that acknowledges LGBT rights as human rights. There is still no treaty guaranteeing equality and nondiscrimination to LGBT individuals, nor one affirming same-sex rights to marriage. Not one of the existing UN human rights conventions specifically upholds LGBT equality nor specifically prohibits homophobic discrimination. In sum, at the global level there is a weak institutional framework to support and protect LGBT people from persecution and abuse.

What type of process at the global level can be established for the creation of a regime to protect LGBT rights? As we saw at the individual level, the process cannot be seen as a way for the North to "preach" to the South about rights and responsibilities. For example, in December 2011 Secretary of State Hillary Clinton proclaimed in Geneva that "gay rights are human rights" and that the Obama administration would push for the decriminalization of homosexuality overseas. She pledged "to ensure that our foreign assistance promotes the protection of LGBT rights." Leaders and newspapers in many African states responded with anger. In Liberia, for example, newspapers condemned the Obama policy and homosexuality in general. In Uganda, an adviser to President Museveni responded to Clinton's remarks by saying, "I don't like her tone, at all. . . . Homosexuality here is taboo, it's something anathema to Africans." And in Kenya, influential church leaders immediately condemned the idea that LGBT people deserved equal rights. "We don't believe in advancing the rights of gays," said Oliver Kisaka, deputy general secretary of the National Council of Churches of Kenya.[56]

This same dynamic played itself out during President Obama's trips to Africa in June 2013 and July 2015. During his stay in Senegal in 2013, Obama urged African leaders to make sure that governments don't discriminate against gays and lesbians. Senegalese president Macky Sall responded by stating that while his country was not homophobic, "we are not ready to decriminalize homosexuality." He went on to chide the United States for maintaining the death penalty. Sall's comments won quick praise from Senegal's press, as seen in the following headlines: "Obama Makes a Plea for the Homos, Macky Says No!" (*Le Pop*); "No, We Can't" (*Liberation*); "President Sall Has Closed the Debate on Homosexuality" (*L'Observateur*). Many Senegalese citizens were offended by Obama's remarks. A retired Senegalese army major spoke proudly of President Sall: "He's courageous to have spoken like that, in front of the greatest power on earth. Even if they turn off the spigots, we won't give in." Others thought Sall could have pushed further. A security guard said: "He should have said, 'This [gay marriage] can never exist in Senegal; this can never happen here.'"[57]

During his 2015 trip to Kenya, President Obama argued that no nation should discriminate against gays and lesbians, comparing it to the segregation of African Americans in the United States. "As an African-American in the United States I am painfully aware of what happens when people are treated differently under the law." Obama continued, "If somebody is a law-abiding citizen who is going about their business and working in a job and obeying the traffic signs and doing all the other things good citizens are supposed to do and not harming anybody, the idea that they are going to be treated differently or abused because of who they love is wrong. Full Stop." But Obama's words had little impact on Kenyan president Uhuru Kenyatta, who responded by stating: "There are some things [like gay rights that] we must admit we don't share; our culture, our society don't accept." Kenyatta's remarks drew applause from the Kenyans attending the news conference. Homosexual acts in Kenya are illegal and punishable by fourteen years in jail.[58]

It is not surprising that, in response to Obama's comments on LGBT rights, President Sall would raise concerns about the United States continuing to administer the death penalty. In international law, the death penalty is considered inhumane and unfairly applied and thus a violation of the fundamental human right, the right to life itself. For example, in its first comprehensive review of the US human rights record, the UN HRC in November 2010 called on the United States to abolish the death penalty, reduce overcrowding in prisons, ratify international treaties on women and children, and take further steps to prevent racial profiling. While the United States expressed a willingness to discuss some of these recommendations, it immediately rejected the international calls to abolish capital punishment.[59] The United States is simply not interested in being "lectured to" by the United Nations or African nations about the death penalty. In fact, such efforts often cause a nationalist backlash inside America and make the struggle to end this merciless practice much more difficult. Just as the death penalty will never be changed in the United States as a result of reprimands from the United Nations or African leaders, LGBT rights will never be enacted in African nations as a result of pleas from outsiders. In fact, as seen in the reaction to Clinton's and Obama's comments on gay rights, such interventions often instill a jingoistic backlash, which makes the struggle for equality more difficult.[60]

Does this mean that the United States, and other nations, should ignore the fact that gay men and lesbians in Senegal or Kenya are abused, beaten, and sometimes tortured by the police with impunity? Should outsiders turn the other way when mobs threaten Senegalese or Kenyan gays, who are mocked in the newspapers and subject to arrest simply for being gay?[61] No. It simply means outside efforts to uphold basic human rights must be coordinated and supported by those fighting inside the country for dignity and equality.

The importance of South Africa's leadership on LGBT issues therefore cannot be understated. The leadership for change in Africa must come from inside Africa, with those living outside the continent lending support. It is similar to the struggle against apartheid in South Africa. The leadership of the fight against apartheid came from the ANC inside the country. The international "mobilization of shame" did contribute to the successful effort of the ANC to end apartheid, yet perhaps the primary reason these international efforts of individuals, nations, and organizations around the world were effective was because they were done in conjunction with a local movement. The international community was following the lead of the people of South Africa and responding to their requests. Outsiders were not imposing sanctions against the will of the people. The key individuals and organizations fighting for human rights in South Africa requested outside support for their efforts. NGOs, the United Nations and other IGOs, national governments, and individual global citizens responded and worked collectively to impose harsh sanctions on the racist regime. And eventually this global effort in support of the ANC's struggle for the protection of basic standards of human dignity and human rights for all the people of South Africa was successful.

It was thus significant that in July 2013 the Office of the UN High Commissioner for Human Rights (OHCHR) launched its "Free & Equal" global public education campaign for LGBT equality in Cape Town, South Africa. The former high commissioner for human rights, Navi Pillay, is herself South African. In Cape Town, Pillay stated that basic human rights protections remain a "hollow promise for many millions of LGBT people forced to confront hatred, intolerance, violence and discrimination on a daily basis."[62] South African Archbishop Emeritus Desmond Tutu likened the fight against gay prejudice to the antiapartheid struggle and said that he would rather go to hell than worship a homophobic God.[63] Hopefully this campaign will inspire millions to discuss these issues locally in their neighborhoods, places of worship, and community organizations.

An Interview with Rev. Dr. Kapya Kaoma

In 2009 Rev. Dr. Kapya Kaoma from Zambia began his investigation of the US Christian Right stoking the flames of homophobia in Africa. Dr. Kaoma's research has been instrumental in revealing to the world how the activities of religious leaders from America actively promote a culture of intolerance toward the African LGBT community. In *American Culture Warriors in Africa: A Guide to the Exporters of Homophobia and Sexism,* Dr. Kaoma documents the ways the Christian Right exports to Africa an agenda of dangerous bigotry.[a]

FELICE. Why should a US citizen feel a human rights duty regarding homophobia in Africa when there are so many other pressing human rights issues at home (including tragically high US poverty levels, bulging prisons, growing food insecurity, and ongoing racial discrimination)? Isn't an individual's primary moral duty to act to prevent human suffering in his or her home community?

REV. DR. KAOMA. Having studied in the best Evangelical schools, my passion for this work comes out of my Evangelical conviction that every human being is a sacred image of God. My research seeks to defend the Evangelical and Christian faith from the misrepresentation of the US Christian Right, whose bigotry in Africa is presented as default Christianity and Evangelicalism in particular. But it also seeks to alert my fellow Christians about the damage being caused in our name.

Back to your questions, there are many levels to them. First, the global–local interaction can't be avoided because the suffering of the LGBT community abroad is connected to America's front door. The American Christian Fundamentalists are going global with their culture wars. They represent the face of the local with their global activism in Africa and elsewhere. They take the local American face to these countries and claim to represent your home community and especially the US Evangelicalism. Thus, at home, Americans and especially Christian Evangelicals have the right to say no; these bigoted and hateful views do not represent my country, my values, and my faith.

It is a question of moral responsibility. We have witnessed the glo-balization of the US "culture wars." Having lost ground at home on gay rights and women's rights, the US Christian Right is now exporting its so-called Christian values—rejected and discredited in the United States—to Africa. The American Christian Right tells its African allies that they should stand up to immoral Western gays who are recruiting Africans into the vice of homosexuality. The Right warns Africans that it has lost the battle on these issues in the United States; hence they focus on helping Africa stop this immorality which seeks to destroy the world and Africa in particular.

For example, these Christian Fundamentalists go into a country like Zambia (my homeland), which has been historically accepting of homosexuality, and they preach that gays are coming to rape your children, and in particular your boys, and this is what causes Africans to react so violently. They are told it's about their children, and that the "homosexual agenda" is a threat to their family, nation, and faith. And further, that if the gays succeed, God will destroy Africa (like the destruction of Sodom and Gomorrah). They state that Christianity is dying in the United States because of the gay rights movement, and thus these so-called Christian values now must be protected in Africa. In Zambia, we never had a prosecution of a gay person until the American Fundamentalists promoted this imaginary "international gay agenda" to destroy the world. It is the American Christian Rightists who are pushing Africa to accept restricted, socially constructed gender roles.

We—Africans and Americans—are interlinked. The American community must understand that the promotion of violent homophobia is coming from your own people, and thus it is impossible to say that it does not affect you locally. The root cause of the brutality of gay men and lesbians in Africa is in your local American communities. We cannot separate our common humanity; the plight of the LGBT com-munity in Africa should be a moral concern of all Americans who care about human rights.

FELICE. How can US citizens act to help end the ongoing oppression of the LGBT community in Africa without appearing to lecture, patron-ize, or judge Africans from afar? How can a foreigner act in support of the African LGBT community without provoking a nationalist backlash or being seen as a cultural imperialist?

REV. DR. KAOMA. You don't have to go to Africa to bring about change. Americans and especially Evangelicals must hold their own people accountable at home. Stop them from promoting lies (which others take as fact) abroad. Evangelicals must not claim that the preachers of hate do not represent them while doing nothing to contain and discredit such preachers. In Africa, the American individuals discredited at home for intolerance and wrong theologies become spokespeople for American foreign policy as well as Christianity. If you expose what these guys are doing first to the American people and then to the world, they won't have the same power in the Global South.

It is important to point out that US Fundamentalists present their dangerous ideologies in the language of human rights aimed at stopping the imperialism of the West on Africa. Besides, they don't consider their actions "imperialist" because cross-cultural sharing of the "Christian" gospel is an important aspect of the Christian faith and mission. Since the Right coats its culture wars with "Christianity," through the media, dominated by US Christian Right operations such as Trinity Broadcasting Network, Daystar, and Christian Broadcasting Network, they have managed to promote their programs and ideology, broadcasting throughout Africa; yet this is not considered imperialism because of its "religious" camouflage. Moreover, the African media follows the arguments of the US Christian Right and its African religious allies in the presentations of LGBT issues.

Instead, it is the American human rights groups that are accused of being "imperialist" and imposing so-called Western human rights and values on Africans. Human rights are not foreign to Africa. Ubuntu, the entire theory of ethical judgments based on "Respect of the Human," was part and parcel of the fight against colonialism and dictatorships throughout Africa in the twentieth century. Ubuntu is based on the fundamental fact that every human being is morally equal and must be protected—what affects one affects all and vice versa. The human rights language is not new to Africa. Across the continent, in the local context, people say that you need to protect the dignity of each human being. So by arguing for basic human rights for the LGBT community, you are not promoting something that is strange and foreign to Africans. Those who claim that LGBT rights are "Western" rights representing "Western" lifestyles are simply making this up as an excuse to oppress others—often for political and financial gain.

Human rights represent universal values found around the world. Across cultures and political boundaries, there is agreement that a human being has some fundamental rights that cannot be ignored without consequences.

Again, LGBT rights are not primarily about sex; and sex is not the defining issue. The African LGBT community is fighting for the space to exist as full human beings; the right to work without discrimination; the right to get on a bus or taxi; the right to walk the streets of Nairobi or Lusaka without fear of attack; the rights to be protected as citizens of African nations. While the Christian Right extremely sexualizes LGBT rights, sex is not the defining issue. The moral issue is to treat this person as a human being with the fundamental human right to be respected and protected. Since we don't assume that sex is the defining human rights issue for heterosexuals, why do we make that assumption for homosexuals?

That said, one of the biggest challenges in African LGBT struggles is to not ignore or dismiss religion. Unlike in the secularized West, Africans are extremely religious; hence the struggle ought to be planted in the religious landscape.

Besides, shouting from America about these issues will backfire. It is problematic to lobby your local representatives to pressure African political leaders on gay rights. This will not only force African politicians to take sides but confirm the US Christian Right claims of neocolonialism. And, even more important, it is possible to stand in solidarity with those LGBT individuals and groups in Africa courageously fighting for acceptance and protection by holding your people accountable at home. You can also stand in solidarity with the people working on the ground in Africa—the local African LGBT community—for no civil rights movement has ever won from outside; the liberation of LGBT individuals ought to grow and come from the African soil.

Further, the biggest problem in the struggle is the lack of visibility of LGBT persons throughout Africa. Legislation has been passed in many countries to stop LGBT organizing and advocacy. Due to these intolerable laws and vicious homophobia, LGBT persons in many African countries remain invisible and don't have the power to speak out. Empowering LGBT persons with education and life skills will not only increase their socioeconomic and political power, but also their social visibility. The moment that LGBT persons are seen as human and contributing to the life of the community, the majority of Africans will change their views. But mostly we don't have the human face to the LGBT. Instead, many consider the movement composed of foreign white people who take advantage of Africans.

The LGBT community is actually part of the life of African nations—in the broadcasting industry, the media, the economic life of the nation. It is only when these many contributions to society and community life are finally appreciated by the majority that we will see progress. When the voices of African LGBT people are heard and respected then the current false perceptions of this community will be overcome.

Africans need solidarity. But change will not come from abroad, only from Africans themselves. Americans can support those groups. But don't go to Africa and lecture people there about these issues. Think about it this way: how would Americans react if Malawians came to the United States to teach America about democracy?

Americans, especially Evangelical Christians, can help expose the Christian Right at home, hold them accountable, and provide information to those fighting for their rights both in the diaspora and in Africa. It is important to support those fighting on the ground. We have a chance to change the tide on the African continent at many levels. By pushing sex into the political discourse on the African continent, the Evangelical Right has given us an opening. While we can now trace the ideological sources of militant homophobia as well as debunk the myths employed in this debate, we must be wary of presenting LGBT struggles as all about sex—it is about fundamental human rights for all people. As the popular saying goes, we have to act locally but think globally. Hold your own people accountable, and stand in solidarity with local African LGBT activists in their home communities. Like in the fight against apartheid in South Africa, the United States can help by raising the plight of LGBT Africans to the US and wider international community.

The metanarrative of LGBT freedom includes the full spectrum of political, civil, economic, and social human rights. It is time for us to humanize the "gay debate" on the continent. We are talking about human beings—men and women—who bleed like I do; have feelings like I possess; and who have the right to live lives of dignity and respect. They deserve their rights as I deserve mine; and to deny them is morally wrong.

[a] Rev. Dr. Kapya Kaoma, *American Culture Warriors in Africa: A Guide to the Exporters of Homophobia and Sexism* (Somerville, MA: Political Research Associates, 2014).

DISCUSSION QUESTIONS

1. Do you agree that individuals today should feel a sense of ethical duty based on the actions of predecessors during periods of colonialism and imperialism? Why should history impact current human rights duties?
2. Should the United States prioritize LGBT rights in Africa given that there are so many other pressing issues of concern (including aid, trade, investment, combatting the growth of extremist terrorist organizations, and so on)?
3. How can the United Nation's OHCHR pressure nations of Africa to change laws and practices that discriminate against the LGBT community without provoking a "nationalist" backlash?
4. Rightly or wrongly, clearly many Africans today see homosexuality as incompatible with traditional "African values." How is this perspective thus countered? What historical and contemporary evidence offers a better view?

WEBSITES

The Center for the Development of People in Malawi supports sexual minorities through civic education, training, capacity building, networking, and research. Website: http://www.cedepmalawi.org.

The Coalition of African Lesbians includes more than thirty organizations in nineteen countries in Africa committed to justice for lesbian and bisexual women. Website: http://www.cal.org.za/new.

Gay and Lesbian Memory in Action (GALA) in South Africa works to protect, preserve, and disseminate knowledge on the history, culture, and contemporary experiences of LGBT people. Website: http://www.gala.co.za/index.htm.

International Lesbian, Gay, Bisexual, Trans and Intersex Association is a worldwide federation of member organizations from 110 countries. Website: http://ilga.org.

OutRight Action International (formerly known as the International Gay and Lesbian Human Rights Commission) advocates on behalf of people who experience discrimination or abuse on the basis of their sexual orientation, gender identity, or gender expression. Website: https://www.outrightinternational.org.

Sexual Minorities Uganda [SMUG], a nonprofit NGO that works toward achieving full legal and social equality for LBGT people, is the umbrella organization of all homosexual organizations in Uganda. Website: https://sexualminoritiesuganda.com.

Chapter Four

Saudi Arabia and the Rights of Women

Saudi Arabia is a decidedly patriarchal society with sex-based discrimination as official state policy. This chapter does *not* explore Islamic rationales for curbing women's rights and relegating women to second-class status. These premodern views on the status of women are contested within Islam. The disagreements and debates among Muslims regarding women's rights are fierce and run the spectrum. For example, Abdullahi Ahmed An-Na'im, the Charles Howard Candler Professor of Law at Emory University, argues that "the state is a political institution that cannot be Islamic."[1] An-Na'im continues: "The Islamic reforms I am calling for are intended to encourage and support efforts to require complete equality for women and non-Muslims from a Shari'a point of view and not simply for political expediency."[2] At the other end of the political spectrum are those Muslims advocating an "Islamic" state, such as Ruhollah (Ayatollah) Khomeini on the Shi'a side or Hizb-ur Tahrir for the Sunnis.[3] These proponents of an Islamic state explore the original sources of Islam, the Qur'an and the example of the Prophet as set forth in the *sunna*, to determine "what Islam originally envisaged as women's roles."[4] In Saudi Arabia, the state employs such "Islamic" rationales to deny basic human rights to women. This hotly contested debate is intense among Muslims. It is only within this community of believers that these foundational debates will be resolved.

The approach here is different. I first explore the "facts on the ground" regarding the status of women's rights in Saudi Arabia and the rules and regulations governing gender divisions in Saudi society. Second, I look at the ways in which these practices align with or violate the internationally recognized corpus of human rights law. And finally, I articulate the human rights duties for individuals, nation-states, and international organizations concerned about women's rights in Saudi Arabia.

THE STATUS OF WOMEN IN SAUDI ARABIA

The *Global Gender Gap Report 2015,* published by the World Economic Forum, ranked Saudi Arabia 134 out of 145 countries for gender parity.[5] Two societies exist in Saudi Arabia, one for men and the other for women. Ann Elizabeth Mayer labels this separation "gender apartheid." Mayer explains,

> [T]he regime resort[s] to appeals to Islamic family values, Arab tradition, and Saudi patriotism in order to maintain the traditional patriarchal family structure and to keep women subordinated and cloistered within its confines. In other words, the Basic Law accommodates the Saudi system of gender apartheid. Not surprisingly, Saudi Arabia was one of only three nations willing to have full diplomatic relations with the Taliban government in Afghanistan, a regime that nearly all states refused to recognize because of its appalling rights abuses, especially its gender apartheid.[6]

What does gender apartheid look like in Saudi Arabia? The organization Saudi Women for Reform reported the following to the United Nations:

1. Absolute prohibitions [for women]:

    - Not allowed in all the government's departments including the administration of women's education, and public institutions such as the Department of Social Insurance. Accordingly women's access to resources is limited and some times denied the right, or abused by men who provide such services.
    - Not allowed to issue an official document that combines the mother's identity information with her children's.
    - Not allowed to drive a car.
    - Not allowed into many shops and public service stores such as video shops, music shops, children's barber shops, travel agencies, or foreign labor recruitment offices (such as drivers).
    - Not allowed to ride any game while accompanying a child in a public place such as a Mall.
    - Not allowed to ride any boats in public parks.
    - Not allowed to use gym rooms in hotels nor having designated hours.

- Not allowed into any sports clubs (all male), sport halls, or attend sport games.[7]

2. Prohibited [for women] except with a Mahram or guardian:

- Not allowed to schools, universities, postgraduate studies except with permission from a guardian.
- Not allowed to travel abroad except with a guardian's permission. If a woman does not have a guardian: a father or a husband or brother, then her SON will be her guardian.
- Not allowed to work except with a guardian's permission.
- Not allowed to take a car that she owns out of the country unless she has a permission of the minister of interior or the governor.
- Not allowed into restaurants or cafés except with a mahram.
- Not allowed to stay in hotels or furnished flats without a mahram.
- Religious discrimination occurs in the two Holy Mosques. In Makkah's Holy Mosque women's share of the main space surrounding the *Kaaba*, which is the holiest place, is about one seventh of the inner circle of the mosque (the circumambulation area), the remaining area is open to men's prayers only.
- In Madina's Holy Mosque, women are not allowed to reach the Rawdah al Sharifah (the holiest part of the mosque) except for a small part of it, a few hours a day, whereas it is open for men the whole time and the remaining area of the Rawdah.
- Not allowed to have an operation without the consent of a guardian, especially when it is a gynaecological operation.
- Not allowed to enter a hospital for delivery except with a guardian's approval, nor can she be discharged from the hospital or prison without a male guardian's signature.
- Not allowed to register her baby's birth notification. Who can register it is only the father, or a male relative over 17 years old.
- According to the regulations of the Saudi Arabian Monetary Agency (SAMA), a woman is not allowed to open a bank account in the name of her son or daughter except with the father's consent, nor is she allowed to carry any transactions on her child's behalf even if it is she who is depositing money in it.[8]

Human Rights Watch documents the human rights violations resulting from male guardianship and sex segregation in education, employment, health care, law, freedom of movement, and marriage. Gender apartheid results in the government denying more than half of its citizens' fundamental human rights and the ability to make decisions for themselves. As Human Rights Watch writes:

> The Saudi government has instituted a system whereby every Saudi woman must have a male guardian, normally a father or husband, who is tasked with making a range of critical decisions on her behalf. This policy, grounded in the most restrictive interpretation of an ambiguous Quranic verse, is the most significant impediment to the realization of women's rights in the kingdom. The Saudi authorities essentially treat adult women like legal minors who are entitled to little authority over their own lives and well-being.[9]

Saudi Women for Reform also details the ways in which women are excluded from both formulating and executing governmental policies. These Saudi women argue that the objective of women's education in the kingdom is "to prepare women for their natural roles as mothers and wives." As such, the number of university seats and the number of scholarship opportunities available for Saudi women are much less than those reserved for men. Illiteracy rates are much higher for Saudi women (29 percent) compared to Saudi men (7 percent).[10]

Eleanor Abdella Doumato documents the ways in which public education in Saudi Arabia serves as both a "major stimulus for women to enter the job market and a major deterrent." On the one hand, schooling has given girls a "legitimate destination outside the home, while also imparting secular knowledge and raising women's expectations about their own capabilities." On the other hand, Saudi education remains tied to a traditional "gender paradigm" linked to mandatory religious studies. The segregation of women has thus become a "moral imperative that is more firmly instilled" throughout the society. The ruling elite opens up educational avenues for women. But this education is "tied to its highly conservative Wahhabi ulama," a worldview that "doesn't welcome women as actors on the public stage."[11]

Saudi women are prevented from working in many sectors of the economy due to the prohibition of women working in sexually "mixed" environments. In banking and journalism women do not receive equal pay or benefits for equal work. According to 2013 government statistics, less than 11 percent of Saudi adult women (680,000) were employed, while 60 percent of adult Saudi men (four million) were at work. About one-third of Saudi women with bachelor's degrees report being unable to find a job and are frustrated by not being able to apply their knowledge and skills at work.[12]

A Saudi woman is a legal appendage to a male person and is unable to conduct legal issues before a judge on her own. A woman who needs to go to court needs two men from her family to identify her. Personal identity cards don't help. Her legal capacity is thus dependent on a man and her legal status resembling that of a minor. A Saudi women's testimony is generally valued at half that of a man. However, in 2004 reforms were implemented that allowed women's colleges and universities to offer degree programs in law. By 2013 four women had been granted law licenses. According to Katherine Zoepf, the "greatest effect of the reforms seems to be a growing awareness, among ordinary Saudi women, of the legal rights they do have, and an increasing willingness to claim these rights, even by seeking legal redress, if necessary."[13]

Unequal treatment continues throughout the society in regards to divorce laws, property laws, domestic violence, union rights, fertility issues, and participation in the political process. The social and political restrictions on Saudi women are extreme. Many Saudi women point to an ingrained male concept of "honor" as the backbone to this patriarchal system.[14] A Saudi man's honor is tied to his position as guardian and protector of the females in his life; his honor is tarnished if these women assert their independence and rights.

Many observers believe that Saudi women have less freedom than women in any other country in the world. Defiance of male authority is punished severely. In addition, a religious police force patrols the kingdom and enforces the veil for women and beats women with sticks in Mecca and Medina if they stray into male-only areas, or if their dress is considered immodest by their conservative standards. The religious police also monitor shops to make sure they do not display "indecent" magazine covers.[15]

Saudi Arabia's heavy use of the death penalty and its harsh treatment of human rights advocates, including arbitrary arrest, detention without trial, and torture, has been criticized in the global media, yet domestically such actions often effectively silence criticism. For example, Ashraf Fayadh, a Palestinian poet who has always lived in Saudi Arabia, was sentenced in 2015 to death by beheading for poems deemed atheistic and blasphemous. After an international outcry appealing for his release, which involved hundreds of leading authors, artists, and actors, and more than sixty international arts and human rights groups, a Saudi court in February 2016 overturned the death sentence and instead imposed an eight-year prison term and eight-hundred lashes for Fayadh.[16] Raif Badawi, a Saudi writer who managed an online forum called "Free Saudi Liberals," was convicted of insulting Islam and promoting unacceptable thoughts electronically and faces ten years in prison and a thousand lashes.[17] In addition, the government tightly controls domestic radio and television stations and pays public relations firms millions to counter reports of the kingdom's abuses of human rights and, in particular, the subjugation of women.[18]

As noted above, sex segregation results in few women being allowed to work in the private sector. Since women are not allowed to drive, transportation becomes a huge problem. In 2014 Saudi officials created a pilot program of transportation subsidies for taxis to allow women to take new jobs at one of Riyadh's shopping malls. But the costs of expanding the program are prohibitive. The government could create more public transit, but the sexes would have to continue to be segregated.[19]

Although buses are segregated, many Saudi men do not allow their wives to use public transportation. The alternatives: have a male family member provide transportation or hire a driver or taxi, which is very costly. The lack of day care facilities also impacts a woman's ability to work. Again, a man's honor is tied to societal norms regarding his wife, whose first duty must be to her husband and family. Working outside the home thus often becomes problematic. However, in 2014 the arrival of car services brought women a new means of travel and freedom of movement. Saudi women have been heavy users of new car service options such as Uber and its Dubai-based competitor, Careem.[20]

The human rights threshold criteria explored in chapter 1 has been surpassed with the denial of basic human rights to the women of Saudi Arabia. The situation has metastasized into a severe human rights crisis limiting the ability of many Saudi women to enjoy life. Saudi women have courageously organized to fight for public policy and legal reforms to change this patriarchal system and establish fundamental protections for girls and women. Analyzing the practices and laws of the Saudi state in relation to internationally affirmed human rights brings clarity to this discussion and casts a bright light on practices that restrict the freedom and well-being of women in Saudi Arabia.

HUMAN RIGHTS LAW

CEDAW provides a global standard on the fundamental rights of women, accepted by 187 states, including many countries in the Arab world.[21]

Through this treaty, the United Nations is able to assess a nation's progress in following through on their word to respect, protect, and fulfill its human rights duties and obligations toward women.

According to Donna Arzt, traditional Islamic law stands in stark contradiction to the rights outlined in CEDAW. Arzt argues that gender inequality under traditional Islamic law is demonstrated by (a) women considered as wards of men, (b) women legally disqualified from holding political or judicial office, and (c) women denied the capacity to initiate a marriage or divorce contract. In addition, a woman's property inheritance is usually about half the share of the male and a woman's testimony in court is worth half of a man's. Furthermore, "[h]usbands have the right to chastise their wives for 'disobedience,' including by 'light beating.'"[22]

Saudi Arabia in ratifying CEDAW made a controversial "general reservation" stating that where there is a conflict between convention principles and Islamic law principles, Islamic law shall have precedence. As a result, the most basic human rights protections guaranteed to women in CEDAW are not upheld in practice in Saudi Arabia. For example, examine CEDAW Article 16 (1):

> States Parties shall take all appropriate measures to eliminate discrimination against women in all matters relating to marriage and family relations and in particular shall ensure, on a basis of equality of men and women:
>
> a. The same right to enter into marriage;
> b. The same right freely to choose a spouse and to enter into marriage only with their free and full consent;
> c. The same rights and responsibilities during marriage and at its dissolution.[23]

Yet in Saudi Arabia none of this is upheld as different rights and duties apply to husband and wife in marriage and divorce. A woman cannot conclude her own marriage contract, but needs a male guardian to act on her behalf. Islamic law recognizes three forms of dissolution of marriage: unilateral repudiation by the husband called *talaq*; divorce by mutual agreement; and judicial dissolution on the basis of specified grounds. Of these three, unilateral repudiation by the husband is the most common. According to Zainah Almihdar: "A husband may exercise this right by pronouncing any words that show his intention to divorce. There are no required formalities; *talaq* by the husband can be done orally or in writing without having to resort to a court or give any reasons for the divorce." This right is guaranteed for the husband.[24]

Another contradiction between the rights accorded women in CEDAW and Saudi law concerns the principles of women's autonomy and freedom. Examine CEDAW Article 15 (2):

> States Parties shall accord to women, in civil matters, a legal capacity identical to that of men and the same opportunities to exercise that capacity. In particular, they shall give women equal rights to conclude contracts and to administer property and shall treat them equally in all stages of procedure in courts and tribunals.[25]

Yet Saudi family law dictates that every woman needs a male family member to act as her guardian and is the one who has decision-making powers over her. In the absence of a father or a husband, this "legal guardian" could even be her son. Zainah Almihdar notes that this principle is a very narrow interpretation of specific Qur'anic verses.[26]

A further violation of internationally affirmed women's rights concerns the guardianship of children. Examine CEDAW Article 16 (f), which gives women

> (f) The same rights and responsibilities with regard to guardianship, wardship, trusteeship and adoption of children, or similar institutions where these concepts exist in national legislation; in all cases the interests of the children shall be paramount.[27]

Yet in Saudi Islamic law "guardianship," which involves decision-making powers affecting the child, such as marriage, education, medical care, and concluding contracts on behalf of the child, is always the responsibility of the father until the child reaches puberty.[28]

Instead of equality, a woman's status is one of a dependent, a minor. A woman needs the consent of a male guardian to take a job, enroll in school, travel, initiate court proceedings, and so on. Even the filing of a report against an abusive guardian requires his approval.[29]

Saudi Arabia's "general reservation" placing Islamic law principles above the human rights principles in CEDAW makes a mockery of their "ratification" of this treaty. As Upendra Baxi writes: "The near-universality of ratification of [CEDAW] . . . betokens no human liberation of women. Rather, it endows the state with the power to tell more Nietzschean lies. . . . 'State' is the name of the coldest of all cold monsters. Coldly, it tells lies, too; and this lie grows out of its mouth: 'I, the state, am the people.'"[30] Saudi Arabia can use its ratification of CEDAW to publicly proclaim a commitment to human dignity for women while simultaneously implementing public policies that undermine women's civil, political, economic, and social human rights. Treaty "ratification" thus gives the Saudi government the ability to "tell more Nietschzean lies." The Saudis attempt to use their ratification of CEDAW as a vehicle to legitimize their international reputation by presenting themselves as a human rights abiding state. Given the severe repression of human rights activists and Saudi women inside the kingdom the hypocrisy is breathtaking.

The Saudi "general reservation" is also illegal. A nation can file a "reservation" to a specific element of a treaty and state that it will not be bound by that provision. However, a nation is not allowed to submit a "reservation" that is incompatible with the overall purpose of the treaty itself. For example, the United States while ratifying the CERD submitted a reservation to Articles 4 and 7, which were felt to violate US laws protecting individual freedom of speech, expression, and association. This reservation was specific and did not undermine the overall purpose of ending racial discrimination. The Saudi reservation to CEDAW, however, is not specific. It rather challenges the whole premise of women's rights articulated so clearly in this treaty. The International Court of Justice (ICJ) has stated that reservations are legitimate as long as they are "compatible" with the purpose of the treaty. An ICJ opinion states:

> The object and purpose of the Convention thus limit both the freedom of making reservations and that of objecting to them. It follows that it is *the compatibility of a reservation with the object and purpose of the Convention* that must furnish the criteria for . . . making the reservation . . . [for] . . . objecting to the reservation . . . [and] the admissibility of any reservation.[31]

The Saudi reservation is clearly not compatible with the purpose of the convention. While the Saudi reservation serves to perpetuate gender inequality, CEDAW demands that ratifying states modify cultural patterns and customary practices that block gender equality. Examine CEDAW Article 5 (a):

> States Parties shall take all appropriate measures:
> (a) To modify the social and cultural patterns of conduct of men and women, with a view to achieving the elimination of prejudices and customary and all other practices which are based on the idea of the inferiority or the superiority of either of the sexes or on stereotyped roles for men and women.[32]

Saudi women have called for the elimination of the principle of "legal guardian" and the removal of all social and cultural patterns that violate women's human rights. In addition, there have been fervent calls for protection of the civil and political rights of human rights advocates. But bringing about such changes will involve a fundamental ideological shift within the Saudi male elite who for decades have resisted accepting universal human rights.

Immediately after World War II, Saudi Arabia opposed the movement to develop global and universal human rights. When the UDHR was approved by the UN General Assembly in 1948 without a dissenting vote, Saudi Arabia was one of the few countries to abstain. The Saudi ambassador to the United Nations objected to Article 18, which states:

> Everyone has the right to freedom of thought, conscience and religion; this right includes freedom to change his religion or belief, and freedom, either alone or in community with others and in public or private, to manifest his religion or belief in teaching, practice, worship and observance.

In its abstention, Saudi Arabia reserved the right to discriminate on the basis of religion, which de facto asserts the principle of gender apartheid. As Abdullahi An-Na'im writes:

> Far from derogating from the universality of the principles of the Declaration, the Saudi abstention, ostensibly based on Islamic religious grounds, in fact demonstrates the equal untenability of discrimination on grounds of either race, in the case of [apartheid] South Africa, or religion, in the case of Saudi Arabia. . . . In other words, Saudi Arabia's allegedly Islamic abstention from joining the international consensus on universal human rights standards is similar to South Africa's racist abstention. [33]

During the late 1940s, Saudi opposed UN provisions on women's rights, arguing that marriage was an area in which "Islamic law was explicit on the smallest details." The Saudi delegates rejected the requirements that wives be of full age and have equal rights, arguing that these obligations reflected Western biases. [34]

The decision by Saudi Arabia to ratify CEDAW in 2000 did not represent a change in the elite's attitudes toward women's rights. According to Mayer, Islamic law in Saudi Arabia "locks women into a system of rigid segregation and subordination that is utterly incompatible with women's equality." The patriarchal Saudi law continues to be enforced ensuring women's ongoing subordinate position. Mayer notes that "[f]eeble measures, such as the 2006 appointment of a few women as advisers to the toothless Consultative Council and plans to allow women to vote in municipal elections in 2015, exemplify Saudi minimalism."[35]

In the 2015 municipal elections, Saudi women were allowed to vote and run for office for the first time. While more than a dozen women won seats on local councils, this represented less than 1 percent of the elected council members nationwide. On the one hand, the participation of women in the vote represented a milestone, an initial step toward bringing women into the public sphere in the kingdom. As Hatoon al-Fassi, a Saudi professor of women's history, stated: "This is a big step that we are making the best of and that we are going to build on to ask for more rights." Yet, on the other hand, the slow, glacial process of reform is frustrating to many women as the government continues to enforce the patriarchal guardianship laws that limit women's agency.[36]

In addition, the government of Saudi Arabia continues to defend its "reservation" to CEDAW while posing as a supporter of human rights. This unsupportable and contradictory position led their representatives to deliver blatant misrepresentations to the United Nations. For example, during their dialogue with the CEDAW Committee in 2007, the committee observed that the Saudi report did not discuss the ban on women driving. The Saudi response was thus: "There is no legal provision banning women from driving cars." While there is technically no statutory law, there is customary law reinforced by a *fatwa* issued in 1990 after a women's driving protest. In fact, Saudi women continue to be arrested and punished for driving. For example, in May 2011, Manal al-Sharif was imprisoned after publicizing her own driving, a punishment designed to deter future mass driving protests.[37] And in April 2014 a Saudi woman was sentenced to 150 lashes and eight months in prison on charges of driving and resisting arrest. These arrests illustrate how extremely dangerous it remains for Saudi women to assert basic rights inside their own country.[38] They also clearly demonstrate that the Saudi delegates were attempting to mislead the CEDAW Committee as it remains a criminal offense for a woman to drive a car in Saudi Arabia.

The CEDAW Committee noted the ways in which the Saudi reservation compromised the objective and purpose of the convention. The committee identified numerous obstacles to the effective implementation of CEDAW. For example, there is no definition of discrimination against women within the state's basic laws, nor provisions for its prohibition. The committee expressed concern about male guardianship over women and the lack of specific laws relating to violence against women.[39] The committee said that Saudi Arabia should end the practice of requiring women to obtain a man's permission to marry, work, travel, or be educated. Overall, the United Nations stated that women in Saudi Arabia should be allowed more basic freedoms and women should be granted equal rights in marriage, divorce, child custody, and inheritance.[40] Yet the impact of these "recommendations" and "statements of concern" by the committee is limited inside the Saudi state. With the ongoing support of the United States and European states, the Saudi elite can continue to pay no attention to the progressive recommendations from the United Nations.

THE UNITED STATES AND EUROPE: IGNORING GENDER APARTHEID

The United States and leading European nations have, in general, ignored gender apartheid in order to pursue economic and geopolitical relations with the Saudi ruling elite. Women's rights just can't compete with oil, arms sales, and security priorities.

Saudi Arabia remains the largest US trading partner in the Middle East. In 2013 Saudi exports to the United States, dominated by oil, were worth more than $51.8 billion. In that same year, US exports to Saudi Arabia, primarily in weapons, machinery, and vehicles, were valued at $18.9 billion.[41]

Both the Bush and Obama administrations have viewed the Saudi government as a vital regional partner with ongoing US arms sales and related training programs. Arms sales to Saudi Arabia include fighter aircraft, helicopters, missile defense systems, missiles, bombs, armored vehicles, and related equipment and services. The estimated total value of these arms sales from 2010 to 2014 is more than $86 billion.[42]

Leaders in both the United States and Saudi Arabia have prioritized continuity in their diplomatic relations over significant change due to policy differences. US criticisms of Saudi's refusal to grant women equal rights have been low-key. Saudi officials describe the differences as "tactical" and claim few disagreements over final objectives.

US expansion of its production of domestic oil has lowered US imports of oil overall and contributed to a significant decline in oil prices. While Saudi officials have expressed some mild concern about these trends, rising demand for oil in South and East Asia has compensated for the decline in sales to the United States. Despite this decline, as of the end of January 2014, the US Energy Information Administration reports that Saudi Arabia was still the second-largest source of US crude oil imports, behind only Canada. The Saudi Kingdom provides more than 1.3 million barrels of oil per day to the United States. These oil exports to the United States represent roughly 15 percent of Saudi exports, while East Asia accounts for more than 50 percent.[43]

The United States and Saudi Arabia have long-standing military training programs and significant, ongoing, high-volume weapons sales. In addition, the Saudi government provides intelligence to the United States on the politics and upheaval in the region; and, perhaps most important, is essentially seen by the United States as a counterweight to Iran. With US oil production surging, oil may no longer be as significant in binding the nations together. Instead, with the growth of ISIS, the nuclear threat in Iran, and political instability across the Middle East, the United States sees the kingdom as essential to stability in the region. Saudi leaders have expressed differences with US foreign policy in Egypt, Iran, and elsewhere. But these differences have not caused either side to fundamentally rethink their strategic relationship; rather, there remains a steadiness and stability in the economic programs and security agreements between the two countries.

Pragmatic considerations of political and economic advantage also shape European foreign policy toward the kingdom. Gerd Nonneman notes a number of distinct areas central to European interests in Saudi Arabia, including strategic calculations with regard to shipping lanes, access to oil, and, since the 1970s, access to the markets of the Persian Gulf and of Saudi Arabia in particular.[44]

In addition, France, Germany, Britain, and Italy have succeeded in capturing shares of the arms market to Saudi Arabia. In the 1980s, France and Britain overtook the United States as arms suppliers. The ascendancy of European countries in the arms market is seen in the following example. In July 1985, after the Saudi attempt to buy F-15 fighter bombers was defeated in the US Congress, the Saudis signed a European contract worth over $30 billion. This was the largest single defense contract in British history, which "shifted the entire structure of the Saudi air force from dependence on the United States to dependence on Britain." By 2000 this agreement had contributed to the establishment of seven joint companies supporting some thirty thousand jobs in Britain.[45]

These extensive ties to Saudi Arabia demonstrate not only economic interdependence but the ethics of interdependence as well. The United States and Europe significantly contribute to the viability of the current Saudi regime. It is impossible to argue that these economic, military, and political links do not also serve elite Saudi interest. The Saudi regime is more easily able to survive and flourish due to the support it receives from the United States and Europe. With their heavy investments and trade agreements, combined with long-standing military, intelligence, and security arrangements, these outside countries are morally culpable for supporting this repressive regime. The relative silence of the United States and Europe on human rights in the kingdom serves the interests of the patriarchal Saudi elite.

Local and Global Conversations: Gender and Honor

Central to the delegated sexual roles in Saudi society is a conception of male and female "honor." Behind gender apartheid is the connection between a male's honor and firm control over the females in his life—his wife and daughters. The privileged status of male family members in this sex-segregated society is based upon the male performing the role of guardian and protector. The male's honor is tarnished if the woman asserts her human rights. Is it possible to foresee a change in this patriarchal system? Is it possible to envision a redefinition of honorable behavior by men and women in Saudi Arabia?

Kwame Appiah notes how "changes in honor codes can reshape honor, mobilizing it in the service of the good." In a discussion of the emancipation of women from honor murder in Pakistan, Appiah writes:

> [W]e may have more success . . . if we work to reshape honor than we will if we simply ring the bell of morality. Shame, and sometimes even carefully calibrated ridicule, may be the tools we need. . . . Honor must be turned against honor killing as it was turned against dueling, against footbinding, against slavery. Keep reminding people, by all means, that honor killing is immoral, illegal, irrational, irreligious. But even the recognition of these truths, I suspect, will not by itself align what people know with what people do. Honor killing will only perish when it is seen as dishonorable. [46]

Appiah continues his discussion with the many ways in which having honor means being entitled to respect. An "honor code," he writes, "says how people . . . can gain the right to respect, how they can lose it, and how having and losing honor changes the way they should be treated." He believes that honor is "well-suited to turn private moral sentiments into public norms. . . . It can help us make a better world."[47]

Yet how do outsiders effectively raise issues of honorable behavior inside another country? Drawing attention, for example, to the ways in which gender apartheid harms Saudi Arabia's international reputation can backfire and produce a nationalist, defensive backlash resulting in an affirmation of these repressive gender roles. What are the human rights duties—at the individual, nation-state, and global levels—for those concerned about women's rights in Saudi Arabia?

HUMAN RIGHTS DUTIES AND WOMEN'S RIGHTS IN SAUDI ARABIA

Duties on Individuals

In March 2014, when President Obama visited Saudi Arabia, he faced a "human rights nightmare." The leading human rights organizations, including Amnesty International and Freedom House, released documentation demonstrating how Saudi Arabia had one of the worst records in the world on protecting civil and political rights. Amnesty documented the kingdom's ongoing "sustained crackdown on human rights activists." Does a US presidential visit at a time like this indirectly facilitate such repression?[48]

To avoid such complicity in oppression, Amnesty International urged Obama to have a female security officer drive his limo while in the country. Fifty-five Republican and Democratic members of Congress and over a dozen NGOs wrote the following to the president before his trip:

> The government of Saudi Arabia has repeatedly engaged in systematic human rights violations targeting women, religious minorities, and peaceful political reformers. Your meetings with King Abdullah and other officials will be an opportunity to publicly integrate human rights concerns, as defined by the Universal Declaration of Human Rights, into the U.S.-Saudi relationship.[49]

The world notices when the United States ignores the arrests of human rights activists and the lashing of women drivers. Most Americans believe that we are a better country when we refuse to sacrifice human rights values for short-term geopolitical or economic gain. An individual US citizen concerned about women's rights in Saudi Arabia could have helped the president in this situation. The president's hand would have been strengthened, for example, if he had gone to Riyadh with the knowledge that millions of US citizens had acted to support women inside the kingdom by coming to the defense of the women arrested for driving in Saudi Arabia.

Overall, American citizens can pressure the US government to reevaluate its close relationship with the elite patriarchy in control of the kingdom. We no longer need to ignore Saudi Arabia's treatment of women in deference to either its geopolitical role in the region or its massive economic power. It is in the US national interest to pursue a more forceful and muscular human rights policy toward Saudi Arabia.

Without citizen pressure, official US foreign policy historically has rarely prioritized human rights and often ignored the most abusive practices. Yet public pressure in support of a strong human rights policy can make a difference. For example, Anthony Lake, former president Bill Clinton's national security advisor, stated that there was little public pressure for the United States to intervene to attempt to stop the Rwandan genocide as the violence escalated in 1994. As a result, Clinton felt no pressure to act and, according to Samantha Power, "did not convene a single meeting of his senior foreign policy advisers to discuss U.S. options for Rwanda." Consequently, during the one hundred days when some eight hundred thousand Tutsi and politically moderate Hutus were murdered, the United States did almost nothing to try to stop the genocide.[50] According to Lake, the United States viewed Rwanda during this period as "a 'sideshow,' but not even a sideshow—a no-show."[51] Lake believes that public pressure could have made a difference here. If Clinton felt that he had public support for intervention to stop the murders, he would have felt pressure to act, and hopefully would have done so. Public pressure in the past has certainly made a difference in bringing about fundamental changes in US policy toward the former apartheid government of South Africa and to ending the Vietnam War.

However, as already noted, pressure from the United States that ignores the vital role of local leadership can backfire. It is definitely not helpful for Europeans and Americans to lecture, patronize, and judge Saudis from afar. In fact, such pressure can embolden the regime and make the struggle for change even more difficult. It is thus essential for those outside the country to follow the lead of women's rights activists inside Saudi Arabia. US citizens can listen to and support the brave Saudi women's rights activists on the ground. These women face a repressive government and a hostile environment. In this dangerous environment, international support can provide essential publicity and protection to these individuals and organizations.

Saudi women's groups that deserve our support include the Association for the Protection and Defense of Women's Rights in Saudi Arabia and the Campaign October 26. Founded by Wajeha al-Huwaider and Fawzia Al-Uyyouni, the association has worked to help women gain the right to drive and to give a voice to the women victims traumatized by ongoing violence. In addition, the Saudi women running the Campaign October 26 also seek to lift the ban on women driving in Saudi Arabia. The actions of these activists are having an impact on Saudi society and deserve the support of individual global citizens around the world. For example, in December 2014, Saudi activists pleaded with the government to free two women, Loujain al-Hathloul and Maysaa al-Amoudi, who were detained after driving to call attention to the absurdity of a Saudi woman not being allowed to drive her own car in her native land. Their actions were part of an ongoing campaign to challenge the kingdom's ban on "driving while female." In late 2014, the Saudi king's advisory council recommended lifting the ban on female drivers, "but only for women over 30, who must be off the road by 8 p.m., cannot wear makeup behind the wheel, and require a male relative's permission."[52]

Another Saudi organization raising women's human rights inside the kingdom is the National Family Safety Program led by Dr. Maha Al Muneef, which focuses on the rights and interests of women and children. Dr. Al Muneef has made personal visits to police stations and courts in Riyadh to meet with officers and judges to educate them on issues of domestic abuse. The National Family Safety Program has held a series of symposiums on domestic violence, in Jeddah, Madinah, and the southern province of Asir, creating a national dialogue on the treatment of women. These Saudi women argue that condoning the physical abuse of women is anathema to all Islamic ideals. As a result of all of her efforts fighting for women's human rights inside Saudi Arabia, Dr. Al Muneef has been described as the "Gloria Steinem of Arabia."[53]

Duties on Nation-States

[T]he brutal oppression of women is a central goal of the terrorists. . . . Civilized people throughout the world are speaking out in horror—not only because our hearts break for the women and children of Afghanistan, but also because in Afghanistan, we see the world the terrorists would like to impose on the rest of us. . . . I hope Americans will join our family in working to ensure that dignity and opportunity will be secured for all the women and children of Afghanistan. —First Lady Laura Bush, November 17, 2001

Following the horrific events of 9/11, the Bush administration linked women's rights to the War on Terror. Yet to many observers such pronouncements seemed as little more than a cynical public relations ploy designed to foster support for the US wars in Afghanistan and Iraq. Feminist scholars note, for example, that the Bush administration refused to support the Union of the Women of Afghanistan and remained silent about gender apartheid in Saudi Arabia. [54] Throughout the twentieth century, the US government used human rights discourse as propaganda to justify morally dubious and illegal military interventions. [55] This pattern of deception in deploying humanitarian and human rights language for geopolitical objectives should give us pause about US claims and military actions taken on behalf of women's rights.

Furthermore, the Bush administration played down the horrendous record of violations against women by US allies in the Northern Alliance, as documented by both Human Rights Watch and Amnesty International. The United States was silent on the rapes and assaults that were widespread in Afghanistan before the Taliban came to power. And the current Afghan regime includes warlords who were complicit in these actions but are now immune from prosecution. [56]

The Obama administration has made support for women's rights in Saudi Arabia a low priority. Negotiations with the kingdom focus on issues of energy, economics, military affairs, and security with human rights issues rarely raised in high-level talks. Publicly, of course, US officials will state overall support for oppressed peoples, and in this case, the rights of women. But if one evaluates a country's foreign policy on the basis of what they do, and not just on what they say, it is hard not to draw the conclusion that women's rights in the Middle East are not a top priority of the United States.

For example, on a visit to Riyadh in November 2013, Secretary of State John Kerry sidestepped an opportunity to support the Saudi women fighting for equal rights. A reporter asked Kerry, "I was wondering what your take is on women driving in Saudi Arabia?" Kerry responded, "[I]t's no secret that in the United States of America we embrace equality for everyone, regardless of gender, race or any other qualification. But it's up to Saudi Arabia to make its own decisions about its own social structure choices and timing for whatever events." [57]

Kerry's comments were also much more lenient than Hillary Clinton's views when she was secretary of state. In June 2011, when asked about the women risking arrest by driving, Clinton replied:

I am moved by it and I support them. We have raised this issue at the highest level of the Saudi Government. We've made clear our views that women everywhere, including women in the Kingdom, have the right to make decisions about their lives and their futures. And mobility, such as provided by the freedom to drive, provides access to economic opportunity, including jobs, which does fuel growth and stability. And it's also important for just day-to-day life, to say nothing of the necessity from time to time to transport children for various needs and sometimes even emergencies.[58]

In his visit to Saudi Arabia in March 2014 President Obama appeared to straddle between the ambivalence of Kerry and the relative forcefulness of Clinton. In his discussions with King Abdullah of Saudi Arabia, Obama chose to not raise the issues surrounding women's human rights in the kingdom. Yet, just hours before he was to leave the country, he presented an International Women of Courage award to a Saudi woman for her work to prevent domestic violence. The president praised Maha Al Muneef's efforts to improve women's human rights in Saudi Arabia and told her: "[I am] so very, very proud of you and grateful for all the work you're doing here."[59]

Obama's actions epitomize US ambivalence about the priority of women's human rights in foreign policy negotiations. The United States has many significant issues to discuss and negotiate with the kingdom, including nuclear negotiations in Iran and the Syrian civil war. Women's human rights are just not seen as equal in significance to these other issues and deserving of the expenditure of US political capital.

As long as women's human rights are in competition with other geopolitical and economic issues, they will lose out. In our conflicted and divided world system, there will always appear to be more pressing and immediate economic and security concerns that are proclaimed to override human rights. However, this is a false choice. During both the Cold War and the struggle against apartheid in South Africa, the incorporation of a consistent policy in support of fundamental human rights not only helped those individuals struggling for human rights, but also improved the US geopolitical and strategic global position. The United States today can consistently and continuously push and prod Saudi Arabia to uphold global human rights standards without jeopardizing other foreign policy priorities. As noted, human rights duties at the national level require that leaders of states uphold principles and instruments of international law and human rights. To fulfill and uphold its human rights duties and obligations, the United States should pursue a more forceful human rights agenda in its foreign policy.

In addition, US national security would be enhanced if the American government confronted and challenged the extremist policies of the Saudi elite. Saudi's current rulers rely on an alliance with a religious clergy that preaches and defends Wahhabism, an ultrapuritanical form of Islam. Wahhabism hopes to restore an Islamic caliphate and has produced fanatical terrorists in pursuit of this mission. Saudi nationals who grew up exposed to this radical extremist propaganda have carried out many of the most violent acts of terrorism against the United States and other countries. Religious television, social media, and Islamist newspapers in the kingdom preach hatred of the West and in particular the United States. ISIS itself is a reflection of this extremist culture. Yet the US government continues to ally with Saudi Arabia, despite the kingdom becoming the location of the chief ideological sponsors of terrorism in the world today.[60]

Due to Saudi Arabia's geopolitical position and vast oil resources, human rights have been consistently subordinated to economic and political interests. In the practice of its foreign policy, the United States unfailingly glosses over the human rights violations in the kingdom. As National Security Advisor Susan Rice stated in a December 2013 speech, "Let's be honest: At times, as a result, we do business with governments that do not respect the rights we hold most dear. We make tough choices." But the "tough choices" in regards to Saudi Arabia never go in the direction of human rights. The "choice" is rather to support economic and geopolitical priorities.[61]

The tragedy of this consistent "realist" foreign policy is that it privileges the views of the Saudi elite over those of Saudi citizens. As with all countries, Saudi society is divided over fundamental issues, including women's rights. It is certainly the case that thousands of Saudi women resent being treated as legal minors, unable to make their own life decisions about travel, education, and certain medical procedures. And the situation is not improving. For example, Adam Coogle, a Middle East researcher at Human Rights Watch, recently reported: "Two women in the Eastern Province were convicted by a Saudi court of 'inciting a woman against her husband' for trying to help a woman who said she had been locked in her home without adequate food."[62]

The United States is misreading both Saudi society and the Saudi ruling structure where there is a "tug-of-war between reformist and conservative factions." Instead of bolstering the position of the reformist, the relative silence of the United States lends vital credibility to the conservatives making it even more dangerous than it already is for activists and reformers to speak out.[63]

Duties on Global Institutions and Organizations

> On the ground, women in the Muslim world are piercing the veil of religious sovereignty. . . . A close study of women activists in the Muslim world demonstrates how they are confronting problems with formal laws that often privilege the viewpoints and interests of traditionalists and patriarchs. Rather than accepting the binary framework of religion (on traditional leaders' terms) or rights (without normative community), activists are developing strategies that enable women to claim both. —Madhavi Sunder[64]

Working primarily through NGOs, women throughout the Muslim world have accepted the human rights duties of global citizenship and are working both in their countries, including Saudi Arabia, and across borders to end systematic discrimination and crafting liberating alternatives to existing gender-bias laws and structures. These women do not accept that either secularism or feminism is "Western" and strive to create a more just world for all. These global and regional organizations and networks created by these Muslim women deserve broad support.

For example, the transnational network Women Living under Muslim Laws (WLUML) is pursuing a human rights strategy designed to both "pierce the veil" of religious sovereignty and articulate and demand freedom and equality within their communities. Through information sharing via Internet, Twitter, and old-fashioned fax machines, WLUML links women in the Muslim world who are seeking to articulate women's human rights within Muslim communities and countries. Madhavi Sunder describes how WLUML is networking and sharing information with women around the world and particularly with women from Muslim countries. This global network of Muslim women challenges the patriarchal claims of the fundamentalists and contests the very idea of monolithic Muslim laws. "To that end, WLUML collected information chronicling the existence of alternative legal systems in Muslim communities that were far less repressive—indeed were progressive—on women's issues." The WLUML thus contests the fundamentalists' depictions of identity and empowers women in their Muslim communities to create a more egalitarian framework embracing women's rights. The WLUML provides a critical source of solidarity and support for women activists in Muslim countries. Strategically, this offers "an important retort to fundamentalists who depict women's rights as 'Western' and un-Islamic."[65]

WLUML stresses that religion and culture are not homogeneous but pluralist, contested, and evolving. Women have the right to participate, challenge, and create their culture and communities. Women have the right to define their identity for themselves and "stop accepting unconditionally and without questions what is presented to them as the 'correct' religion, the 'correct' culture, or the 'correct' national identity." The WLUML writes, "The essential issue is who has the power to define what women's identities should be. . . . It is time to challenge both politically as well as personally—those who define what the identity of women should be as Muslims."[66]

Muslim women in Egypt are also utilizing modern technologies to mobilize action on women's rights at home and abroad. HarassMap is a project incubated by the Egyptian NGO Nahdet El Mahrous and was created in response to persistent sexual harassment on the streets of Egypt. In 2005 the cofounders of HarassMap were overwhelmed by the appalling sexual harassment they encountered on a daily basis. These women decided not to wait for the government to act, but to "do something on the ground" to change society's acceptance of sexual harassment. After conducting a survey, they realized that most women in Egypt were affected by sexual harassment and many people wanted to do something about it. With other volunteers they started a campaign, which eventually was adopted by the Egyptian Center for Women's Rights.[67]

Frontline SMS and Ushahidi are free software that can be linked together to make an anonymous reporting and mapping system. The cofounders realized that this new technology was perfect for mapping sexual harassment, since about 97 percent of Egyptians own a mobile phone. HarassMap was launched in December 2010 utilizing "online reporting and mapping technology to support an offline community mobilization effort to break stereotypes, stop making excuses for perpetrators, and to convince people to speak out and act against harassment."[68]

HarassMap tracks and maps incidents of sexual harassment through text message or computer reports and utilizes the Ushahidi open source platform. It is of note that Ushahidi—which means "testimony" in Swahili—was first developed in 2008 in Kenya to map reports of postelection violence. These traumatic incidents of violence in Kenya were submitted via the web and mobile phones, which gave "citizen journalists" a "map" of the terror on the ground.[69] The HarassMap initiative has helped to break the fear and taboo of openly discussing sexual harassment in Egypt. There is now open discussion of these issues, and a variety of new initiatives to combat sexual harassment have been launched. HarassMap is an exciting example of how "crowdsource mapping" initiatives are being effectively utilized for progressive organizing within and between nations. Activists from twenty-eight different countries have asked for HarassMap to assist and guide them in establishing similar initiatives in their home countries. Some of these initiatives include Ramallah Street Watch, Resist Harassment (Lebanon), Safe Streets (Yemen), Bijoya (Bangladesh), Name and Shame (Pakistan), Women under Siege (Syria), Akshara/HarassMap India, and SawtNsaa (Algeria). In addition, women from Saudi Arabia are also working to set up their version of HarassMap. [70]

WLUML and HarassMap are examples of women's NGOs working both locally and globally on women's rights in Muslim countries. These organizations are in the lead in the struggle to protect women's basic rights and freedoms in the Middle East. The NGOs are acting to fulfill human rights duties at the global level.

The construction of international laws and institutions to promote women's rights is also central at the world level. The most significant instrument of international law concerning the rights of women is CEDAW. As noted above, the CEDAW Committee has had little success in holding Saudi Arabia accountable to the human rights protections for women articulated so clearly in this treaty. The CEDAW Committee needs more financial and administrative support to be effective. The world's major powers, including the United States, have made the human rights compliance mechanisms at the OHCHR in Geneva a low priority. If the global community is serious about fulfilling its human rights duties toward women, these institutions and compliance mechanisms must be strengthened. [71]

In chapter 2, I noted how important it was for the United Nations to speak out about mass incarceration and police brutality in the United States and in other countries around the world. It often takes an outside voice of experts, who are not politically invested in the country, to be able to accurately assess state practice in regards to human rights fulfillment. The denial of women's rights in Saudi Arabia is another clear example where international action is essential. The imposition of gender apartheid by the ruling male elite of Saudi society has radically transformed the lives of millions inside the kingdom. Yet the most powerful states, and the United Nations itself, lightly criticize this systemic discrimination against women. By bolstering the Saudi regime through its economic and political policies, the developed, rich nations become morally complicit in perpetuating gender discrimination in the kingdom. This creates an ethic of interdependence generating human rights duties for global citizens to support and follow the leadership of the Saudi women struggling for basic rights.

The issue here is not one of "rescuing women from Islam."[72] Patriarchy in Saudi Arabia is the bulwark of an authoritarian political state that uses

---

Saudi Women's Struggle to Drive

Saudi Arabia remains the world's only country where women are not allowed to drive a car. Yet in October 2014 Saudi women activists declared their online campaign for women's right to drive a success. The campaign, which began in 2013, has been encouraging women to post online images of themselves driving. Dozens of women responded positively and posted images of themselves behind the wheel of a car. As one organizer commented: "A day hasn't gone by without receiving one or two videos" of Saudi women driving. In addition, more than 2,800 people signed the online petition asking Saudi authorities to lift the ban on women driving.

But women remain afraid and those who post videos and images risk arrest and worse. Despite the support from religious and academic leaders to give women the right to drive, there has been no change in the kingdom's legislation. According to a Saudi woman activist, who spoke on condition of anonymity, a Saudi woman driver received a hundred lashes for violating local customs and norms. The interior ministry responding to this current campaign for women's human rights warned that it would continue to "strictly implement" measures against anyone who "contributes in any manner or by any acts, towards providing violators with the opportunity to undermine the social cohesion." Saudi women activists responded by saying that they thought this meant the campaign was having a successful impact. One Saudi activist put it this way: "I think it's pretty successful. If we're getting a reaction, that means we're effective."[a]

---

[a] "Saudi Women's Driving Campaign Seen as 'Successful,'" *Business Insider*, October 26, 2014. Available at http://www.businessinsider.com/afp-saudi-womens-driving-campaign-a-success-2014-10 (accessed December 30, 2015); "Saudi Arabia: 2,800 Women Take Up the Driving Challenge, *Ansamed* (Dubai), October 27, 2014. Available at http://www.ansamed.info/ansamed/en/news/sections/generalnews/2014/10/27/saudi-arabia-2800-women-take-up-the-driving-challenge_20d19861-936d-4180-a41f-e5121cb1d2cb.html (accessed December 30, 2015).

religion to hide this oppression and bolster male rule. These dynamics are not unique to the Islamic world. Repressive governments around the world promote authoritarian structures that perpetuate the systematic discrimination of women. These governments, not any particular religion, are responsible for the oppression of women. Glaring inequities based upon gender, and hideous violence against women, are a global phenomenon. It is not helpful to stereotype one religion or one region as extremely different from other religions and regions in regards to the violation of the basic rights of women. Women in Saudi Arabia, and women everywhere, deserve lives free of bias, exploitation, discrimination, and domestic abuse, where the human dignity of all is upheld.

DISCUSSION QUESTIONS

1. How is the language of universal human rights potentially helpful to the women of Saudi Arabia who seek to end gender-biased laws and institutions? How could such an approach potentially produce a nationalist and cultural backlash and thus hinder the struggle for women's rights? Is it possible to thread this needle?
2. How can those who live outside Saudi Arabia raise issues of gender equality inside the kingdom without appearing to be on a crusade to "save" Muslim women?
3. Do citizens in Europe and the United States have a human rights duty to act in support of women's organizations dedicated to women's rights in Saudi Arabia? Why or why not? Explore the degree of ethical interdependence between the Saudi government and the United States and Europe.
4. How do long-standing cultural customs defining honorable male and female behavior evolve and change? What causes a society to redefine gender roles?

WEBSITES

Musawah ("equality" in Arabic) is a global movement led by Muslim women dedicated to equality and justice in the Muslim family. Website: http://www.musawah.org.

Muslimah Media Watch provides a space for Muslim feminists to speak for themselves and critique how their images appear in the media and popular culture. Website: http://www.patheos.com/blogs/mmw/about-2.

Sisters in Islam promotes gender equality, justice, freedom, and dignity in Islam by empowering women to be advocates for change. Website: http://www.sistersinislam.org.my.

Women's Islamic Initiative in Spirituality and Equality (WISE) empowers Muslim women globally to become full participants in their communities. Website: http://www.wisemuslimwomen.org.

Women Living under Muslim Laws (WLUML) is a global network of support for women whose lives are governed by laws and customs said to derive from Islam. Website: http://www.wluml.org.

Chapter Five

Environmental Rights in China

Is China's consumption of coal the "scariest environmental fact in the world?" After the US Energy Information Administration (EIA) reported that in 2011 China's coal consumption surged for a twelfth consecutive year, alarms were sounded by a variety of scientists from around the world. In 2011 China was burning 2.3 billion metric tons of carbon-emitting coal to run its power plants and support its economic growth and thus was burning almost as much coal as the rest of the world combined. Bryan Walsh clearly states the alarm these statistics provoked: "Coal already accounts for 20% of global greenhouse-gas emissions, making it one of the biggest causes of man-made climate change. Combine that with the direct damage that air pollution from coal combustion does to human health, and there's a reason why some have called coal the enemy of the human race."[1]

Unfortunately, the situation is even worse than these earlier reports indicated. The Chinese government released new data in late 2015, which disclosed that China had been burning up to 17 percent more coal a year than had previously been reported. This updated report stated that China burned or otherwise consumed 4.2 billion metric tons of coal in 2013, far exceeding that of any other country, and emitted almost a billion more tons of carbon dioxide into the atmosphere than had previously been estimated. This new data indicated that Chinese coal consumption had been underestimated since 2000. The new data, for example, added about 600 million tons to China's coal consumption in 2012.[2]

Behind this huge increase in coal consumption is China's need to generate enough electricity to meet the demands of a robust economy, which grew on average 9 percent per year from 2000 to 2010. Coal remains popular not only in China, but around the world, because it is very cheap. With clean energy alternatives (solar, wind, and so on) still expensive relative to coal, poor and developing nations will continue to burn coal to meet pressing economic and humanitarian energy needs.[3]

By 2013 China became the world's leader in the release of greenhouse gases in the atmosphere, especially carbon dioxide, and still holds this dubious distinction today. In 2013 China released 29 percent of the world's carbon dioxide emissions, twice the amount released by the United States.[4]

The United States has reduced its domestic coal usage, but has been dubbed the "Saudi Arabia of Coal" due to its abundant coal resources. Demand for US coal remains high in China. The EIA, for example, notes a 107 percent jump from 2011 to 2012 in US coal shipments to China, from 4 million tons in 2011 to 8.3 million tons in 2012. China became both the world's largest coal producer (3.7 billion metric tons) and the world's top buyer of foreign coal (270 million tons of imports), according to the China Coal Transportation and Distribution Association. The EIA executive director describes the "troubling paradox" of coal: "To the degree that affordable coal has allowed hundreds of millions of people in emerging economies to enjoy the conveniences that the industrialized world began taking for granted long ago, its proliferation is a blessing. Yet for a society increasingly concerned about the amount of carbon it is sending into the atmosphere, the surge in coal burning is not good news."[5]

The Union of Concerned Scientists has concluded that with the countries of the world continuing to burn coal at these levels, "it will be impossible to achieve the reductions in carbon emissions needed to have a reasonable chance of preventing the worst consequences of global warming." Since it is relatively abundant and cheap, coal remains the most widely used fuel for generating electricity around the world. Yet it is the most carbon intensive of the fossil fuels. As is widely documented, global warming is largely due to human emissions of carbon into the atmosphere, with coal consumption the single biggest source of carbon discharges from human activities. In addition, coal power plants require approximately 25 gallons of water for each kilowatt-hour generated, contributing to water scarcity. There are also health consequences from coal burning, including illnesses caused by poor air quality and mercury poisoning.[6]

In addition, the World Resources Institute (WRI) describes a huge potential expansion of coal-fired power plants, despite the dire warnings that carbon emissions will lead to unstoppable climate change. The WRI identified plans for twelve hundred new coal plants around the world, with three-quarters to be located in India and China. The author of the report, WRI's Ailun Yang, stated: "This is definitely not in line with a safe climate scenario—it would put us on a really dangerous trajectory." To avoid this outcome, nations would have to move to replace coal with renewable energy and tighten air pollution regulations. While there has been movement in this direction in China, it has not been enough to forestall or prevent the devastating climate change consequences.[7]

"The coal that has powered China's economic growth," according to Elizabeth C. Economy, "is also choking its people." China's reliance on coal "is devastating" its environment. According to Economy, by 2007 China was home to sixteen of the world's twenty most polluted cities, with four of the worst in the coal-rich province of Shanxi, in northeastern China. Economy continues:

> As much as 90 percent of China's sulfur dioxide emissions and 50 percent of its particulate emissions are the result of coal use. Particulates are responsible for respiratory problems among the population, and acid rain, which is caused by sulfur dioxide emissions, falls on one-quarter of China's territory and on one-third of its agricultural land, diminishing agricultural output and eroding buildings.[8]

The 130 million new cars that China is expected to have on the roads by perhaps as early as 2020 will exacerbate this air pollution crisis. Experts note that levels of airborne particulates are already six times higher in Beijing than in New York City. Without a significant change in its urbanization policies, China's environmental conditions will only worsen. According to the Chinese Academy of Environmental Planning, the cost of environmental degradation in China was about $230 billion in 2010, or 3.5 percent of the nation's GDP, three times that in 2004. This figure ($230 billion) is calculated on the costs that arise from pollution and overall damage to the ecosystem as a result of its rapid industrialization. In January 2013, outrage boiled over when air pollution in north China reached record levels. The public fury forced officials to allow news organizations to report more accurately and with candor on the pollution. Yet economic growth remains the top governmental priority. China officially estimated its GDP in 2012 at $8.3 trillion and projected a 7.5 percent rate of growth for 2013 and an average of 7 percent a year growth in its subsequent five-year plan. This planning will result, according to a Deutsche Bank report released in February 2013, in a continuing steep environmental decline, especially given the expected high level of coal consumption and the boom in automobile sales.[9]

In April 2013, a summary of data from a scientific study of the leading causes of death worldwide concluded that outdoor air pollution contributed to 1.2 million premature deaths in China. The researchers called "ambient particulate matter pollution" the fourth-leading risk factor for deaths in China, behind dietary risks, high blood pressure, and smoking. The calculations of premature deaths because of air pollution are politically sensitive and Chinese officials in the past have censored reports that documented such premature deaths.[10] In Beijing, "levels of deadly pollutants up to 40 times the recommended exposure limit . . . struck fear into parents." As Edward Wong reports, "Few developments have eroded trust in the Communist Party as quickly as the realization that the leaders have failed to rein in threats to children's health and safety." The "fury over air pollution" is widespread and "just beginning to gain momentum." Parents are confining their children to home, scrambling to buy air purifiers, and facemasks "are now part of the urban dress code."[11]

In December 2015 Beijing for the first time issued two "red alerts" for air pollution indicating emergency levels of airborne toxins harmful to human health. These highest-level emergency pollution actions for China's capital city of 22 million people included "a shutdown of more than 3,200 schools, the pulling of about half the city's five million cars off the road each day and the temporary closing of factories and construction sites in the municipal area." Few missed the irony of this spell of poisonous air taking place at the exact moment when Chinese president Xi Jinping was meeting in Paris with world leaders to discuss the dangers of fossil fuel use. The world press coverage of China's toxic air crisis was exceedingly embarrassing to the Chinese government.[12]

CHINA'S GLOBAL "SPILLOVER" OF ENVIRONMENTAL PROBLEMS

Pollution, of course, does not respect national boundaries. China's environmental problems cannot be confined to its geographical space, but "spill over" into surrounding countries and throughout the world's ecosystem. Jianguo Liu and Jared Diamond note that China is already the largest contributor of sulfur oxides and chlorofluorocarbons in the atmosphere and its dust and aerial pollutants are transported eastward to neighboring countries and even to North Africa. A major cause of these developments leading to this worsening of global air pollution and the global warming crisis is China's consumption of coal. As noted above, China is now the world's leader in the production and consumption of coal. Coal remains the country's primary energy source and the main cause of its air pollution. [13]

In addition, dirty emissions from China's export industries are carried by powerful global winds called westerlies across the Pacific and within days contribute to air pollution in the western United States. These filthy discharges have caused dangerous spikes in contaminants in California as dust, ozone, and black carbon from China accumulate in the valleys and basins of western states. According to a scientific study published in *Proceedings of the National Academy of Sciences*, black carbon is a particular problem because rain does not wash it out of the atmosphere, and it thus persists across long distances. Diseases associated with black carbon include asthma, cancer, emphysema, and heart and lung disease. [14] The scientists wrote:

> Rising emissions produced in China are a key reason global emissions of air pollutants have remained at a high level during 2000–2009 even as emissions produced in the United States, Europe, and Japan have decreased. Outsourcing production to China does not always relieve consumers in the United States— or, for that matter, many countries in the Northern Hemisphere—from the environmental impacts of air pollution. [15]

Furthermore, China's rapid economic growth has led to other areas of environmental "spillover." For example, as the world's second leading importer of tropical rainforest timber, China is a leading force behind tropical deforestation. And China's new position in the global economy has made global environmental conditions worse. As Liu and Diamond write: "A factor exacerbating many environmental problems in China is that, as a 'world factory,' China exports products but consumes natural resources and leaves pollutants behind." For example, according to Liu and Diamond, "China's coal-based production of ammonia, required for fertilizer and textile manufacture, consumes 40–80 times more water than natural-gas-based ammonia production." [16]

Pollution from China is also claimed to be having a dramatic impact on the trees in the primeval forests in the surrounding Japanese islands leaving behind "the bleached, skeletal remains of dead trees" throughout the dark green mountainsides. According to environmental engineer Osamu Nagafuchi, this devastation is a product of airborne pollutants from China. While officials in Japan and China examine and debate Nagafuchi's conclusions, citizens of the islands argue that the pollutants are already threatening their health. "We are starting to feel like the canary in the coal mine," said Yakushima island mayor Koji Araki. "Our island is right downwind from China, so we get the brunt of it." In addition, a unique species of pine found only on Yakushima and a neighboring island is now endangered. [17]

While China's environmental problems spill over to its neighbors and the world, the opposite is true as well. The high volume of trade and investment with China has led to unequivocal harm to China's environment. According to Liu and Diamond, developed countries export untreated garbage to China, including waste containing toxic material. In addition, foreign companies transfer pollution-intensive industries, including technologies illegal in the country of origin, to China. Furthermore, most of China's exports abroad are primary goods or manufactured products that create pollution and require intensive resource use. While China's integration into the global economy contributed to its economic growth, it also created enormous environmental devastation inside and outside its borders. [18]

CHINA'S ENVIRONMENTAL POLICIES

Since at least 2003, China had declared a commitment to achieve sustainable development and "harmony" between "man" and nature. China has also participated in UN environmental conferences and legal regimes, and passed over a hundred environmental policies, laws, and regulations. However, many of these laws lack effective implementation and monitoring mechanisms and an overall systemic approach that focuses on long-term consequences. In addition, until recently, public environmental awareness remained low and political pressures to address environmental issues remained weak. Current outrage over the extreme levels of air pollution may push the government toward policies to move China away from coal as an energy source. [19]

China's economic and environmental institutions and structures are remarkably similar to those in capitalist countries, including the United States. The powerful pressures for economic growth result in institutions and policies to promote China's dramatic growth rates, while the institutions and policies to mitigate the environmental "externalities" accompanying that growth are weak.[20] Wang Chunmei and Lin Zhaolan summarize this dynamic:

> As Local leaders, who have both environmental and production responsibilities, have no incentive to increase the weight of protection goals in their decision-making calculus. Indeed, they face demanding production targets which offer monetary and promotion bonuses when completed and penalties when not. Unlike production targets, there are almost no rewards or punishments explicitly tied to success or failure in executing environmental laws. In case of a trade-off between production and the environment, the rational official expectantly will sacrifice environmental goals, or even make decisions that lead to greater environmental degradation, to meet production targets.[21]

In addition, corruption and infighting inside the government bureaucracy have further limited strong action to strengthen environmental policies. According to Edward Wong, "Even as some officials push for tighter restrictions on pollutants, state-owned enterprises—especially China's oil and power companies—have been putting profits ahead of health in working to outflank new rules." Wong further points out that the three biggest power companies in the country "are all repeat violators of government restrictions on emissions from coal-burning plants; offending power plants are found across the country, from Inner Mongolia to the southwest metropolis of Chongqing." State-owned power companies regularly ignore government orders to upgrade coal-burning electricity plants.[22]

Yet according to a report released by the Pew Charitable Trusts, in 2012 China became the world's leader in clean energy investments, surpassing US spending on renewables. The report states, "The center of gravity in the clean energy world has shifted from the United States and Europe to China." China pursued an aggressive renewable energy policy and the government financed the rapid growth of the country's solar and wind industries. As a result, according to the Pew report, China attracted $65 billion in clean energy investment in 2012, or 30 percent of all renewable investment in the world's top twenty economies. The Pew report states: "Given its world-leading long-term goals and record for meeting or exceeding mileposts en route to these goals, China is likely to be a world leader throughout this decade." China is now a leading manufacturer of wind turbines and solar products. These investments reflect that Chinese leadership feels pressure to address the horrible air quality in the country and recognize the dangers of its reliance on coal.[23]

The environmental crisis in China demonstrates how the human rights threshold criteria elaborated in chapter 1 has been exceeded. The continued burning of coal, in particular, has led to widespread suffering and severe human deprivations resulting in clear violations of established global human rights. In addition, with economic growth as the overall Chinese priority, these environmental degradations have metastasized and grown ominously. Fortunately, as will be shown below, environmental activists in China have taken the lead by pressuring the government to change directions and adopt clean energy policies. Individuals, states, and nonstate actors around the world have a human rights duty to support the efforts of these Chinese environmental activists to create viable alternatives to a coal-based energy system. What are the human duties of individuals, nation-states, and global actors concerned about the suffering caused by environmental degradation in China?

HUMAN RIGHTS DUTIES AND ENVIRONMENTAL RIGHTS IN CHINA

Duties on Individuals

China's integration into the global economy has been accompanied by severe environmental damage and decay. This economic interdependence has created a degree of ethical interdependence between the peoples of the world, in both developed and underdeveloped nations, and China in relation to the protection of the Chinese environment. The spillover of environmental problems has occurred in both directions. China's rapid economic development has contributed to air pollution and global warming that spills over into the planet's environment. And foreign firms and nations trading and investing in China have led to explicit harm to China's environment (as outlined above).

It is in the interests of individuals everywhere to help China protect its environment. But what can an individual citizen do to impact China? One pathway is for individuals to support Chinese environmental NGOs, which are essential to helping the government build the capacity to address the growing monumental environmental problems. There are more than thirty-five hundred registered NGOs in China, and many unregistered organizations active in universities and rural areas. While environmental activism and NGO organizing is still a relatively new phenomenon in China, according to Deng Guosheng, director of the NGO Research Center at Tsinghua University, "NGOs today have many good facilities, which those of the 1990s didn't have access to." For example, the Chinese NGO Green Beagle was established in 2009. It has access to state-of-the-art technology and reports on air and water quality in Beijing. In 2011 Green Beagle's report of Beijing's levels of PM2.5—fine particles in the air that are hazardous to people's health—generated controversy and prompted local authorities to begin reporting their own PM2.5 data. One of the major goals for Green Beagle and other environmental NGOs is to raise awareness to the public and the government. The director of the environmental NGO Green Earth Volunteers, Wang Yongchen, put it this way: "The longer we work on environmental protection, the more we want to influence government decision making and policies. We have to bridge environmental issues with the government and the people."[24]

Chinese environmental NGOs in the 1990s successfully organized long-lasting campaigns across regions in China to save the golden monkey and Tibetan antelope. In 2003, environmentalists protested the construction of golf courses sponsored by the municipal government in Shanghai. In 2004, over a dozen environmental NGOs joined together in Beijing to launch the "26°C Campaign," designed to monitor air conditioning use and conserve electricity. Working with international NGOs, environmentalists in China have also campaigned against plans for dam construction on the Nu River in northeastern Yunnan. Furthermore, during China's bid for the 2008 Olympic Games, environmental NGOs worked together to criticize governmental environmental policies and suggest "green" paths forward. These successful efforts of Chinese environmental NGOs and activists deserve the support of individual citizens around the world.[25]

In addition to supporting the work of environmental NGOs, citizens in other nations can pressure their home governments to accept binding quotas on the emissions of carbon into the atmosphere. While both China and the United States have agreed to adopt national environmental plans with "goals," they have refused to adopt binding national targets to limit the emissions of carbon dioxide responsible for global warming. Scientists have been clear about the devastating consequences of inaction. In May 2013 the world passed a long-feared milestone as scientists reported that the "level of the most important heat-trapping gas in the atmosphere, carbon dioxide" had reached "a concentration not seen on earth for millions of years." "Scientific instruments showed that the gas had reached an average daily level above 400 parts per million," a level that had "not been this high for at least three million years, before humans evolved." While many believe that 350 parts per million is the point of no return, many countries have adopted an official target of 450 parts per million as the maximum level compatible with sustainability. We will soon be at 450. According to environmental expert Ralph Keeling, who runs a monitoring program at the Scripps Institution of Oceanography in San Diego, "Unless things slow down, we'll probably get there [450 ppm] in well under 25 years." Keeling continues: "It means we are quickly losing the possibility of keeping the climate below what people thought were possibly tolerable thresholds."[26]

It is hard to imagine how good citizenship would not include an acceptance of the need for binding commitments to limit the amount of carbon dioxide one's home country emits into the atmosphere. The stakes could not be higher. It is unfortunately not an exaggeration to suggest that without action to limit carbon emissions, the sustainability of life itself is threatened.[27]

Duties on Nation-States

Environmentalists in China highlight a variety of crucial governmental actions, including four fundamental priorities: (1) implement and enforce the laws that already exist on paper, which would involve an increase in the number of environmental enforcement officials and an increase in funding for environmental investments; (2) eliminate subsidies for environmentally damaging industries, beginning with coal; (3) impose environmental consumption taxes on cars and begin to set a price on ecosystem services; and (4) significantly increase investments in education in environmental awareness and ecosystem vulnerability.[28]

However, since 70 percent of total smoke and 70 percent of total carbon dioxide released into China's atmosphere are the result of burning coal, the elimination of this dirty energy source remains a fundamental environmental priority. Coal currently provides 75 percent of electric power, 60 percent of chemical industry fuel, and 80 percent of industrial fuel in China. Unless drastic action is taken, China's dangerous emissions from coal burning will continue to grow for many years to come.[29]

Elizabeth Muller, executive director of Berkeley Earth, argues that the only way for China to address its increasing energy needs and to lower its greenhouse gas emissions is to switch from coal to natural gas as its primary energy source.[30] Unfortunately, such a strategy is too often based on extracting large amounts of shale gas through hydraulic fracturing. The increasingly documented ecological risks of "fracking," including the pollution of groundwater and the release of methane gas, suggest that China should pursue a different direction. In fact, China should be supported in an attempt to "leapfrog" to new technologies and move away from fossil fuels altogether. Collectively, the international community can work together to bring down the costs of alternatives, including solar and wind energy. China should not face a trade-off between either funding environmentally safe energy sources or improving the health and well-being of its people. Countries can help each other switch from coal to renewable sources of energy.

While the United States has been a reluctant world leader on many global environmental issues, including energy efficiency, it has begun to move away from coal.[31] According to the Energy Information Agency, in 2012 "US utilities burned 815 million tons of coal for electricity, down from over 1 billion tons in 2005, and the lowest utility coal consumption since 1990." While as recently as 2009, 53 percent of electricity in the United States came from coal, by 2012 it was less than 38 percent. Furthermore, the EIA projects that a further 15 percent of existing coal-fired capacity in the United States will be retired by 2019. It is wind energy that accounted for 42 percent of the nation's new electrical-generating capacity, more than coal and natural gas combined. "Texas, of all places, generates 20 percent of its electricity with 12,200 megawatts of installed wind capacity."[32]

In addition, in June 2013 Obama reaffirmed at a Georgetown University speech that the United States would reduce its emissions by 17 percent from 2005 levels by 2020. He will do this by imposing limits on carbon emissions from power plants, which account for approximately 40 percent of US greenhouse gas emissions. As a result of these actions, the hope is that some power companies will close old coal-fired plants and look to lower-emission alternatives. To further curb emissions abroad, Obama also stated that the United States would no longer finance the building of conventional coal-fired plants overseas.[33]

Ontario, Canada's most populous province, provides a stunning example of how a community can put an end to coal-burning power plants. Ontario acted as a true international global citizen when it implemented measures to dramatically reduce the region's "environmental footprint" on the world's atmosphere. In the first quarter of 2014, Ontario closed the last of its big coal-fired generators, bringing to a halt a total of nineteen boilers that had been fueled by coal. According to the International Institute for Sustainable Development: "The coal phase out in Ontario has become 'the single largest

GHG reduction measure in North America.' Since 2007, when coal accounted for about 25 per cent of its electricity generation, the province has reduced its greenhouse gas (GHG) emissions by approximately 34 mega-tonnes (Mt) or 17 per cent."[34] Ontario succeeded in this effort by implementing an ambitious low-carbon-generating strategy. This was no small undertaking. Coal-fired electricity provided a quarter of Ontario's power and was Ontario's largest source of toxic chemical, heavy metal, sulfur, and nitrogen air pollution. This pollution, including smog, dust, and mercury emissions, became a hot political issue in 2003, and the newly elected provincial government pledged strong action to close down Ontario's coal-generated electricity business. The government's Green Energy Act promoted renewable sources, which included "feed-in tariff provisions" that offered twenty-year contracts to purchase wind-, solar-, biomass-, and biogas-fueled electricity at generous prices. These policies created a "rush of big wind farms," with hundreds of windmills built on farmland along the highway corridor from Windsor to Toronto. Keith Schneider writes: "Wind generating capacity now [in 2013] measures 2,000 megawatts. That will double in the next 18 months, according to the Energy Ministry, which would mean wind power would produce more than 10 percent of the total generating capacity of 36,000 megawatts. The provincial government estimates that 30,000 jobs are connected to the Ontario Green Energy Act and the manufacturing and installation of wind parks."[35]

Renewable energy sources are also a priority in Europe. Statistics from the European Union show that in 2010 electricity generated from renewable energy sources contributed almost one-fifth of EU's electricity. "From 2000 to 2010 the number of gigawatts of electricity generated from biomass in EU nations more than tripled. During the same decade, the number of gigs generated by wind turbines increased almost seven-fold. A gigawatt is 1 billion watts."[36] Ontario and the European Union exemplify how at the national and regional levels states can change priorities and accept a human rights duty to promote and protect environmental sustainability.

Duties on Global Institutions and Organizations

In November 2014, China and the United States announced a joint plan to curb carbon emissions. The United States pledged to emit 26 to 28 percent less carbon in 2025 than it did in 2005, double the pace of reduction it targeted for the period from 2005 to 2020. China pledged to stop its emissions from growing by 2030 by boosting clean energy sources, like solar power and windmills, to account for 20 percent of China's total energy production.[37]

This climate deal between the world's No. 1 (China) and No. 2 (US) carbon polluters was noteworthy. China had earlier maintained that since the developed world's consumption of resources and creation of pollutants on a per capital basis was still much higher than China's, China could continue to claim a moral right to develop. Beijing previously held the position "that the developed countries must take the main responsibility for past greenhouse gas emissions."[38] However, public anger inside China over high levels of toxic smog, combined with some of the worst air pollution levels in the world, pushed the government to change this position and adopt a more proactive environmental policy.

As a result, China now appears to accept the need for effective public policy to curb environmentally destructive practices. For example, in its agreement with the United States, China also promised to cap its burning of coal by 2020. As documented above, coal burning is the country's primary source of severe air pollution, which "spills over" to surrounding countries. In June 2015, China announced a new goal designed to reduce the country's "carbon intensity," which is a measure of how much pollution is generated for every percentage point of economic growth. The Chinese government had earlier promised to cut its carbon intensity by 40 to 45 percent from its 2005 level by 2020. The new Chinese goal extends the cut to 60 to 65 percent by 2030.[39]

China's example of tougher actions to limit carbon emissions helped to stimulate global progress at an environmental conference in Lima, Peru, in December 2014, where developing countries for the first time agreed to limit their own emissions. It is impossible to imagine this Lima global accord being approved without the leadership of both China and the United States.

In Paris in December 2015, China and the United States worked together at a UN conference to help forge a new global agreement and action plan on climate change. For the first time 195 nations committed themselves to lowering emissions of greenhouse gases to prevent a further dangerous rise in the world's temperature. The governments from each of these nations agreed to establish national plans showing how they will reduce their greenhouse gas emissions. Action is required of all countries, rich and poor. The agreement establishes the goal of limiting the rise in the world's temperature to 1.5 degrees Celsius, in order to protect island states threatened by the rise in sea levels. The aim of the Paris agreement is to gradually have all countries stop using the most polluting fossil fuels, including coal. However, according to scientists who have analyzed it, the agreement may only cut global greenhouse gas emission by about half enough to prevent an increase in atmospheric temperatures of 2 degrees Celsius or 3.6 degrees Fahrenheit. At that point the world will be trapped into a future of potentially devastating consequences, such as rising sea levels, severe droughts, and widespread food and water shortages. Already 186 nations have put forward their nation's individual plans on how they will cut carbon emissions through 2025 or 2030. However, these plans will not be enough to cut emissions by half the levels required to prevent the worst effects of global warming. To address this shortfall, the pact includes a series of legally binding requirements for countries to ratchet up their policies every five years with updated plans that would tighten their emissions cuts. In addition, countries are legally required to monitor and report on their emission levels with a universal accounting system. While this system is voluntary, the hope is that by publicly monitoring and verifying a country's compliance with the accord, a system of "name and shame" via peer pressure would produce results. No state wants to be seen as a polluter and international laggard.[40]

The Paris agreement also acknowledges in a preamble the need for $100 billion to be raised each year to help poor countries mitigate and adapt to climate change. The agreement endorses the international environmental law principle of "common but differentiated responsibilities" in relation to climate change. The industrialized countries, historically responsible for emitting the most carbon into the atmosphere, thus have an obligation to fund climate finance for poor countries, while developing countries can contribute on a voluntary basis.[41]

Skeptics note that China has agreed to goals that are not actually that ambitious. China is already poised to draw 15 percent of its energy from renewables by 2020, and thus aiming for 20 percent by 2030 is straightforwardly attainable. Scholars at the Economist Intelligence Unit[42] had already forecast coal use in China to plateau by 2020. (China reports that in 2014 coal consumption fell by 2.9 percent due to slow growth and a drop in consumption resulting in China's first fall in emissions of carbon dioxide in fifteen years.[43]) There are also serious questions about the effectiveness of the Chinese national "carbon-trading" system to be set up by 2016. Initial pilot programs have been disappointing and ineffective. Furthermore, China has long-standing issues with transparency and statistical accuracy. Self-reporting, in China and elsewhere, is notoriously unreliable and slippery.[44]

In addition, China's commitment in Paris to stop the growth of greenhouse emissions by 2030 is undermined by Chinese state-owned companies, with state loans, building coal-fired power plants across the developing world. Chinese companies have embarked on ninety-two coal-fired power plant projects in twenty-seven countries with a combined capacity of 107 gigawatts, the equivalent of increasing China's own coal-fired electricity output by more than 10 percent. Concerns about global warming and air pollution have been shelved, as these ninety-two projects, for example, will have enough capacity to completely offset the planned closing of coal-fired plants in the United States thorough 2020. These Chinese state-run firms unfortunately are building less efficient plants that generate more carbon dioxide emissions. The China Export-Import Bank, China Development Bank, and other big state-owned commercial banks have provided at least $25 billion to these projects. According to Michael Forsythe, "China's support for coal can be seen across Asia, from Indonesia, where Chinese firms have built and announced plans for more coal-fired plants since 2010 than any other country, to India, where the sprawling Sasan Ultra Mega Power Project in the central state of Madhya Pradesh was completed this year using boilers, turbines and generators manufactured by the state run Shanghai Electric Group."[45]

The Paris accord creates a framework that requires all nations to put forward individual state plans to cut their own emissions. However, this will result in the domestic politics of each nation negotiating the content of those plans rather than science determining the actions necessary to save the planet. Furthermore, many of these plans will not be enacted until 2025 or 2030. The Paris agreement is a healthy start but in itself is unfortunately inadequate to meet the many challenges of global warming.

International monitoring and global compliance mechanisms of the national emissions-reduction plans are essential. A global authority is needed to make sure that all nations that submit national emissions reduction plans, including China and the United States, follow through on their word. For example, in addition to the US–China deal, the European Union has an ambitious plan to reduce emissions by 40 percent of 1990 levels by 2030. Will there be a neutral observer, a global international organization that can effectively pursue European compliance with these goals?

Consider the case of India. As the third largest emitter of greenhouse gases (just behind China and the United States), India's participation in this global effort is critical. India's economy is growing fast and the Indian government has pushed for solar energy. But, India continues to rely on coal and in the last five years increased its coal capacity by 73 percent. Scholars note that India's unregulated coal plants already kill up to 115,000 Indians yearly and that India's air is among the world's dirtiest. In fact, according to the World Health Organization, India has now surpassed China as the world's smoggiest country with thirteen of the top twenty most polluted cities on the planet. Despite these horrible outcomes, India currently plans to triple coal production to an astounding 1.5 billion tons a year. India, facing unacceptable levels of poverty, destitution, and suffering for millions of its poorest citizens, has consistently prioritized economic growth over environmental protection. India will need international help to bridge this chasm. As noted above regarding China, economic development does not have to be at the expense of the environment. But India will need support and help from the international community to successfully transition out of coal and toward sustainable energy alternatives. For example, India does have an ambitious plan for renewable energy, especially solar and wind power. With assistance these impressive targets have a chance to come into fruition; without global cooperation it will be difficult for India to produce an environmental plan on par with China's.[46]

Global institutions are needed to help all nations, including China and India, fulfill their global environmental duties and avoid further harmful environmental practices. For example, Liu and Diamond point to a number of joint paths for China, the United States, and international organizations to pursue, including: "training environmental planners and managers; sharing methods for conflict resolution; transferring environmentally benign technologies, such as ones for cleaner manufacturing, water conservation and waste treatment; and transferring high-efficiency technologies, which would yield the additional advantage of reducing the already growing competition between China and other countries for energy and other global resources."[47] However, the success of such policies hinges on agreed upon norms, rules, procedures, and compliance mechanisms. The sharing of technology, in particular, will require honest neutral administrators to make sure that the benefits truly go to the countries' citizens and not elites.

Another example of the need for global environmental governance is the proposal for "carbon tariffs" to be levied against the exports of countries that refuse to limit their emissions of greenhouse gases. Such tariffs would create a powerful incentive for nations to follow through on their commitment in

Paris for a national emissions reduction plan (and could probably be upheld within current trade law).

The success of such carbon tariffs, or the cooperative efforts outlined by Liu and Diamond, depends upon effective global environmental governance. Nations must be able to work collectively on these pressing environmental issues and programs in an atmosphere of trust with individual responsibility and accountability verified. The creation of global environmental management through international organization is thus central to achieving a healthy environment. While there exists no single institution in control of the management of the global environment, international organizations dedicated to the "right to a healthy environment" have grown in scope since the two key UN conferences on the environment and development (Stockholm 1972 and Rio de Janeiro 1992).

However, the existing international environmental organizations, including the United Nations Environment Program, remain weak and underfunded. There is no global organization, for example, with the power to create financial incentives for countries like China to move away from coal. There is no global agency with the power to fine and tax irresponsible behavior and no global authority to coordinate and integrate global environmental programs. Global environmental IOs lack the resources and power to really help a country like China make a transition away from an energy system based on the burning of fossil fuels.[48]

The Obama administration in November 2014 announced that the United States would contribute $3 billion to a new global fund to help the world's poorest countries address the effects of climate change. A senior US official stated: "We're doing this because it is in our national interest to build resilience in developing countries to climate change." This contribution will go to the Green Climate Fund, a UN-created financial institution with headquarters in Incheon, South Korea, and is intended to spur other developed countries to make similar pledges. At least ten other countries, including France, Germany, and South Korea, have already pledged an additional $3 billion. Such actions by the world's richest countries will help to create a global framework through which the world can tackle these massive environmental problems. The world's poorest and least developed nations have insisted that the richest economies and largest greenhouse gas polluters accept the ethical duty to pay the billions of dollars needed to help the world's poorest adapt to climate change. The Green Climate Fund appears to be a small step in the right direction.[49]

As noted throughout this book, human rights duties at the world level focus on the construction of laws and institutions to promote global human rights. The construction of neutral global environmental organizations, dedicated to scientific objectivity and committed to the survival needs of the global community overall, is responsive to the high level of ethical and environmental interdependence existing in our world today.

DISCUSSION QUESTIONS

1. What is the legal and ethical foundation to the human "right to a healthy and balanced environment"? What are the human rights duties for individuals, nations, and the global community that flow from this proclaimed right?
2. The United States and the richest countries have historically created the most damage to our environment. In particular, the industrialized nations have emitted massive quantities of greenhouse gases contributing to global warming and climate change. On a per capita basis, the United States remains the world's leading emitter of carbon into the atmosphere. Given this history and ongoing practice, why should China (or India) feel an ethical duty to limit their carbon emissions? Since coal is a cheap energy source for their relatively poor people, why should they limit coal burning?
3. Has Ontario set an example that other nations can emulate? If Ontario can successfully phase out and close down all of its coal-fired power plants, why can't other nations act accordingly?
4. In what ways could global trade agreements be written to help the environment and not harm it? Could the relocation of factories to countries with lower environmental protections be banned? What other steps could be taken?

WEBSITES

Friends of the Earth Hong Kong promotes sustainable and equitable development and environmental policies. Website: http://www.foe.org. hk/e.

Friends of Nature (FON) is the oldest environmental NGO in China and works on some of the most pressing environmental problems, includ-

"Under the Dome": Environmental Activism in China

After her baby daughter was born with a lung disease, former China Central Television (CCTV) anchor Chai Jing produced a self-funded 104-minute feature-length environmental documentary titled *Under the Dome*. This hard-hitting film, narrated by Chai Jing in the style of a public talk, describes in detail the "airpocalypse" smog problem in China. After the film quickly became a sensation in China with more than 150 million online views, Chinese authorities blocked further viewings. The film was removed from distribution and the link to the film on the Chinese video site Youku returns the message: "We apologize, but Youku couldn't find the page you requested."[a]

The film has been dubbed China's *Silent Spring* or *Inconvenient Truth* and was originally released in partnership with official media. The film's documentation of negligent government supervision and lenient penalties for polluters was decidedly politically sensitive. Environmentalists note that while China has promising environmental protection legislation, the close ties between industry and government officials often results in a lack of local enforcement. The deteriorating levels of air and water pollution have brought many Chinese citizens into environmental activism. Unfortunately, these citizen protests are often seen as a threat to the ruling Communist Party and environmental activists are consistently detained and threatened. Human rights lawyer Tang Jitlian put it this way: "The government sees the exercise of power by its citizens as a threat to its authority, and to its existence. That's why they won't let any [activist] slip through the net."[b]

Yet the documentary succeeded in dramatically illustrating the costs of China's massive pollution problem, which prompted passionate discussions and governmental action. When asked to respond to the film's criticisms, even Premier Li Keqiang stated: "We need to make the cost for pollution too high to bear."[c]

The compelling documentary, *Under the Dome*, can be seen on YouTube with English subtitles at https://www.youtube.com/watch?v=T6X2uwlQGQM.

---

[a] "Smog Protesters Detained as China Censors Hard-Hitting Pollution Film," Radio Free Asia, March 9, 2015. Available at http://www.rfa.org/english/news/china/detention-03092015110138.html (accessed March 21, 2015).

[b] "Smog Protesters Detained."

[c] *Foreign Policy*, November/December 2015, 75.

ing protecting endangered species. Website: http://old.fon.org.cn/channal.php?cid=774&.

Global Village of Beijing (GVB) promotes the concept of a "green community" and since 1998 has been a close partner of China's Ministry of the Environment. Website: http://www.c-can.cn/en/node/652.

The Institute of Public & Environmental Affairs (IPE), located in Beijing, has developed a pollution database to monitor corporate environmental performance. Website: http://www.ipe.org.cn/en/index.aspx.

Conclusion

Global Governance and Human Rights

From a perspective of universal human rights, as noted in chapter 1, the distinction between domestic and foreign suffering is often spurious. The economic, political, and social links between all countries is now so extensive that it is impossible to draw a clear line of ethical duty at the border. The case studies explored in this book are vivid illustrations of human rights duties beyond borders and reveal ways in which we are ethically interdependent. In each of these case studies, a "human rights threshold" was surpassed and human rights duties emerged at the individual, nation-state, and global levels. Severe violations of international human rights occurred in each of these case studies resulting in a growing metastasizing of violations causing widespread suffering.

This concluding chapter examines how a framework of "global governance" helps conceptualize individual and group rights, responsibilities, and duties in this new cosmopolitan era. These approaches to global governance should not be viewed as alien to Americans. In fact, as noted at the end of this chapter, the ethics illuminating Franklin Delano Roosevelt's "Four Freedoms" embody this vision of global human rights and duties.

THE NATIONALIST CHALLENGE

In response to then-senator Barack Obama's Berlin speech on August 3, 2008, syndicated columnist George Will wrote:

"Citizen of the world" and "global citizenship" are, strictly speaking, non-sense. Citizenship is defined by legal and loyalty attachments to a particular political entity with a distinctive regime and culture. Neither the world nor the globe is such an entity.[1]

In this quote, Will captures the essence of the nationalist critique of the idea of global citizenship, which presents a competing conception of the relationship between the individual, the state, and humankind overall. From Aristotle to Hegel, the state was seen as the essence of the idea of the sanctity of the polis with the nation serving as the vehicle to provide the safety and security that allows individuals to lead moral lives. An individual citizen's loyalty and identity is thus tied to the nation and not to the "world" or distant strangers. The modern state system demonstrates the power of nationalism and how an often "invented" or "imagined" common culture and tradition can create a strong patriotic allegiance to a nation defined in terms of a specific geographical space.[2] This powerful socialization process creates entrenched political ties from which the rights and responsibilities of citizenship are defined and accepted. The nation-state becomes central to how the individual, and the community as a whole, understand ethical action, justice, rights, and responsibilities. From this perspective, it is nonsense to talk about citizenship and governance outside of the context of the nation-state.

National patriotism continues as a driving force in world affairs in the twenty-first century. The challenge to those attempting to articulate a framework of global governance and global human rights duties is to overcome the arguments of the nationalists and communitarians on the importance of the nation-state as the singular vehicle for democratic politics and security. In the abstract, the ideas of global human rights may rhetorically present a framework that binds the peoples of the world together; but in reality, according to nationalists, it is local identities and traditions that truly bind people. Political philosopher Michael Walzer argues that rights need a location just as individuals need a home. Since the nation-state remains the central actor in world affairs, it remains the critical arena of political life.[3] Walzer is correct: the nation-state can protect the rights of its citizens while the United Nations and international organizations are frequently unable to act in a similar manner. Furthermore, individuals residing in failed states and stateless persons not only do not have a government to protect them from abuse, but also often have no access to global human rights institutions and programs to come to their assistance.

Some communitarians argue further that the growth of globalist and cosmopolitan ways of thinking can undermine loyalty to the state and leave individuals with nothing to protect them, resulting in isolation and anomie. As Edmund Burke famously wrote in *Reflections on the French Revolution*:

> To transfer humanity from its natural basis, our legitimate and home-bred connection—to lose all feelings, for those who have grown up by our sides, in our eyes, the benefit of whose cares and labours we have partaken from our birth, and meretriciously to hunt abroad after foreign affections, is such a disarrangement of the whole system of our duties, that I do not know whether benevolence so displaced is not almost the same thing as destroyed, or what effect bigotry could have produced that is more fatal to society. [4]

Kwame Appiah addresses this anxiety directly by demonstrating how cosmopolitanism and patriotism can coexist in harmony and be mutually beneficial. But some nationalists respond that Appiah ignores the dangers inherent in a globalist project and claim that transferring loyalties above the state can undermine patriotism and lead to social disintegration. Furthermore, some nationalists argue that a "global identity" will not attract the same loyalty that individuals find in their nations. Global governance is thus both undesirable and impractical. [5]

Other nationalists note the ways in which the people of the world are divided by geography, language, culture, religion, and politics. They question whether there are global conceptions of justice and morality. While local cultural communities and nations have developed over hundreds of years, global citizenship and global governance is not so clearly rooted in historical experience. Does this mean that few people in the world can really think in terms of global human rights and duties? Some nationalists would answer yes and assert that there is little world species consciousness to drive global governance forward.

Derek Heater summarizes three arguments put forward by critics of schemes of global governance and global citizenship. First, it is the nation-state "that remains for the vast majority of people their 'community of fate.'" Second, any weakening of the state has come from below with the creation of "regional cultural identities, more than any succumbing to supranational forces." And third, the "homogenizing thrusts of globalization have been exaggerated" and the world's peoples remain in distinct civilizations with differing national interests and cultural priorities. [6]

Yet the world's major religions assert a common humanity across culture; biologically human beings are the same no matter where they are born; philosophers from the Greek Stoics through the Enlightenment have asserted the importance of acting on a framework of global citizenship; since World War II globally recognized human rights are based on the premise of the essential oneness of humankind; and economic and technological globalization has brought all of humanity closer together than ever before. In addition, an environmental consciousness has blossomed since the 1970s as the fragile state of the world's ecosystem has brought a new awareness of common ecological vulnerabilities impacting all cultures. Solutions to these ecological dilemmas demand a global approach to sorting out environmental rights and responsibilities.[7]

Perhaps the issue becomes: what difference does it make? If our goal is to create a just world system that addresses the root causes of human suffering, which is more helpful—a nationalist approach or a global human rights and global governance framework? In this era of complex interdependence with mutual vulnerabilities and sensitivities inside individual states to global economic, environmental, and political events, is the framework of global citizenship and global governance helpful in sorting out human rights and duties in the twenty-first century? Or is the existing nationalist approach based upon communitarian principles of justice and morality the most viable framework to achieve justice?

The case studies of mass incarceration in the United States, LGBT rights in Africa, women's rights in Saudi Arabia, and environmental rights in China demonstrate the utility of a global governance framework constructed around human rights and duties with individual, nation-state, and world dimensions. As discussed in chapter 1, at the individual level, human rights duties revolve around consciousness and awareness of moral interdependence. Such consciousness pushes individuals to expand their ethical circles of rights and responsibilities from family to nation to humanity as a whole. At the nation-state level, human rights duties involve the incorporation of international law, universal human rights, and global environmental accords into national policy formation. Such a commitment recognizes the ways in which this cooperative normative framework boosts national security by grounding the international system on principles that enhance peace. At the global level, institutions and "regimes" of cooperation are pivotal to the creation of a world system responsive to conditions of ethical interdependence and the global human rights duties. Such global institutions give state and nonstate actors the ability to interact and engage with one another, building mechanisms of trust and verification. Neutral global institutions are better positioned to apply human rights norms fairly across boundaries and help to construct regimes of global governance responsive to the rights of the most vulnerable among us.

This tripartite (individual, nation-state, global) understanding of global human rights duties and ethical interdependence is not a radical position calling for an end to national affiliations or national patriotism. In fact, there is a long lineage of conservative and "mainstream" philosophers and practitioners who argue that patriotism and globalism go hand in hand. Aristotle, for example, viewed human affection growing through a hierarchy of attachments—family, household, village, and finally the polis itself. The conservative philosopher Edmund Burke wrote: "To be attached to the subdivision, to love the little platoon we belong to in society, is the first principle (the germ as it were) of public affections. It is the first link in the series by which we proceed toward a love to our country and to mankind."[8]

Both national and global institutions are central to the protection of basic human rights and human flourishing. There is thus no contradiction in recognizing both a moral justification for allegiance to one's nation-state and a moral justification for global institutions and regimes. In fact, the ability of the nation's leader to protect her citizens from global economic, technological, and environmental forces depends upon such global institutions working toward common, equitable solutions to these global problems. To be clear, the argument here is not for a single world government or world state. In fact, it is the narrower political communities of nation-states that allow for both cultural diversity to flourish and for democratic participation and popular control of societies. Global governance is designed to complement not replace national governance systems, and protect not squelch cultural differences. In fact, the safeguarding of local communities is dependent upon a viable, global framework of norms and institutions designed to protect individuals and groups from the common global vulnerabilities confronting all individuals and states around the world.

Democratic participation through a framework of national citizenship is only partially empowering in the twenty-first century. State power is limited by global economic, political, and technological forces, which individual nations cannot control. As many scholars have noted, these global forces demand that we rethink our traditional understandings of "sovereignty." The legitimacy of the liberal state lies in its ability to protect basic human rights.

Global dynamics—from ecological destruction to financial turmoil to aggressive war and genocide—point toward the need to augment the liberal state with a framework of global governance.

David Held, for example, argues for a "cosmopolitan model of sovereignty." Held writes:

> Cosmopolitanism is, contrary to popular criticism, the triumph of difference and local affiliations. Insofar as a cosmopolitan institutional project aims at the entrenchment of law-governed relations, it creates the requirements for political autonomy that each person and group needs in order to foster its ideas of the good life. Without such a framework, solutions will not be adopted on the basis of deliberation and law, but on the basis of power and economic strength. A world without cosmopolitan principles is not a world in which communal differences are entrenched and valued for their own sake, but rather a world in which power (in its different manifestations) drives the resolution of what I have called the pressing issues of our time.[9]

Held points to the "difficulties of managing global risks associated with human interdependence" in "three policy domains of finance, security and the environment." There is now widespread understanding and recognition of how "complex interdependence" and "globalization" have created common economic, security, and environmental vulnerabilities beyond the control of individual communities and nation-states. Almost daily the media is filled with examples of nations confronting these types of global problems. The most widely recognized and acknowledged vulnerabilities arise from the integrated way in which the global economy now functions. And there is further recognition that each state acting alone will be unable to resolve these issues and thus unable to provide human security to its citizens. Yet despite this recognition, our global international institutions are unfortunately often inadequately structured to provide much help. As Held writes: "Each of these three domains [finance, security, and the environment] suffers from what can be called a 'capacity problem'—existing institutions which address the global nature of risk are not fit for purpose."[10]

As early as 1994, moral philosopher Martha Nussbaum claimed that global citizenship, with its focus on universal rights and reason, should be the basis for civic education. Nussbaum justified this position with three main points. First, "by looking through the lens of the other," Nussbaum argued, "we learn more about ourselves." "[W]e come to see what in our practices is local and nonessential, what is more broadly or deeply shared." Second, she believes that a cosmopolitan education promotes a constructive dialogue toward solving the world's most pressing problems. "We make headway solving problems that require international cooperation." And third, with a cosmopolitan education "we recognize moral obligations to the rest of the world that are real and that otherwise would go unrecognized." Global citizens are more disposed to recognize moral obligations not only to one's family and nation but also to humanity as a whole. Already in our democracy, citizens are instructed to "join hands across boundaries of ethnicity, class, gender, and race." A cosmopolitan perspective would encourage young people to 'join hands' across national borders as well, which may help to curb aggressive jingoism.[11]

Many UN diplomats and human rights activists in New York City and Geneva perceive a growing acceptance of the ideas of global governance, the universality of human rights, and the need for international organizations around the world. The success of key global organizations since World War II, including the Office of the High Commissioner for Refugees, the United Nations Development Programme, and so on, is now widely recognized in Europe, Latin America, and elsewhere. In contrast, inside the United States there is deep skepticism toward the possibility of building regimes of cooperation and resistance to the ideas of global governance. The media's fixation on perceived UN failures and scandals[12] enhances this distrust within the United States toward the United Nations and other key global organizations.

In addition, inside the academic community there is resistance to many of these ideas as well. The field of international relations remains focused on traditional approaches to national security, often with an emphasis on "hard power"—that is, military and economic resources. While there is wide acceptance in the academy of "economic interdependence," only a few human rights scholars have the temerity to outline and document the ways in which we have become ethically interdependent as well. The "commonsense" approach is to see distinct cultures and "civilizations" as unique, embedded communities, each having its own sense of right and wrong, its own definition of "justice," its own framework of rights and responsibilities. Michael Walzer's response to Nussbaum is perhaps a clear example. Walzer writes,

> I am not a citizen of the world, as she would like me to be. I am not even aware that there is a world such that one could be a citizen of it. No one has ever offered me citizenship, or described the naturalization process . . . or provided me with a list of benefits and obligations of citizenship, or shown me the

world's calendar and the common celebrations and commemorations of its citizens.[13]

Yet, as previously explored, the ideas of global citizenship do not depend upon the existence of a "world state." In fact, Walzer's dismissive polemic ignores the reality on the ground. In the twenty-first century, the term "global citizenship" captures the ways in which individuals and states already act on principles of global human rights and global duties. Global citizenship reflects elements of how the world actually "is" and not just how it "ought" to be.

The tensions between globalism and nationalism are often exaggerated for political purposes.[14] Many, if not most, people take both sets of values seriously and do not view them as alien, contradictory, or impossible to align. This does not mean that these normative approaches never conflict. Rather it is to argue that even when uncomfortable tensions exist, the resolution of those conflicts often involves compromise. The new "commonsense" approach to citizenship is thus not to view "global" and "national" understandings of the term as in conflict. Rather it is to understand that in this era of ethical interdependence, a holistic approach, with national and global dimensions, to the crafting of individual rights and responsibilities is a useful framework for addressing the common ethical problems confronting all of humanity.

GLOBAL GOVERNANCE AND HUMAN RIGHTS

The idea of "governance" is distinct from "government." A government imposes a system of rule over a state and is legally "sovereign" in that there is no authority with the ability to override its decisions. Governance systems, on the other hand, often rely on formal and informal acceptance of rules, norms, and decision-making procedures by a variety of local, national, and global actors. While there is no global sovereign, the current functioning system of global governance is composed of nation-states, IOs, NGOs, civil society movements, philanthropists, organized labor, and other powerful global actors, including multinational corporations, private military and security companies, and financial markets. To a large degree, these national and global organizations operate within an agreed upon system of rules and laws. This "global governance system" thus creates effective rule and policy, and, most important, *the ideas framing human rights and duties undergird the legitimacy of this governance system.*

International organizations, of course, remain key to global governance functioning. According to Margaret Karns and Karen Mingst, there were 238 intergovernmental organizations at the start of the new century.[15] Many of these IOs focus specifically on a human rights agenda, including the Office of the High Commissioner for Human Rights, Office of the High Commissioner for Refugees, World Health Organization, International Labor Organization, UN Environment Program, and so on.

International law is composed of treaties, customary practices, and general principles that govern relations between nation-states, impacting nonstate actors and individuals as well. In addition to the extensive corpus of human rights law reviewed above, nation-states have agreed to norms governing arms control, environmental sustainability, and the law of the sea.

The focus of many NGOs remains on human rights norms, including Amnesty International, Human Rights Watch, Transparency International, and Oxfam. In addition, environmental rights are pursued by many organizations, including the World Wide Fund for Nature, Greenpeace, and others.

Such a voluntary system of global governance may be better able to adapt to the environmental, financial, technological, and economic security challenges of the twenty-first century than a more centralized, top-down approach. Individuals, private organizations, and nation-states see the value of cooperative action around a human rights agenda. Their voluntary agreement and action creates a potentially more robust and long-lasting governance structure than one imposed by a hegemonic power. This jumble of formal and informal arrangements has opened up new avenues for addressing human rights issues across boundaries. There has thus been noteworthy progress since World War II toward the creation of an operational system of global governance based on human rights norms.

A UN priority has been to reframe global rights and responsibilities in relation to the following areas reflective of the ethics of interdependence: aggressive war and war crimes; environmental sustainability; crimes against humanity and genocide; terrorism; and basic civil and political rights. In fact, "sovereignty" has been reconceptualized to include a "responsibility to protect"; for example, the state has the primary responsibility for the protection of its population from genocide, war crimes, crimes against humanity, and ethnic cleansing. However, if the state fails to fulfill this responsibility, the international community is to be prepared to assist not only with diplomatic, humanitarian, and other peaceful means, but also with stronger actions, including the use of force, to protect innocent populations. [16] This framing of the "responsibility to protect" demonstrates the symbiotic relationship between national and global governance. The protection of the basic rights of citizens, including the right to life itself, around the world depends upon not only a humane national government, but also global institutions dedicated to upholding norms of compassionate governance and the protection of human rights.

The sovereign power and political authority of nation-states is thus circumscribed within this human rights framework of global governance. A nation today finds itself embedded within complex and overlapping regimes of political authority. The nation-state remains resilient, but it is no longer the sole center of legitimate power. And thus, the concept of "citizenship" shifts from the idea of exclusive membership within a territorial community to include the acceptance of global rules and principles also defining each individual's rights and duties—that is, global citizenship. As Held writes: "The meaning of citizenship thus shifts from membership in a community which bestows, for those who qualify, particular rights and duties to an alternative principle of world order in which all persons have equivalent rights and duties in the cross-cutting spheres of decision-making which can affect their vital needs and interests." What this implies is that individuals come to "enjoy multiple citizenships—political membership, that is, in the diverse political communities which significantly affect them." Individuals become not only citizens of their immediate political community based on geography, but also members of the regional and global networks that impact their lives. [17]

Seyla Benhabib, for example, identifies a transition in the modern period from international to "cosmopolitan norms of justice." Cosmopolitanism is based on the idea of a single global ethical community, with all humans under the same moral standards. While traditional international rules emerge from treaty obligations and multilateral agreements among states, cosmopolitan norms of justice "accrue to individuals as moral and legal persons in a worldwide civil society." The international legal and normative framework accompanying economic globalization, based on state consent, often fails to capture this new moral interdependence. Benhabib articulates the challenge that cosmopolitan norms of justice pose to democratic principles of self-determination. The distinctiveness of cosmopolitan norms is that they "endow *individuals* rather than states and their agents with certain rights and claims." The uniqueness of the human rights system established after World War II is that it represents "an eventual transition from a model of international law based on treaties among states to cosmopolitan law understood as international public law that binds and bends the will of sovereign states."[18]

A humane framework of global governance is thus linked fundamentally to the creation of a more democratic and equitable world system based on an understanding of the ethics of interdependence. Humane and benevolent global governance is designed to break down existing privileges and enhance individual human rights for all. As noted throughout this text, human rights flow from principles of equality, the idea that each person should enjoy impartial treatment based on rules, and principles that can be universally applied.

In sum, due to economic, technological, and environmental interdependence, the nation-state acting alone is often unable to provide human security for its citizens. The movement for humane governance and human rights thus has a global dimension, a loosely integrated form of world order that coexists with rich cultural and political diversity between and within nation-states. In response to the growing inability of individual states to protect citizens from new global threats, the ideas of global governance and global citizenship have emerged to redefine boundaries and affirm the priority of individual and group rights in the development of national and global humane governance. In this era of globalized capital, an embryonic world society based on normative principles of the equal moral standing of all human beings has also materialized.

President Franklin Delano Roosevelt (FDR) certainly embraced this perspective and sought to link American nationalism to a globalist human rights agenda.

FDR'S GLOBALIST APPROACH TO HUMAN RIGHTS

On January 1, 1941, in his small study on the second floor of the White House, FDR slowly dictated his famous declaration of hope for "a world founded upon four essential human freedoms": freedom of speech and expression, freedom of religion, freedom from want, and freedom from fear. FDR believed these were not a vision for "a distant millennium" but "a definite basis for a kind of world attainable in our own time and generation." Newspaper editors declared that the president had given the world "a new Magna Carta of democracy," and the Four Freedoms became the moral cornerstone of the United Nations.[19] Accordingly, the Four Freedoms formed the basis of the internationalist ethical principles found in the United Nations Charter and the UDHR that arose out of the Great Depression and the world wars of the twentieth century.[20]

In their original context, the Four Freedoms were designed as a global moral framework, on which to base the restructuring of international relations after World War II. While FDR's New Deal was primarily a domestic program of reform intended to protect the weak and vulnerable in the United States, the Four Freedoms addressed a larger stage. FDR realized that national security and economic prosperity for our country depended upon the creation of a cooperative world system based upon ethical principles. FDR recognized the reality of ethical interdependence between peoples and nations everywhere. FDR thus called for freedom of speech and religion "everywhere in the world." He sought freedom from want in "world terms," meaning "economic understandings which will secure to every nation a healthy peacetime life for its inhabitants everywhere in the world." And, finally, freedom of fear translated into world terms meant "a worldwide reduction of armaments to such a point and in such a thorough fashion that no nation will be in a position to commit an act of physical aggression against any neighbor—anywhere in the world." FDR called for a "new moral order" based upon the "supremacy of human rights everywhere."

FDR thus provides us with an example of a strong leader pursuing an agenda of global human rights framed within the concepts of global citizenship and global governance. In essence, he made the claim that it is morally and politically unacceptable to ignore global human rights concerns, including the plight of the world's poor. This ethical conclusion is based not only upon abstract moral principles, but also upon a new understanding of national security and national citizenship. FDR realized that security for US citizens (freedom from fear) could not be attained through a sole focus on the assertion of military power. He recognized that a state of constant fear, fueled by the arms race, does not create secure rule, but rather a condition of instability and insecurity. Global security, on the other hand, can be built upon principles including freedom and democracy, instead of an overreliance on military power. FDR's first freedom, "freedom of speech and expression—everywhere in the world," is thus central to the creation at home of a secure and just America.

It is interesting to note the many ways in which FDR's vision was later articulated in the UDHR and international human rights treaties. FDR's actions demonstrate how nationalist patriotism can align with a vision of global citizenship. In fact, the success of American principles of personal responsibility, hard work, and individual initiative depend upon the protection of basic human rights and duties at home and abroad. FDR's globalism provides an inspiring historical example useful to draw on for the formulation of policies and programs responsive to the ethics of interdependence in the twenty-first century.

Notes

INTRODUCTION

1. Whereas it is commonly believed that there is some distinction between the terms "ethical" and "moral," to many philosophers they are synonyms, with the former derived from the Greek and the latter from the Latin. I will thus use "moral" and "ethical" as essentially equivalent terms.

2. Well-known individuals who embrace this awareness and the individual global duties that flow from ethical interdependence include Dr. Martin Luther King Jr., Bishop Desmond Tutu, and Thich Nhat Hanh.

3. "Regimes are principles, norms, rules, and decision-making procedures around which actor expectations converge." Stephen D. Krasner, *Structural Conflict: The Third World against Global Liberalism* (Berkeley: University of California Press, 1985), 4.

4. Steven Raphael and Michael A. Stoll, *Why Are So Many Americans in Prison?* (New York: Russell Sage Foundation, 2013), 10; Michelle Alexander, *The New Jim Crow: Mass Incarceration in the Age of Colorblindness* (New York: New Press, 2012), 6–7.

5. Alan Cowell, "Ugandan President Signs Antigay Law," *New York Times*, February 24, 2014.

6. Human Rights Watch, *Perpetual Minors: Human Rights Abuses Stemming from Male Guardianship and Sex Segregation in Saudi Arabia* (New York: Human Rights Watch, 2008), 2.

7. Daniel Cusick and ClimateWire, "China's Soaring Coal Consumption Poses Climate Challenge," *Scientific American*, January 30, 2013.

1. GLOBAL HUMAN RIGHTS AND DUTIES: A PRIMER

1. See, for example, Philip Alston and Ryan Goodman, "Rights, Duties and Dilemmas of Universalism," *International Human Rights*, by Philip Alston and Ryan Goodman (Oxford:

Oxford University Press, 2013), 489–681; Michael Freeman, *Human Rights*, 2nd ed. (Cambridge: Polity Press, 2011).

2. William F. Felice, *Taking Suffering Seriously* (Albany, NY: SUNY Press, 1996), 17.

3. See Thomas Pogge, *World Poverty and Human Rights* (Malden, MA: Polity, 2002).

4. See Jack Donnelly, *The Concept of Human Rights* (New York: St. Martin's Press, 1985); Richard Falk, *Human Rights and State Sovereignty* (New York: Holmes & Meier, 1981); David Forsythe, *The Internationalization of Human Rights* (Toronto: Lexington Books, 1991); Louis Henkin, *The Age of Rights* (New York: Columbia University Press, 1990).

5. Articles 1–21, "Universal Declaration of Human Rights."

6. Articles 22–28, "Universal Declaration of Human Rights."

7. Felice, *Taking Suffering Seriously*, 31–32; Article 28, "Universal Declaration of Human Rights." Karl Vasak, formerly UNESCO's legal adviser, popularized this framework as "three generations" of rights reflecting norms of liberty, equality, and fraternity. See Roland Rich, "The Right to Development: A Right of Peoples," in *The Rights of Peoples*, ed. James Crawford (Oxford: Clarendon Press, 1988), 41.

8. See, for example, Alston and Goodman, "Conflict in Culture, Tradition and Practices: Challenges to Universalism," 531–681.

9. See Amartya Sen, "Human Rights and Asian Values," presented at the Sixteenth Morgenthau Memorial Lecture on Ethics and Foreign Policy, sponsored by the Carnegie Council on Ethics and International Affairs, in New York City on May 1, 1997. Available at http://www.nyu.edu/classes/gmoran/SEN.pdf (accessed November 7, 2015).

10. Freeman, *Human Rights*, 53.

11. "Cairo Declaration on Human Rights in Islam, Aug. 5, 1990, U.N. GAOR, World Conf. on Hum. Rts., 4th Sess., Agenda Item 5, U.N. Doc. A/CONF.157/PC/62/Add.18 (1993)." Available at https://www1.umn.edu/humanrts/instree/cairodeclaration.html (accessed November 7, 2015). See also Turan Kayaoğlu, "It's Time to Revise the Cairo Declaration of Human Rights in Islam," Brookings Institute, April 23, 2012. Available at http://www.brookings.edu/research/opinions/2012/04/23-cairo-kayaoglu (accessed November 7, 2015).

12. Alston and Goodman, *International Human Rights*, 531–33.

13. Rosalyn Higgins, *Problems and Process: International Law and How We Use It* (Oxford: Clarendon Press, 1994), 96.

14. For an evaluation of the work of the treaty bodies, country reports, and individual compliant procedures, see the evaluation of the Committee on the Elimination of All Forms of Racial Discrimination in William F. Felice, "Race and Economic and Social Human Rights," in *The Global New Deal: Economic and Social Human Rights in World Politics*, 2nd ed., by William F. Felice (Lanham, MD: Rowman & Littlefield, 2010), 157–77.

15. Julia Hausermann, "The Realisation and Implementation of Economic, Social and Cultural Rights," in *Economic, Social and Cultural Rights: Progress and Achievement*, eds. Ralph Beddard and Dilys M. Hill (New York: St. Martin's 1992), 49.

16. Felice, *Taking Suffering Seriously*, 6.

17. Richard Falk, "Foreword," in Felice, *Taking Suffering Seriously*, xi.

18. Felice, *Taking Suffering Seriously*, 1–14.

19. Felice, *Taking Suffering Seriously*, 2, 36–40.

20. Madhavi Sunder, "Piercing the Veil," in *Just Advocacy? Women's Human Rights, Transnational Feminisms, and the Politics of Representation*, eds. Wendy S. Hesford and Wendy Kozol (New Brunswick, NJ: Rutgers University Press, 2005), 266.

21. See Felice, *The Global New Deal*, 206.

22. Central liberal principles include civil and political rights, such as free expression, due process, and the right to participate in government directly or through free elections. See M.

McDougal, H. Lasswell, and L. Chen, *Human Rights and World Public Order* (New Haven, CT: Yale University Press, 1980).

23. Henry Shue, *Basic Rights: Subsistence, Affluence, and U.S. Foreign Policy* (Princeton, NJ: Princeton University Press, 1980), 32.

24. Freeman, *Human Rights*, 83.

25. Freeman, *Human Rights*, 84.

26. Seyla Benhabib, *Another Cosmopolitanism* (Oxford: Oxford University Press, 2006), 16–17.

27. Kwame Anthony Appiah, *Cosmopolitanism: Ethics in a World of Strangers* (New York: Norton, 2006), xviii–xix.

28. These levels are an interpretation of Luis Cabrera's categories of global citizenship, which he defines as good international citizenship, global citizenship as a global ethic, and institutional global citizenship. See Luis Cabrera, *The Practice of Global Citizenship* (Cambridge: Cambridge University Press, 2010), 21–33.

29. Cabrera, *The Practice of Global Citizenship*, 26–27.

30. Richard Falk, "The Making of Global Citizenship," in *Global Visions: Beyond the New World Order*, eds. Jeremy Brecher, John Brown Childs, and Jill Cutler (Boston: South End Press, 1993), 39.

31. Hans Schattle, *The Practices of Global Citizenship* (Lanham, MD: Rowman & Littlefield, 2008), 28.

32. Oxfam, "Education for Global Citizenship: A Guide for Schools," 2015, p. 5. Available at http://www.oxfam.org.uk/education/global-citizenship/global-citizenship-guides (accessed March 4, 2016).

33. After nearly a decade's worth of research on global citizenship, including extensive interviews around the world, Hans Schattle writes: "More so than any other concept, the persons interviewed for this study framed global citizenship as dependent on awareness of oneself and the outside world. Especially when individuals were asked challenging questions about how anyone could possibly be a global citizen without a centralized world government, without recognized world passports, or without national and ethnic identities giving way to a widely acknowledged civic identity shared across humanity, a common reply in the interviews was that anyone can be a global citizen through awareness or a state of mind. In fact several respondents brought up a related word: consciousness." Schattle, *The Practices of Global Citizenship*, 26–27.

34. Cabrera, *Practice of Global Citizenship*, 21.

35. Barack Obama, "Transcript: Obama's Speech in Berlin," *New York Times*, July 24, 2008. Quoted in Cabrera, *Practice of Global Citizenship*, 21–22.

36. Barack Obama, "On a New Beginning," Cairo University, June 4, 2009. Available at http://www.whitehouse.gov/the_press_office/Remarks-by-the-President-at-Cairo-University-6-04-09 (accessed January 2, 2015).

37. "President Obama Offers a Statement on the Attacks in Paris," *White House Blog*, November 13, 2015. Available at https://www.whitehouse.gov/blog/2015/11/13/watch-president-obamas-statement-attacks-paris (accessed December 1, 2015).

38. Cabrera, *Practice of Global Citizenship*, 24–25.

39. The UDHR is available at http://www.ohchr.org/EN/UDHR/Pages/Introduction.aspx (accessed January 6, 2016).

40. Ratification information for the CCPR and the CESCR is available at http://treaties.un.org/Pages/Treaties.aspx?id=4&subid=A&lang=en (assessed January 6, 2016).

41. See William F. Felice, *How Do I Save My Honor? War, Moral Integrity, and Principled Resignation* (Lanham, MD: Rowman & Littlefield, 2009), 69–71.

42. Joh Kyl, Douglas Feith, and John Fonte, "The War of Law," *Foreign Affairs* 92, no. 4 (July/August 2013): 115–25.

43. David Rieff, "Goodbye, New World Order," *Mother Jones*, July 1, 2003. Quoted in Schattle, *Practices of Global Citizenship*, 142.

44. Cabrera, *Practice of Global Citizenship*, 33.

45. Functionalist theorists in international relations pioneered globalization and integration theories based on the common interests and needs of all states. See David Mitrany, *A Working Peace System* (Chicago: Quadrangle Books, 1966).

46. For information on the federalists approach to global institution building see the World Federalist Movement: http://www.wfm-igp.org (accessed January 2, 2015).

47. Richard Falk, "Theory, Realism, and World Security," in *World Security: Trends & Challenges at Century's End*, by Michael T. Klare and Daniel C. Thomas (New York: St. Martin's Press, 1991), 21–22. For an overview history of the World Order Models Project, see http://www.worldpolicy.org/blog/2012/03/07/world-order-models-project (accessed June 20, 2013).

48. Cabrera, *Practice of Global Citizenship*, 66.

49. See Felice, *The Global New Deal*, 257–87.

50. Probably the most well-known definition of subsidiarity is in the 1993 Treaty on European Union (Treaty of Maastricht), Article 3B: "In areas which do not fall within its exclusive competence, the [European] Community shall take action, in accordance with the principle of subsidiarity, only if and in so far as the objectives of the proposed action cannot be sufficiently achieved by the Member States and can therefore, by reason of the scale or effects of the proposed action, be better achieved by the Community." Treaty on European Union (Treaty of Maastricht) is available online at http://eur-lex.europa.eu/en/treaties/dat/11992M/htm/11992M.html#0095000020 (accessed January 21, 2015).

51. For information on the "individual complaint procedures" see Felice, *The Global New Deal*, 81–83, 101–3, 108–9, 163–65, 187.

52. States are responsible to exercise "due diligence" in monitoring and controlling the behavior of nonstate actors, including multinational corporations, in their jurisdiction to protect citizens' economic and social human rights. Multinational corporations can exhibit "good international citizenship" by upholding the rights and duties found in international human rights law, including the International Labor Organization's basic human rights conventions, which form the corpus of minimum international labor standards or internationally recognized worker rights. See also *Maastricht Guidelines on Violations of Economic, Social and Cultural Rights*, available at http://www1.umn.edu/humanrts/instree/Maastrichtguidelines_.html (accessed January 3, 2016).

53. See Felice, *The Global New Deal*, 81–83; 163–65; 265–68.

54. *Black's Law Dictionary* defines "duty" as follows: "In its use in Jurisprudence, this word [duty] is the correlative of right. Thus, wherever there exists a right in any person, there also rests a corresponding duty upon some other person or upon all persons generally. But it is also used, in a wider sense, to designate that class of moral obligations which lie outside the jural sphere; such, namely, as rest upon an imperative ethical basis, but have not been recognized by the law as within its proper province for purposes of enforcement or redress. Thus, gratitude towards a benefactor is a duty, but its refusal will not ground an action. In this meaning 'duty' is the equivalent of 'moral obligation,' as distinguished from a 'legal obligation.'" *Black's Law Dictionary Free Online*, 2nd ed., available at http://thelawdictionary.org/duty (accessed December 23, 2015).

55. See International Council on Human Rights Policy, "Taking Duties Seriously: Individual Duties in International Human Rights Law," 1998. Available at http://www.ichrp.org/files/reports/10/103_report_en.pdf (accessed October 23, 2014).

56. "African Charter on Human and Peoples' Rights," ASU Doc. CAB/LEG67/3 rev.5, I.L.M. 58 (1982), entered into force October 21, 1986. Available at http://www.achpr.org/files/instruments/achpr/banjul_charter.pdf (accessed October 18, 2014).

57. "American Declaration of the Rights and Duties of Man," adopted by the Ninth International Conference of American States, 1948. Available at http://www.cidh.org/Basicos/English/Basic2.American%20Declaration.htm (accessed October 18, 2014).

58. See *Schenck v United States*, 249 US 47 (1919) where the US Supreme Court upheld certain limitations on the freedom of expression rights in the First Amendment.

59. The texts of the UDHR, CCPR, and the CESCR are available at the website of the UN Office of the High Commissioner for Human Rights, at http://www.ohchr.org/Documents/Publications/FactSheet2Rev.1en.pdf (accessed December 23, 2015).

60. International Council on Human Rights Policy, "Taking Duties Seriously: Individual Duties in International Human Rights Law," 1998.

61. Kofi Annan, "In Larger Freedom: Towards Development, Security and Human Rights for All," 2005. Available at http://www.un.org/largerfreedom (assessed July 30, 2013). Quoted in Felice, *The Global New Deal*, 97.

62. Mary Robinson, "Statement by the United Nations Commissioner for Human Rights to the Round-Table on Human Rights and Extreme Poverty," Geneva, March 24, 1998. Quoted in Felice, *The Global New Deal*, 97.

63. Committee on Economic, Social and Cultural Rights, "The Incorporation of Economic, Social and Cultural Rights into the United Nations Development Assistance Framework (UNDAF) Process," 1998.

64. See Felice, *The Global New Deal*, 77–85. See also William Felice and Diana Fuguitt, "International Organization and Poverty Alleviation," *Human Rights and Human Welfare* 12 (2012).

65. *Our Global Neighborhood: The Report of the Commission on Global Governance* (New York: Oxford University Press, 1995), 56.

66. Businessdictionary.com. Available at http://www.businessdictionary.com/definition/threshold-effect.html (accessed October 19, 2014).

2. MASS INCARCERATION IN THE UNITED STATES

1. Lauren Glaze, Danielle Kaeble, Todd Minton, and Anastasios Tsoutis, "Correctional Populations in the United States, 2014," Bureau of Justice Statistics. Available at http://www.bjs.gov/index.cfm?ty=pbdetail&iid=5519 (accessed March 13, 2016).

2. Lauren E. Glaze and Erinn J. Herberman, "Correctional Populations in the United States, 2012," Bureau of Justice Statistics. Available at http://www.bjs.gov/index.cfm?ty=pbdetail&iid=4843 (accessed August 5, 2014).

3. Becky Pettit, *Invisible Men: Mass Incarceration and the Myth of Black Progress* (New York: Russell Sage Foundation, 2012), 15.

4. E. Ann Carson and Daniela Golinelli, "Prisoners In 2012: Trends in Admissions and Releases, 1991–2012," Bureau of Justice Statistics. Available at http://www.bjs.gov/index.cfm?ty=pbdetail&iid=4910 (accessed August 5, 2014).

5. Pettit, *Invisible Men*, 11.

6. Steven Raphael and Michael A. Stoll, *Why Are So Many Americans in Prison?* (New York: Russell Sage Foundation, 2013), 58.

7. Raphael and Stoll, *Why Are So Many Americans in Prison?*, 8–9.

8. Michelle Alexander, *The New Jim Crow: Mass Incarceration in the Age of Colorblindness* (New York: New Press, 2012), 6–7.

9. Raphael and Stoll, *Why Are So Many Americans in Prison?*, 10.

10. Raphael and Stoll, *Why Are So Many Americans in Prison?*, 10.

11. Alexander, *New Jim Crow*, 9, 180.

12. Alexander, *New Jim Crow*, 180.

13. Pew Research Center on the States, "One in 100: Behind Bars in America 2008" (Washington, DC: Pew Charitable Trusts, 2008); quoted in Pettit, *Invisible Men*, 14.

14. Pettit, *Invisible Men*, 18.

15. Pettit, *Invisible Men*, 18.

16. Becca Bohrman and Naomi Murakawa, "Remaking Big Government: Immigration and Crime Control in the United States," in *Global Lockdown: Race, Gender, and the Prison-Industrial Complex*, ed. Julia Sudbury (New York: Routledge, 2005), 113.

17. Julia Sudbury, "Introduction: Feminist Critiques, Transnational Landscapes, Abolitionist Visions," in *Global Lockdown*, xiv.

18. Bohrman and Murakawa, "Remaking Big Government," 113.

19. Ruth Wilson Gilmore, *Golden Gulag: Prisons, Surplus, Crisis, and Opposition in Globalizing California* (Oakland: University of California Press, 2007), 18.

20. Raphael and Stoll, *Why Are So Many Americans in Prison?*, 113–14.

21. Gilmore, *Golden Gulag*, 18–19.

22. Gilmore, *Golden Gulag*, 19.

23. Andrew D. Black, "'The War on People': Reframing 'The War on Drugs' by Addressing Racism within American Drug Policy through Restorative Justice and Community Collaboration," *University of Louisville Law Review* 46 (2007–2008): 188.

24. The statistics in the following section on the US economy are taken directly from my book *The Global New Deal: Economic and Social Human Rights in World Politics*, 2nd ed. (Lanham, MD: Rowman & Littlefield, 2010), 251–53. See also William Felice, "Human Rights Disparities between Europe and the United States: Conflicting Approaches to Poverty Prevention and the Alleviation of Suffering," *Cambridge Review of International Affairs* 19, no. 1 (March 2006).

25. Jason DeParle, "Reports, Delayed Months, Says Lowest Income Groups Grew," *New York Times*, May 12, 1992, 15(A).

26. "Children in Poverty: 1 Million More in 80's," *New York Times*, July 8, 1992, 20(A).

27. Alan B. Krueger, "The Truth about Wages," *New York Times*, July 31, 1997, 23(A).

28. Lynnley Browning, "U.S. Income Gap Widening, Study Says," *New York Times*, September 25, 2003, 2(C).

29. Andrew Hacker, "The Underworld of Work," *The New York Review of Books*, February 12, 2004.

30. Sarah Burd-Sharps, Kristen Lewis, and Eduardo Borges Martins, *The Measure of America: American Human Development Report 2008–2009* (New York: Columbia University Press, 2008), 12.

31. Burd-Sharps, Lewis, and Martins, *The Measure of America*, 19.

32. Anna Bernasek, "The Typical Household, Now Worth a Third Less," *New York Times*, July 26, 2014.

33. Joseph E. Stiglitz, "Inequality Is Not Inevitable," *New York Times*, June 27, 2014.

34. "Table 7.1: Inequality of Labor Income across Time and Space," "Table 7.2: Inequality of Capital Ownership across Time and Space," and "Table 7.3: Inequality of Total Income (Labor and Capital) across Time and Space," in Thomas Piketty, *Capital in the Twenty-First Century* (Cambridge, MA: Belknap Press of Harvard University Press, 2014), 247–49, 264.

35. Raphael and Stoll, *Why Are So Many Americans in Prison?*, 173.

36. Raphael and Stoll, *Why Are So Many Americans in Prison?*, 173.

37. PRWORA, "Personal Responsibility and Work Opportunity Reconciliation Act," (1996) Pub.L. 104–193, 110 Stat. 2105.

38. The analysis of PRWORA is taken directly from my book *The Global New Deal*, 245–46.

39. See, for example, David Willman, "$40-Billion Missile Defense System Proves Unreliable, *Los Angeles Times*, June 15, 2014. Available at http://www.latimes.com/nation/la-na-missile-defense-20140615-story.html (accessed December 6, 2015).

40. Eduardo Porter, "The Myth of Welfare's Corrupting Influence on the Poor," *New York Times*, October 20, 2015. Available at http://www.nytimes.com/2015/10/21/business/the-myth-of-welfares-corrupting-influence-on-the-poor.html.

41. Porter, "The Myth of Welfare's Corrupting Influence on the Poor."

42. Loïc Wacquant, *Punishing the Poor: The Neoliberal Government of Social Insecurity* (Durham, NC: Duke University Press, 2009), 78, 85.

43. See Michael B. Katz, *The Undeserving Poor: From the War on Poverty to the War on Welfare* (New York: Pantheon Books, 1989).

44. Alexander, *New Jim Crow*, 100.

45. Alexander, *New Jim Crow*, 103.

46. Alexander, *New Jim Crow*, 102.

47. Alexander, *New Jim Crow*, 101.

48. Alexander, *New Jim Crow*, 103.

49. Cornel West, foreword to Alexander, *New Jim Crow*, x.

50. Glenn C. Loury, *Race, Incarceration, and American Values* (Cambridge, MA: MIT Press, 2008), 8.

51. Cited in Loury, *Race, Incarceration, and American Values*, 18.

52. Joy James, ed., *The New Abolitionists: (Neo)Slave Narratives and Contemporary Prison Writings* (Albany: State University of New York Press, 2005), xiii.

53. Alexander, *New Jim Crow*, 2.

54. Laleh Ispahani, *Out of Step with the World: An Analysis of Felony Disenfranchisement in the U.S. and Other Democracies* (New York: American Civil Liberties Union, 2006), 4. Also, quoted in Alexander, *New Jim Crow*, 158–59.

55. Brent Staples, "Florida Leads the Pack—in Felon Disenfranchisement," *New York Times*, November 7, 2014.

56. Pamela S. Karlan, "Forum," in *Race, Incarceration, and American Values*, 43–44.

57. Quoted in Karlan, "Forum," 44.

58. For an excellent analysis of the War on Drugs, see Black, "'The War on People,'" 179–99.

59. Ronald Reagan, "Remarks at the Conservative Political Action Conference Dinner," February 18, 1983. Available at http://www.presidency.ucsb.edu/ws/?pid=40948 (accessed July 31, 2015); also quoted in Wacquant, *Punishing the Poor*, 10.

60. George H. W. Bush, "Address to the Nation on the National Drug Control Strategy," September 5, 1989. Available at http://www.presidency.ucsb.edu/ws/?pid=17472 (accessed July 31, 2015).

61. George H. W. Bush, "Remarks at a Briefing on Law Enforcement for United States Attorneys," June 16, 1989. Available at http://www.presidency.ucsb.edu/ws/?pid=17160 (accessed July 31, 2015); also quoted in Wacquant, *Punishing the Poor*, 9.

62. Raphael and Stoll, *Why Are So Many Americans in Prison?*, 114.

63. Raphael and Stoll, *Why Are So Many Americans in Prison?*, 114–15.

64. Linda Evans, "Playing Global Cop: U.S. Militarism and the Prison-Industrial Complex," in *Global Lockdown: Race, Gender, and the Prison-Industrial Complex*, ed. Julia Sudbury (New York: Routledge, 2005), 216.

65. Wacquant, *Punishing the Poor*, 62.

66. Wacquant, *Punishing the Poor*, 62.

67. Raphael and Stoll, *Why Are So Many Americans in Prison?*, 97–98; Wacquant, *Punishing the Poor*, 65.

68. Michael Javen Fortner, "The Real Roots of 70s Drug Laws," *New York Times*, September 28, 2015. Available at http://www.nytimes.com/2015/09/28/opinion/the-real-roots-of-70s-drug-laws.html (accessed December 5, 2015).

69. Fortner, "The Real Roots of 70s Drug Laws." See also Michael Javen Fortner, *Black Silent Majority: The Rockefeller Drug Laws and the Politics of Punishment* (Cambridge, MA: Harvard University Press, 2015).

70. Raphael and Stoll, *Why Are So Many Americans in Prison?*, 101.

71. Wacquant, *Punishing the Poor*, 66.

72. Wacquant, *Punishing the Poor*, 66.

73. Raphael and Stoll, *Why Are So Many Americans in Prison?*, 102.

74. Wacquant, *Punishing the Poor*, 66.

75. Raphael and Stoll, *Why Are So Many Americans in Prison?*, 102–3.

76. Wacquant, *Punishing the Poor*, 66.

77. Raphael and Stoll, *Why Are So Many Americans in Prison?*, 103.

78. Raphael and Stoll, *Why Are So Many Americans in Prison?*, 110.

79. Robert A. Ferguson, *Inferno: An Anatomy of American Punishment* (Cambridge, MA: Harvard University Press, 2014), 2.

80. Ferguson, *Inferno*, 14–15.

81. Anthony M. Kennedy, "Speech at the American Bar Association Annual Meeting," August 9, 2003: An Address by Anthony M. Kennedy, Associate Justice, Supreme Court of the United States, 1–11. Quoted in Ferguson, *Inferno*, 17–18.

82. Amnesty International, *Annual Report: United States of America 2013*, May 29, 2014. Available at http://www.amnestyusa.org/research/reports/annual-report-united-states-of-america-2013?page=4 (accessed October 9, 2014).

83. Amnesty International, *Annual Report: United States of America 2013*.

84. Amnesty International, "Our Mission." Available at http://www.amnestyusa.org/about-us/our-mission (accessed October 9, 2014).

85. Anne Applebaum, *Gulag: A History* (New York: Anchor Books, 2004); "Gulag: Soviet Forced Labor Camps and the Struggle for Freedom," online exhibit available at http://gulaghistory.org/nps/onlineexhibit/stalin/crimes.php (accessed March 13, 2016).

86. Ferguson, *Inferno*, 16.

87. David Kaiser and Lovisa Stannow, "The Shame of Our Prisons: New Evidence," *The New York Review of Books*, October 24, 2013; Allen J. Beck et al., *Sexual Victimization in Prisons and Jails Reported by Inmates, 2011–2012: National Inmate Survey, 2011–2012*, Bureau of Justice Statistics, available at http://www.bjw.gov; Allen J. Beck et al., *Sexual Victimization in Juvenile Facilities Reports by Youth, 2012: National Survey of Youth in Custody, 2012*, Bureau of Justice Statistics, available at http://www.bjw.gov.

88. Quoted in Ferguson, *Inferno*, 26.

89. "End 40 Years of Solitary," Amnesty International. Available at http://www. amnestyusa.org/our-work/cases/usa-the-angola-3; "International Coalition to Free the Angola 3." Available at http://angola3.org. David Cole, "Albert Woodfox's Forty Years in Solitary Confinement," *The New Yorker*, June 16, 2015.

90. Campbell Robertson, "Last 'Angola 3' Inmate Freed after Decades in Solitary," *New York Times*, February 19, 2016; Campbell Robertson, "For 45 Years in Prison, Louisiana Man Kept Calm and Held Fast to Hope," *New York Times*, February 20, 2016.

91. Human Rights Committee, "Concluding Observations on the Fourth Periodic Report of the United States of America," April 23, 2014, CCPR/C/USA/CO/4. Available at http://www. ushrnetwork.org/sites/ushrnetwork.org/files/iccpr_concluding_obs_2014.pdf (accessed October 11, 2014).

92. American Civil Liberties Union, "Prison Conditions." Available at https://www.aclu. org/prisoners-rights/prison-conditions (accessed October 11, 2014).

93. Erik Eckhom, "A.C.L.U. in $50 Million Push to Reduce Jail Sentences," *New York Times*, November 6, 2014. Available at http://www.nytimes.com/2014/11/07/us/aclu-in-dollar50-million-push-to-reduce-jail-sentences.html (accessed November 8, 2014).

94. Trymaine Lee, "Holder Officially Backs Reduced Prison Sentence Proposal," MSNBC.com, April 10, 2014. Available at http://www.msnbc.com/msnbc/doj-eric-holder-urges-reduced-prison-sentence-plan#52619 (accessed October 11, 2014).

95. Lee, "Holder Officially Backs Reduced Prison Sentence Proposal."

96. Lee, "Holder Officially Backs Reduced Prison Sentence Proposal."

97. Inimai M. Chettiar, "Why President Obama Must Act on Mass Incarceration," MSNBC.com, April 20, 2014. Available at http://www.msnbc.com/msnbc/obama-mass-incarceration-commission (accessed October 11, 2014).

98. Eckholm, "A.C.L.U. in $50 Million Push to Reduce Jail Sentences."

99. Erik Eckholm, "California Convicts Are Out of Prison after Third Strike, and Staying Out," *New York Times*, February 26, 2015.

100. "California Leads on Justice Reform," *New York Times*, October 29, 2014; Paige St. John and Marisa Gerber, "Prop. 47 Jolts Landscape of California Justice System," *Los Angeles Times*, November 5, 2014. Available at http://www.latimes.com/local/politics/la-me-ff-pol-proposition47-20141106-story.html (accessed November 8, 2014).

101. Marc Mauer and David Cole, "How to Lock Up Fewer People," *New York Times*, May 23, 2015.

102. Jennifer Steinhauer, "Push to Scale Back Sentencing Laws Gains Momentum," *New York Times*, July 28, 2015.

103. "President Obama Takes on the Prison Crisis," *New York Times*, July 16, 2015; Peter Baker, "Obama, in Oklahoma, Takes Reform Message to the Prison Cell Block," *New York Times*, July 16, 2015.

104. Kaiser and Stannow, "The Shame of Our Prisons."

105. Jamil Dakwar, "After Ferguson, U.N. Calls on U.S. to Get Its Act Together on Race Discrimination," American Civil Liberties Union (ACLU), August 29, 2014. Available at https://www.aclu.org/blog/human-rights-racial-justice/after-ferguson-un-calls-us-get-its-act-together-race-discrimination (accessed October 9, 2014).

106. Dakwar, "After Ferguson."

107. Dakwar, "After Ferguson."

3. HOMOPHOBIA AND ANTI-GAY VIOLENCE IN AFRICA

1. Alan Cowell, "Ugandan President Signs Antigay Law," *New York Times*, February 24, 2014.

2. David Smith, "Gay African Refugees Face Abduction, Violence and Rape in Uganda and Kenya," *Guardian*, May 18, 2012; Eric Sande, "Homophobic Attacks on the Rise in Africa," *News from Africa*, February 4, 2011; "Anti-Gay Abuse Rife in Africa," *Washington Times*, April 22, 2010.

3. Alexis Okeowo, "Out in Africa: A Gay-Rights Struggle with Deadly Stakes," *The New Yorker*, December 24, 2012.

4. Cowell, "Ugandan President Signs Antigay Law"; Serge Schmemann, "Gains and Grave Setbacks for Gay Rights," *New York Times*, February 28, 2014.

5. Saad Abedine and Elizabeth Landau, "Ugandan Tabloid Prints List of 'Homosexuals,'" CNN.com, February 25, 2014. Available at http://www.cnn.com/2014/02/25/world/africa/uganda-anti-gay-law (accessed October 30, 2014).

6. "Ugandan Court Invalidates Anti-Gay Law," *New York Times*, August 1, 2014.

7. "Gay Man's 3-Year Sentence Upheld by Cameroon Court," *New York Times*, December 17, 2012.

8. "Nigerian Leader Signs Law Banning Gay Associations," *New York Times*, January 13, 2014.

9. Damian Ugwu, "As the Flames of Homophobia Burn around the World, Understanding Nigeria's Anti-Gay Bill," *Huffington Post*, December 3, 2012.

10. BBC News Africa, "Ghana Refuses to Grant Gays' Rights Despite Aid Threat," November 2, 2011. Available at http://www.bbc.co.uk/news/world-africa-15558769 (accessed February 11, 2013).

11. Andrew Solomon, "In Bed with the President of Ghana?," *New York Times*, February 9, 2013; Malaysian National News Agency, "Ghana Constitution Frowns upon Gay Rights— Justice Minister." Available at http://www.bernama.com/bernama/v6/newsworld.php?id=926999 (accessed February 11, 2013).

12. Tamasin Ford and Bonnie Allen, "Nobel Peace Prize Winner Defends Law Criminalizing Homosexuality in Liberia," *Guardian*, March 19, 2012. Available at http://www.guardian.co.uk/world/2012/mar/19/nobel-peace-prize-law-homosexuality (accessed February 12, 2013).

13. Mabvuto Banda, "Malawi Pardons Gay Couple during UN Chief's Visit," *Reuters*, May 30, 2010. Available at http://www.reuters.com/article/2010/05/30/idUSLDE64T0CK (accessed February 12, 2013).

14. See, for example, OutRight Action International at http://www.iglhrc.org/cgi-bin/iowa/article/takeaction/resourcecenter/1634.html (assessed December 14, 2015); Human Rights Watch at http://www.hrw.org/en/africa (assessed December 14, 2015); Amnesty International at http://www.amnestyusa.org/our-work/countries/middle-east-and-north-africa (assessed December 14, 2015).

15. See, for example, the 2011 State Department Human Rights report on the treatment of LGBT individuals in Uganda at http://www.state.gov/j/drl/rls/hrrpt/humanrightsreport/index.htm?dlid=186254 (assessed March 5, 2016).

16. Marc Epprecht, *Hungochani: The History of a Dissident Sexuality in Southern Africa* (Ithaca, NY: McGill-Queen's University Press, 2004), 4–5.

17. Kapya Kaoma, *Globalizing the Culture Wars: U.S. Conservatives, African Churches, & Homophobia* (Somerville, MA: Political Research Associates, 2009), 3.

18. Kaoma, *Globalizing the Culture Wars*, 3–4.

19. Kapya Kaoma, *Colonizing African Values: How the U.S. Christian Right Is Transforming Sexual Politics in Africa* (Somerville, MA: Political Research Associates, 2012), vi.

20. Kaoma, *Colonizing African Values*, vi.

21. See, for example, Gordon Isaacs and Brian McKendrick, *Male Homosexuality in South Africa: Identity Formation, Culture and Crisis* (Cape Town: Oxford University Press, 1992); Matthew Krouse and Kim Berman, eds., *The Invisible Ghetto: Lesbian and Gay Writing from South Africa* (Johannesburg: COCAW, 1993); Mark Gevisser and Edwin Cameron, eds., *Defiant Desire: Gay and Lesbian Lives in South Africa* (Johannesburg: Ravan, 1994); Rudi Bleys, *The Geography of Perversion: Male-Male Sexual Behaviour outside the West and the Ethnographic Imagination* (New York: New York University Press, 1995); Stephen Murray and Will Roscoe, *Islamic Homosexualities: Culture, History and Literature* (New York: New York University Press, 1997); Stephen Murray and Will Roscoe, *Boys Wives and Female Husbands: Studies in African Homosexualities* (New York: St. Martin's Press, 1998); Neville Hoad, "Arrested Development or the Queerness of Savages," *Postcolonial Studies* 3, no 2 (2000).

22. See Paul Semugoma, Steave Nemande, and Stefan D. Baral, "The Irony of Homophobia in Africa," *The Lancet* 380, no. 9839 (July 28, 2012); David F. Greenberg, *The Construction of Homosexuality* (Chicago: University of Chicago Press, 1990); Brent L. Pickett, *Historical Dictionary of Homosexuality* (Lanham, MD: Scarecrow Press, 2009).

23. Epprecht, *Hungochani*; Marc Epprecht, *Heterosexual Africa? The History of an Idea from the Age of Exploration to the Age of AIDS* (Athens: Ohio University Press, 2008).

24. Makau Mutua, "Sexual Orientation and Human Rights: Putting Homophobia on Trial," in *African Sexualities: A Reader*, ed. Sylvia Tamale (Oxford: Pambazuka Press, 2011), 452–62.

25. There is no one Islamic, nor one Christian, view of homosexuality. Instead there are contested views on homosexuality within both religions. For example, as a counter to the views of Tariq Ramadan cited above, see the interview with Muhsin Hendricks of South Africa, believed to be the first openly gay Muslim imam in the world. Available at http://www.trust.org/item/20130613082540-l91b8 (accessed July 1, 2013). See also http://www.glaad.org/blog/openly-gay-imams-serve-affirming-gleam-hope-muslim-lgbt-community (accessed July 1, 2013).

26. Tariq Ramadan, "Islam and Homosexuality," May 29, 2009. Available at http://www.tariqramadan.com/spip.php?article10683&lang=fr (accessed June 30, 2013).

27. David F. Greenberg, *The Construction of Homosexuality* (Chicago: University of Chicago Press, 1990).

28. Epprecht, *Hungochani*, 9.

29. Epprecht, *Hungochani*, 7.

30. Epprecht, *Hungochani*, 225.

31. Michael Schulman, "Generation LGBTQIA," *New York Times*, January 9, 2013.

32. Schulman, "Generation LGBTQIA."

33. Aamer Madhani and Jim Norman, "51% Agree with Obama's Endorsement of Gay Marriage," *USA Today*, May 11, 2012. Available at http://usatoday30.usatoday.com/news/washington/story/2012-05-11/USA-TODAYGallup-poll-Obama-gay-marriage/54905424/1 (accessed February 15, 2013).

34. "Gay Marriage Approved in Two States on a Good Night for US Liberals," *Guardian*, November 7, 2012. Available at http://www.guardian.co.uk/world/2012/nov/07/gay-marriage-votes-us-election (accessed February 15, 2013).

35. Adam Liptak, "Supreme Court Bolsters Gay Marriage with Two Major Rulings," *New York Times*, June 27, 2013.

36. Lizette Alvarez and Nila Do Simon, "Same-Sex Pairs in Florida Say Jubilant 'I Dos,'" *New York Times*, January 6, 2015; "U.S. to Recognize Same-Sex Marriage in 6 More States," *New York Times*, October 25, 2014.

37. "A Profound Ruling Delivers Justice on Gay Marriage," *New York Times*, June 26, 2015.

38. "The Challenges That Remain after Marriage Equality," *New York Times*, July 29, 2015; Liptak, "Supreme Court Bolsters Gay Marriage"; Danaya C. Wright, "The Fast Track to Gay Marriage," *Tampa Bay Times*, June 30, 2013.

39. See Desiree Lewis, "Representing African Sexualities," in *African Sexualities: A Reader*, ed. Sylvia Tamale (Oxford: Pambazuka Press, 2011), 199–216.

40. Damian Ugwu, "As the Flames of Homophobia Burn," *Huffington Post*, December 3, 2012.

41. "SA Signs UN Gay Violence Statement," mambaonline.com, March 22, 2011. Available at http://mambaonline.com/article.asp?artid=5447 (accessed February 15, 2013).

42. See Louis Henkin, Gerald Neuman, Diane Orentlicher, and David Leebron, "Judicial Enforcement against Foreign Violations," *Human Rights* (New York: Foundation Press, 1999), 856–81.

43. Center for Constitutional Rights, "LGBTI Uganda Fights Back: The Case against Scott Lively." Available at http://ccrjustice.org/LGBTUganda (accessed February 18, 2013). NBCNews.com, "Lawsuit: US Evangelist Inspired Deadly Hate against Uganda Gays," March 15, 2012. Available at http://worldnews.nbcnews.com/_news/2012/03/15/10695690-lawsuit-us-evangelist-inspired-deadly-hate-against-uganda-gays?lite (accessed February 18, 2013).

44. Adam Liptak, "Justices Bar Nigerian Human Rights Cases from U.S. Courts," *New York Times*, April 17, 2013. The court ruled that Nigerian plaintiffs who said foreign oil companies had been complicit in violating their human rights may not sue in American courts.

45. "Plaintiff's Response to Defendant's 'Notice of Supplemental Authority Requiring Dismissal of Plaintiff's Federal Law Claims,'" *Sexual Minorities Uganda v. Scott Lively*, Civil Action, 3:12-CV-30051, May 7, 2013. Available at http://ccrjustice.org/files/SMUG_Pl-ResponsetoDefSupplAuthority_05_13.pdf (accessed June 20, 2013).

46. See, for example, Douglas Sanders, "Human Rights and Sexual Orientation," May 16, 2007. Available at http://ilga.org/ilga/en/article/1078 (accessed June 21, 2013).

47. Office of the High Commissioner for Human Rights, "Born Free and Equal," Geneva, 2012 (HR/PUB/12/06), 7.

48. Douglas Sanders, "Human Rights and Sexual Orientation in International Law," WORLD, May 25, 2007, 13.

49. Neil MacFarquhar, "In a First, Gay Rights Are Pressed at the U.N.," *New York Times*, December 18, 2008. Available at http://www.nytimes.com/2008/12/19/world/19nations.html (accessed February 20, 2013).

50. Associated Press, "U.N. Gay Rights Protection Resolution Passes, Hailed as 'Historic Moment,'" June 17, 2011. Available at http://www.huffingtonpost.com/2011/06/17/un-gay-rights-protection-resolution-passes-_n_879032.html (accessed February 20, 2013).

51. *Ontopmagazine*, "Obama Administration Signs onto United Nations Gay Rights Resolution," March 23, 2011. Available at http://www.ontopmag.com/article.aspx?id=7891 (accessed February 20, 2013). See also International Lesbian, Gay, Bisexual, Trans and Intersex Association, "South Africa Signs UN Gay Violence Statement," June 2011. Available at http://ilga.org/ilga/en/article/mwRtf9j1gW (accessed February 20, 2013).

52. San Diego Gay and Lesbian News, "UN Makes History: First-Ever Condemnation of Killings Based on Gender Identity," November 21, 2012. Available at http://sdgln.com/news/ 2012/11/21/un-makes-history-first-ever-condemnation-killings-based-gender-identity   (accessed February 20, 2013).

53. WORLD, "19th Human Rights Council: Panel Discussion on "Human Rights, Sexual Orientation and Gender Identity," March 8, 2012. Available at http://ilga.org/ilga/en/article/ nr5t6qZ1Jy (accessed on February 20, 2013).

54. "South Africa Leads United Nations on Gay Rights, *Mail & Guardian*, March 9, 2012. Available at http://mg.co.za/print/2012-03-09-sa-leads-un-on-gay-rights (accessed March 4, 2013).

55. "South Africa Leads United Nations on Gay Rights."

56. Robbie Corey-Boulet, "The Obama Administration's Bold but Risky Plan to Make Africa Gay-Friendly," *The Atlantic*, March 2012. Available at http://www.theatlantic.com/ international/print/2012/03/the-obama-administrations-bold-but-risky-plan-to-make-africa-gay-friendly/254086 (accessed March 4, 2013). Mike Pflanz, "Africa Reacts to Obama's Pro-Gay Rights Foreign Policy with Ire," *Jewish World Review*, March 4, 2013. Available at http:// www.jewishworldreview.com/1211/clinton_gay_africa.php3#.UTUmA6VptjN   (accessed March 4, 2013).

57. Adam Nossiter, "Senegal Cheers Its President for Standing Up to Obama on Same-Sex Marriage," *New York Times*, June 28, 2013.

58. Carol E. Lee and Heidi Vogt, "President Barack Obama Condemns Kenya on Gay Rights," *Wall Street Journal*, July 25, 2015; Peter Baker and Marc Santora, "Obama in Kenya: An Upbeat Tone, but Notes of Discord, Too," *New York Times*, July 25, 2015. See also Norimitsu Ohishi, "Africans to Welcome Obama, but Not a Scolding on Gay Rights," *New York Times*, July 21, 2015.

59. Human Rights Council, 16th Session, "Report of the Working Group on the Universal Periodic Review: United States of America," A/HRC/16/11 (January 4, 2011). See also Frank Jordans, "US Rejects UN Death Penalty Proposal," *Huffington Post*, November 9, 2010.

60. See, for example, Norimitsu Onishi, "U.S. Suppport of Gay Rights in Africa May Have Done More Harm Than Good," *New York Times*, December 20, 2015.

61. Adam Nossiter, "Senegal Cheers." See also Jori Lewis, "Senegal's Gay Men Suffer Violence," *Human Rights Watch*, November 29, 2010. Available at http://www.hrw.org/audio/ 2010/11/29/senegals-gay-men-suffer-violence (accessed July 1, 2013).

62. "UN Human Rights Office Launches Unprecedented Global Campaign for Lesbian, Gay, Bisexual and Transgender Equality," UN High Commissioner for Human Rights, Cape Town, South Africa, July 26, 2013. Available at http://www.ohchr.org/EN/NewsEvents/Pages/ DisplayNews.aspx?NewsID=13583&LangID=E (accessed August 2, 2013).

63. "Tutu Says He Cannot Worship 'Homophobic' God," Aljazeera, July 26, 2013. Available at http://www.aljazeera.com/news/africa/2013/07/201372619342804519.html (accessed August 2, 2013).

4. SAUDI ARABIA AND THE RIGHTS OF WOMEN

1. Abdullahi Ahmed An-Na'im, *Islam and the Secular State* (Cambridge, MA: Harvard University Press, 2008), 280.

2. An-Na'im, *Islam and the Secular State*, 110.

3. Sean Oliver-Dee, *Muslim Minorities and Citizenship* (London: I. B. Tauris, 2012), 11–17.

4. Ann Elizabeth Mayer, *Islam and Human Rights: Tradition and Politics*, 5th ed. (Boulder, CO: Westview Press, 2013), 99–100.

5. *The Global Gender Gap Report* (Geneva, Switzerland: World Economic Forum, 2015). Available at http://reports.weforum.org/global-gender-gap-report-2015/economies/#economy= SAU (accessed December 29, 2015).

6. Mayer, *Islam and Human Rights*, 122. See also Ruth Roded, ed., *Women in Islam and the Middle East: A Reader* (New York: Tauris, 2008).

7. Saudi Women for Reform, *Shadow Report for the Committee on the Elimination of All Forms of Discrimination against Women* (CEDAW), December 2007, 2. Available at http:// www2.ohchr.org/english/bodies/cedaw/docs/ngos/womenreform40.pdf (accessed December 17, 2015).

8. Saudi Women for Reform, *Shadow Report*, 2–3.

9. Human Rights Watch, *Perpetual Minors: Human Rights Abuses Stemming from Male Guardianship and Sex Segregation in Saudi Arabia* (New York: Human Rights Watch, 2008), 2. Available at http://www.iwraw-ap.org/resources/pdf/40_shadow_reports/Saudi_Arabia_ Report_by_HRW.pdf (accessed February 22, 2014).

10. Saudi Women for Reform, *Shadow Report*, 8–9.

11. Eleanor Abdella Doumato, "Education in Saudi Arabia: Gender, Jobs, and the Price of Religion," in *Women and Globalization in the Arab Middle East*, eds. Eleanor Abdella Doumato and Marsha Pripstein Posusney (Boulder, CO: Lynne Rienner, 2003), 240, 243.

12. Dionne Searcey, "A Conundrum for Saudis: Women at Work," *New York Times*, November 28, 2014. See also Saudi Women for Reform, *Shadow Report*, 9.

13. Katherine Zoepf, "Sisters in Law: Saudi Women Are Beginning to Know Their Rights," *The New Yorker*, January 11, 2016; Saudi Women for Reform, *Shadow Report*, 9.

14. Peter W. Wilson and Douglas F. Graham, *Saudi Arabia: The Coming Storm* (New York: Sharpe, 1994), 240.

15. Ed Husain, "Saudis Must Stop Exporting Extremism," *New York Times*, August 22, 2014.

16. David Batty and Mona Mahmood, "Palestinian Poet Ashraf Fayadh's Death Sentence Quashed by Saudi Court," *Guardian*, February 2, 2016. Available at http://www.theguardian. com/world/2016/feb/02/palestinian-poet-ashraf-fayadhs-death-sentence-overturned-by-saudi-court (accessed March 7, 2016).

17. Rick Gladstone, "Literary Group Asks Obama to Intercede for Condemned Writers in Saudi Arabia," *New York Times*, December 16, 2015.

18. Jan Goodwin, *Price of Honor: Muslim Women Lift the Veil of Silence on the Islamic World* (New York: Plume, 2003), 200.

19. Searcey, "A Conundrum for Saudis."

20. Zoepf, "Sisters in Law"; Wilson and Graham, *Saudi Arabia: The Coming Storm*, 245.

21. Ratification information available at http://tbinternet.ohchr.org/_layouts/ TreatyBodyExternal/Treaty.aspx?Treaty=CEDAW&Lang=en (accessed December 29, 2015).

22. Donna E. Arzt, "The Application of International Human Rights Law in Islamic States," *Human Rights Quarterly* 12, no. 2 (May 1990): 208.

23. *International Convention on the Elimination of All Forms of Discrimination against Women* (CEDAW). Concluded at New York, December 18, 1979. Entered into force, September 3, 1981.

24. Zainah Almihdar, "Human Rights of Women and Children under the Islamic Law of Personal Status and Its Application in Saudi Arabia," *Muslim World Journal of Human Rights* 5, no. 1 (2008): 3–4.

25. CEDAW.

26. These are verse 228 of chapter 2, which states, *inter alia*: *"And women shall have rights similar to the rights against them, according to what is equitable; but men have a degree above them";* and verse 34 of chapter 4, which states, *inter alia: "Men are the protectors and maintainers of women because God has given the one more strength than the other, and because they support them from their means."* Almihdar, "Human Rights of Women and Children under the Islamic Law," 5.

27. CEDAW.

28. Almihdar, "Human Rights of Women and Children under the Islamic Law," 7.

29. Human Rights Watch, *Perpetual Minors: Human Rights Abuses Stemming from Male Guardianship and Sex Segregation in Saudi Arabia* (New York: Human Rights Watch, 2008), 2. Available at http://www.iwraw-ap.org/resources/pdf/40_shadow_reports/Saudi_Arabia_Report_by_HRW.pdf (accessed February 22, 2014).

30. Upendra Baxi, "Voices of Suffering, Fragmented Universality, and the Future of Human Rights," in *The Future of International Human Rights*, eds. Burns H. Weston and Stephen P. Marks (Ardsley, NY: Transnational, 1999), 123; Walter Kaufmann, *The Portable Nietzsche* (New York: Viking Penguin, 1959), 160–61.

31. International Court of Justice, *Reservations to the Convention on Genocide*, 1951, *ICJ Reports* 15, in *Fundamental Perspectives on International Law*, 3rd ed., edited by William R. Slomanson (Belmont, CA: West International Law, 2000), 336.

32. CEDAW.

33. Abdullahi An-Na'im, "Religious Minorities under Islamic Law and the Limits of Cultural Relativism," *Human Rights Quarterly* 9, no. 1 (February 1987): 7n17. Quoted in Arzt, "The Application of International Human Rights Law in Islamic States," 217.

34. Arzt, "The Application of International Human Rights Law in Islamic States," 218.

35. Mayer, *Islam and Human Rights*, 123.

36. Ben Hubbard, "Saudi Elections Are First to Include Women as Voters and Candidates," *New York Times*, December 13, 2015; Ben Hubbard, "In Milestone, Saudis Elect First Women to Councils," December 13, 2015.

37. Mayer, *Islam and Human Rights*, 124.

38. "Saudi Woman Gets 150 Lashes for Driving," Press TV, April 25, 2014; "Lashes for Saudi Female Driver," *Tampa Bay Times*, April 26, 2014 (9A).

39. Nisrine Abiad, *Sharia, Muslim States and International Human Rights Treaty Obligations: A Comparative Study* (London: British Institute of International and Comparative Law, 2008), 114.

40. Frances Harrison, "UN Call for Saudi Women's Rights," *BBC News*, February 1, 2008.

41. Christopher M. Blanchard, "Saudi Arabia: Background and U.S. Relations," *Congressional Research Service Report*, February 12, 2014, 8–9. Available at http://www.fas.org/sgp/crs/mideast/RL33533.pdf (accessed March 15, 2014).

42. Blanchard, "Saudi Arabia: Background and U.S. Relations."

43. Blanchard, "Saudi Arabia: Background and U.S. Relations," 9.

44. Gerd Nonneman, "Saudi–European Relations 1902–2001: A Pragmatic Quest for Relative Autonomy," *International Affairs* 77, no. 3 (2001): 636.

45. Nonneman, "Saudi–European Relations 1902–2001," 649–50.

46. Kwame Anthony Appiah, *The Honor Code: How Moral Revolutions Happen* (New York: Norton, 2010), 170, 171–72.

47. Appiah, *The Honor Code*, 178.

48. "Obama Should Highlight Human Rights Concerns during Saudi Visit, *Freedom House*, March 27, 2014. Available at http://www.freedomhouse.org/country/saudi-arabia#. U0rixMeXtdg (accessed April 12, 2014). "Annual Report: State of the World's Human Rights 2013: Saudi Arabia," *Amnesty International*. Available at http://www.amnesty.org/en/region/saudi-arabia/report-2013 (accessed April 12, 2014).

49. Josh Rogin, "Congress: Obama Must Press Saudi Arabia on Human Rights," *Daily Beast*, March 25, 2014.

50. Samantha Power, *"A Problem from Hell": America and the Age of Genocide* (New York: Basic Books, 2002), 335.

51. Power, *"A Problem from Hell,"* 364.

52. Robert Mackey, "Saudi Activists Call for the Release of Women Detained for Driving," *New York Times*, December 8, 2014; Associated Press, "Saudi Arabia: Advisers Urge King to Let Women Drive, *New York Times*, November 7, 2014.

53. Qanta Ahmed, "Invisible Women at Work: Meet Maha Al-Muneef, the Gloria Steinem of Arabia," *World Post*, May 25, 2011. Available at http://www.huffingtonpost.com/qanta-ahmed/invisible-women-at-work-m_b_206759.html (accessed December 29, 2015).

54. Wendy S. Hesford and Wendy Kozol, introduction to *Just Advocacy? Women's Human Rights, Transnational Feminisms, and the Politics of Representation*, eds. Wendy S. Hesford and Wendy Kozol (New Brunswick, NJ: Rutgers University Press, 2005), 3.

55. See Stephen Kinzer, *Overthrow: America's Century of Regime Change from Hawaii to Iraq* (New York: Holt and Company, 2006); Chalmers Johnson, *The Sorrows of Empire: Militarism, Secrecy, and the End of the Republic* (New York: Holt and Company, 2004).

56. Lila Abu-Lughod, *Do Muslim Women Need Saving?* (Cambridge, MA: Harvard University Press, 2013), 42.

57. Patrick Goodenough, "Kerry Sidesteps Opportunity to Support Saudi Women's Freedom to Drive," CNSnews.com, November 5, 2013. Available at http://www.cnsnews.com/news/article/patrick-goodenough/kerry-sidesteps-opportunity-support-saudi-women-s-freedom-drive (accessed March 15, 2014).

58. Michael Crowley, "Kerry Takes Softer Line Than Hillary on Saudi Women Drivers," *Time*, November 5, 2013. Available at http://swampland.time.com/2013/11/05/kerry-takes-softer-line-than-hillary-on-saudi-women-drivers (accessed March 16, 2014).

59. Michael D. Shear, "Obama Ends Overseas Trip with Award for Saudi," *New York Times*, March 29, 2014.

60. See Kamel Daoud, "Saudi Arabia, an ISIS That Has Made It," *New York Times*, November 20, 2015.

61. Adam Coogle, "The Deafening U.S. Silence on Saudi Rights," *Foreign Policy*, January 28, 2014. Available at http://mideastafrica.foreignpolicy.com/posts/2014/01/28/the_deafening_us_silence_on_saudi_rights (accessed April 12, 2014).

62. Coogle, "The Deafening U.S. Silence on Saudi Rights."

63. Coogle, "The Deafening U.S. Silence on Saudi Rights."

64. Madhavi Sunder, "Piercing the Veil," in *Just Advocacy? Women's Human Rights, Transnational Feminisms, and the Politics of Representation*, 271.

65. Sunder, "Piercing the Veil," 272.

66. Sunder, "Piercing the Veil," 275–76.

67. See HarassMap.org at http://harassmap.org/en/who-we-are/how-and-why-we-began (accessed April 19, 2014). My thanks to Eckerd College student Greg Johnson for calling my attention to HarassMap.

68. See http://harassmap.org/en/who-we-are/how-and-why-we-began (accessed April 19, 2014).

69. See Ushahidi.com at http://ushahidi.com/about-us (accessed April 19, 2014).

70. See http://harassmap.org/en/what-we-do/around-the-world (accessed April 19, 2014).

71. William Felice, *The Global New Deal: Economic and Social Human Rights in World Politics*, 2nd ed. (Lanham, MD: Rowman & Littlefield, 2010), 179–204.

72. See Abu-Lughod, *Do Muslim Women Need Saving?*

5. ENVIRONMENTAL RIGHTS IN CHINA

1. Bryan Walsh, "The Scariest Environmental Fact in the World," *Time: Science and Space*, January 29, 2013. Available at http://science.time.com/2013/01/29/the-scariest-environmental-fact-in-the-world (accessed March 11, 2013). Daniel Cusick and ClimateWire, "China's Soaring Coal Consumption Poses Climate Challenge," *Scientific American*, January 30, 2013. Available at http://www.scientificamerican.com/article.cfm?id=chinas-soaring-coal-consumption-poses-climate-challenge (accessed March 11, 2013).

2. Chris Buckley, "China Burns Much More Coal Than Reported, Complicating Climate Talks," *New York Times*, November 3, 2015.

3. Cusick and ClimateWire, "China's Soaring Coal Consumption."

4. Chris Buckley, "China Pledges to Halt Growth of Carbon Emissions in Climate Plan," *New York Times*, June 30, 2015.

5. Cusick and ClimateWire, "China's Soaring Coal Consumption."

6. Union of Concerned Scientists, "What Are the Options for the Vast Stores of Coal around the World?" Available at http://www.ucsusa.org/global_warming/science_and_impacts/science/coal-and-global-warming-faq.html (accessed March 11, 2013).

7. Damian Carrington, "More Than 1,000 New Coal Plants Planned Worldwide, Figures Show," *Guardian*, November 19, 2012. Available at http://www.guardian.co.uk/environment/2012/nov/20/coal-plants-world-resources-institute (accessed March 12, 2013). Brad Plumer, "The Big Climate Question: Will the World Build 1,200 New Coal Plants?," *Washington Post*, November 20, 2012. See also Terry Macalister, "Coal's Resurgence Undermines Fight against Global Warming," *Guardian*, June 13, 2012. Available at http://www.guardian.co.uk/environment/2012/jun/13/coal-resurgence-global-warming (accessed March 12, 2013).

8. Elizabeth C. Economy, "The Great Leap Backward?," *Foreign Affairs*, September/October 2007.

9. Edward Wong, "Cost of Environmental Damage in China Growing Rapidly Amid Industrialization, *New York Times*, March 29, 2013.

10. Edward Wong, "Air Pollution Linked to 1.2 Million Premature Deaths in China," *New York Times*, April 1, 2013.

11. Edward Wong, "In China, Breathing Becomes a Childhood Risk," *New York Times*, April 22, 2013.

12. Edward Wong, "Beijing Issues a Second 'Red Alert' on Pollution," *New York Times*, December 17, 2015.

13. Jianguo Liu and Jared Diamond, "China's Environment in a Globalizing World," *Nature*, June 30, 2005, 1179–80.

14. Edward Wong, "China Exports Pollution to U.S., Study Finds," *New York Times*, January 20, 2014.

15. Tony Barboza, "China's Industry Exporting Air Pollution to U.S., Study Says," *Los Angeles Times*, January 20, 2014.

16. Liu and Diamond, "China's Environment in a Globalizing World," 1179–80.

17. Martin Fackler, "Scientist Says Pollution from China Is Killing a Japanese Island's Trees," *New York Times*, April 24, 2013. Available at http://www.nytimes.com/2013/04/25/world/asia/japanese-scientist-blames-china-for-yakushimas-dying-trees.html (accessed May 28, 2013).

18. Liu and Diamond, "China's Environment in a Globalizing World," 1184.

19. Gørild Heggelund, "China's Climate Change Policy: Domestic and International Developments," *Asian Perspective* 31, no. 2 (2007): 155.

20. See Heggelund, "China's Climate Change Policy," 155–91.

21. Wang Chunmei and Lin Zhaolan, "Environmental Policies in China over the Past 10 Years: Progress, Problems and Prospects, *Procedia Environmental Sciences* 2 (2010): 1708.

22. Edward Wong, "As Pollution Worsens in China, Solutions Succumb to Infighting," *New York Times*, March 21, 2013.

23. Keith Johnson, "China Surpasses U.S. in Clean-Energy Investment," *Wall Street Journal*, April 17, 2013. Available at http://blogs.wsj.com/washwire/2013/04/17/china-surpasses-u-s-in-clean-energy-investment (accessed April 19, 2013). "New Leader in Clean Energy: China," *Tampa Bay Times*, April 17, 2013.

24. Liu Sha, "Environmental NGOs Grow across China but Still Struggle for Support," *Global Times*, December 6, 2012. Available at http://www.globaltimes.cn/content/714330.shtml (accessed December 19, 2015).

25. Fengshi Wu, "Environmental Activism in China: 15 Years in Review, 1994–2008," Harvard-Yenching Institute Working Paper Series 2009, 8.

26. Justin Gillis, "Heat-Trapping Gas Passes Milestone, Raising Fears," *New York Times*, May 10, 2013. Available at http://www.nytimes.com/2013/05/11/science/earth/carbon-dioxide-level-passes-long-feared-milestone.html (accessed May 28, 2013).

27. Elizabeth Kolbert, *The Sixth Extinction: An Unnatural History* (New York: Henry Holt, 2014).

28. See Benjamin van Rooij, "The People vs. Pollution: Understanding Citizen Action against Pollution in China," *Journal of Contemporary China* 19, no. 63 (2010): 55–77.

29. Chunmei and Zhaolan, "Environmental Policies in China over the Past 10 Years," 1706.

30. Elizabeth Muller, "China Must Exploit Its Shale Gas," *New York Times*, April 12, 2013.

31. For an interesting analysis of how China and the United States might work together to support effective climate change programs, see Deborah Seligsohn, Robert Heilmayr, Xiaomei Tan, and Lutz Seischer, "China, the United States, and the Climate Change Challenge, *World Resource Institute Policy Brief*, October 2009.

32. Keith Schneider, "How Ontario Is Putting an End to Coal-Burning Power Plants," *Christian Science Monitor*, April 3, 2013.

33. Mark Landler, "Obama Seeks to Reassert U.S. Role in Climate Debate," *New York Times*, July 2, 2013.

34. Melissa Harris, Marisa Geck, and Ivetta Gerasimchuk, "The End of Coal: Ontario's Coal Phase-out," International Institute for Sustainable Development, June 2015. Available at https://www.iisd.org/sites/default/files/publications/end-of-coal-ontario-coal-phase-out.pdf (accessed December 20, 2015). "Thunder Bay Generating Station Stops Burning Coal," CBCnews, April 15, 2014. Available at http://www.cbc.ca/news/canada/thunder-bay/thunder-bay-generating-station-stops-burning-coal-1.2610782 (accessed December 20, 2015).

35. Schneider, "How Ontario Is Putting an End to Coal-Burning Power Plants."

36. Schneider, "How Ontario Is Putting an End to Coal-Burning Power Plants."

37. Mark Landler, "U.S. and China Reach Climate Deal after Months of Talks," *New York Times*, November 11, 2014.

38. Heggelund, "China's Climate Change Policy," 156.

39. Chris Buckley, "China Pledges to Halt Growth of Carbon Emissions in Climate Plan," *New York Times*, June 30, 2015.

40. United National Conference on Climate Change, COP21/CMP11. Details on the agreement available at http://www.cop21.gouv.fr/en/more-details-about-the-agreement (accessed December 19, 2015). Coral Davenport, "Nations Approve Landmark Climate Accord in Paris," *New York Times*, December 12, 2015.

41. Davenport, "Nations Approve Landmark Climate Accord in Paris."

42. Economist Intelligence Unit reports available at http://www.eiu.com/home.aspx (accessed December 23, 2014).

43. Edward Wong and Chris Buckley, "Chinese Premier Vows Tougher Regulation on Air Pollution," *New York Times*, March 3, 2015.

44. Martin Adams, "China's Double-Edged Pact," *New York Times*, December 15, 2014. See also Edward Wong, "Questions over China's Climate Change Plan," *New York Times*, November 12, 2014.

45. Michael Forsythe, "China's Emissions Pledges Are Undercut by Boom in Coal Projects Abroad," *New York Times*, December 11, 2015.

46. Gardiner Harris, "Coal Rush in India Could Tip Balance on Climate Change," *New York Times*, November 17, 2014; Keith Johnson, "Green Gamble: Can India Avoid Repeating China's Dirty-Energy Mistakes?," *Foreign Policy*, November/December 2015.

47. Liu and Diamond, "China's Environment in a Globalizing World," 1186.

48. Felice, *The Global New Deal*, 125–56.

49. Coral Davenport and Mark Landler, "U.S. to Give $3 Billion to Climate Fund to Help Poor Nations, and Spur Rich Ones," *New York Times*, November 14, 2014.

CONCLUSION

1. George Will quoted in Luis Cabrera, *The Practice of Global Citizenship* (Cambridge: Cambridge University Press, 2010), 83.

2. See Benedict Anderson, *Imagined Communities* (London: Verso Press, 1991).

3. See Michael Walzer, "The Moral Standing of States: A Response to Four Critics," *Philosophy and Public Affairs* 9, no. 3 (Spring 1980): 209–29.

4. Edmund Burke, *Reflections on the French Revolution*, ed. A. J. Grieve (London: Dent, 1910), 82.

5. It is important to note that there are differences between individual philosophers linked to communitarianism. While both Charles Taylor and Alasdair MacIntyre, for example, are associated with the communitarian critique, Taylor would be much more sympathetic to aspects of an emerging global identity than would MacIntyre.

6. Derek Heater, *World Citizenship: Cosmopolitan Thinking and Its Opponents* (London: Continuum, 2002), 63.

7. Heater, *World Citizenship*, 63–64.

8. Edmund Burke quoted in Michael W. McConnell, "Don't Neglect the Platoons," in *For Love of Country: Debating the Limits of Patriotism*, eds. Martha C. Nussbaum and Joshua Cohen (Boston: Beacon Press, 1996), 79.

9. David Held, *Cosmopolitanism: Ideals and Realities* (Cambridge: Polity Press, 2010), 19–20.

10. Held, *Cosmopolitanism: Ideals and Realities*, 24.

11. Martha Nussbaum, "Patriotism and Cosmopolitanism," in *For Love of Country*, eds. Nussbaum and Cohen, 11–15. See also Martha Nussbaum, "Toward a Globally Sensitive Patriotism," *Daedalus* 137, no 3 (2008): 78–93.

12. See, for example, the media coverage of the UN's "oil for food" program in Iraq. A summary is available at Sharon Otterman, "Iraq: Oil for Food Scandal," Council on Foreign Relations, October 28, 2005. Available at http://www.cfr.org/iraq/iraq-oil-food-scandal/p7631 (accessed December 31, 2015).

13. Michael Walzer, "Spheres of Affection," in *For Love of Country*, 125.

14. For a seminal contribution on these issues, see Ian Shapiro and Lea Brilmayer, *Global Justice (NOMOS XLI)* (New York: New York University Press, 1999).

15. Margaret P. Karns and Karen A. Mingst, *International Organizations: The Politics and Process of Global Governance*, 2nd ed. (Boulder, CO: Lynne Rienner, 2009), 7.

16. See *International Coalition for the Responsibility to Protect.* Available at http://responsibilitytoprotect.org (accessed June 5, 2013).

17. Held, *Cosmopolitanism: Ideals and Realities*, 101–2.

18. Seyla Benhabib, *Another Cosmopolitanism* (Oxford: Oxford University Press, 2006), 16–17.

19. Townsend Hoopes and Douglas Brinkley, *FDR and the Creation of the UN* (New Haven, CT: Yale University Press, 1997), 26–27.

20. This concluding section on FDR is drawn directly from my article: William Felice, "Introduction: Ethical Dimensions to American Foreign Policy," in *A Study Guide to the Four Freedoms* (New York: Carnegie Council for Ethics in International Affairs, 2005). Available at http://www.carnegiecouncil.org/education/001/four_freedoms/5221.html (accessed June 5, 2013).

Index

About the Author

William F. Felice is professor of political science at Eckerd College. Dr. Felice was named the 2006 Florida Professor of the Year by the Carnegie Foundation for the Advancement of Teaching. In addition, Felice has received Eckerd College's Lloyd W. Chapin Award for Excellence in Scholarship and Art (2011) and the John M. Bevan Teaching Excellence and Campus Leadership Award (2005), as well he has been recognized by the students as Professor of the Year (2003) and by the faculty as the Robert A. Staub Distinguished Teacher of the Year (1999).

Felice is the author of *The Global New Deal: Economic and Social Human Rights in World Politics* (second edition, 2010); *How Do I Save My Honor? War, Moral Integrity and Principled Resignation* (2009); *Taking Suffering Seriously: The Importance of Collective Human Rights* (1996); and numerous articles on the theory and practice of human rights. He has published articles in the *Cambridge Review of International Affairs*, *Ethics and International Affairs*, *Human Rights Quarterly*, *International Affairs*, *Social Justice*, and other journals.

Felice received his PhD from the Department of Politics at New York University. He has served as a trustee on the board of the Carnegie Council for Ethics in International Relations. He was also the past president of the International Ethics Section of the International Studies Association.

Dr. Felice can be reached via his website: http://www.williamfelice.com.